The Descendants of José Antonio Guerra

With information on his ancestors
to the 1570s in Spain

by

David G. Conklin

Please direct all correspondence and book orders to:

David G. Conklin
965 Ranch Lane
Kalispell, MT 59901
Tel: 406-210-4989
conklind@hotmail.com

Library of Congress Control Number: 2020951187

ISBN 978-1-7362441-0-4

Printed for the author by
Moore Graphics
11200 W. Wisconsin Ave. #6
Youngtown, AZ 85363

Cover photos:

Front: center-*Guerra family Coat of Arms;*
from left to right-*José Antonio Guerra; Tecla Guerra;*
Victoria Guerra; Abel Guerra

Back: top-*David G. Conklin*; from left to right-
Juan Bautista Chapa; Maria Andrea Peña;
Maria Teresa Longoria; Blas Maria Falcón III

Acknowledgments

I would first like to thank my wife Mary Guerra, her late father Guadalupe, sister Tecla, and her Guerra cousins for giving me permission to interview them, capture their memories on tape, and to use their family memories and photos. These recollections provided almost all of the information on Antonio and Tecla Guerra that did not come from official government records available in the public domain. I also want to further acknowledge the work of my wife Mary, who as always, is my editor-in-chief and biggest supporter.

I also wish to thank my good friend and former college roommate Arnold Browning, who co-authored the very interesting family history "*The Descendants of Emory R. Wilder*" (Browning, Arnold J. & Justin W. Wilder, 2009) and provided the format and impetus for this family history. Also many thanks to my West Valley Genealogical Society volunteer proof readers Patricia Amado, Susan Beckmann, Mary DeMers, Patricia Harrington and Jody Johnson for their valuable corrections and comments.

Thanks to all of you who have provided me with your family information, stories, documents and photos. All illustrations not credited were provided by the author or from public domain sources. In a way, you, members of the Guerra family, are the authors of this book. I am just the recorder of the information that was provided. You encouraged me by your interest in learning more about the origins of the Guerra family. Any errors or omissions, however, are mine alone. Please send me your corrections and any additional information, and I will include them in a future edition of this book.

It is my hope that this first edition will encourage someone in this branch of the Guerra family to update this book in the future. Perhaps one of the cousins or their children will want to update their branch of the family. I would be happy to provide files and advice to any family member who would like to write a book and extend the Guerra family history.

December 2020

About the Author

A Montana resident for more than forty years, David G. "Dave" Conklin is a retired park ranger who lives in the Flathead Valley. Although he has B.S. and M.S. degrees in Forestry and Wildlife Management, and an M.B.A., one of his first professional assignments was writing the *Montana Historic Preservation Plan* (Conklin D. , 1975) and nominating historic sites to the National Register of Historic Places. As a park ranger, he worked to preserve historic parks associated with people who made the country what it is today. While in Helena, Montana Dave built a log cabin where he lived with his family near the old mining town of Unionville. After retiring he published his first book, *Montana History Weekends* (Conklin D. , 2002).

Dave began gathering information about his family and his wife Mary's family in 1978 while still working in Helena, Montana, to include local and family oral histories on audio and videotape as well as photos, documents and notes. After retiring he trained as a Broadcast Journalist for the Army National Guard and served two years in Iraq during Operation Iraqi Freedom where he was awarded the Bronze Star during combat operations. In 2015 Dave retired again, began taking Genealogy Classes, and started work on his memoirs and family histories. He published his first genealogy book, *Conklin-Marinković Family History* (Conklin D. G., 2018), in 2018, which is available at major genealogical libraries in the U.S., Amazon.com, or from the author himself. He is a member of the West Valley Genealogical Society, Peoria, Arizona and splits his time between Kalispell, Montana and Sun City, Arizona.

The Author
David Gene "Dave" Conklin, Jan 2016

CONTENTS

Introduction

My purpose in compiling this information is to promote an appreciation of the Guerra family history and appreciation of both those born into the family, and those like me, who married into it. I have centered this book on Mary Guerra's paternal grandparents, José Antonio Guerra and Tecla Guerra, whom I did not even see a photo of until I began this project. I am thankful that I knew Mary's late father, Guadalupe Guerra, and mother, Nettie Taylor, who were still alive to meet their grandchildren; our daughter Dacia and son Christopher.

When we look at our parents and grandparents we often catch glimpses of ourselves, and it's not just from shared DNA. The people who raise us shape us, almost invisibly, through the values they convey, their convictions, and especially through their actions. I hope that this book will inspire you to think about the legacy that you leave your children. Our grandparents passed on to us a strong work ethic, moral values, self-discipline, concern for neighbors, the importance of hospitality, and the importance of love and family.

I have included brief information about each person's education, occupation, military, public service, and burial location when that information was available. I would hope that Antonio and Tecla would be pleased to know that many in the family seek to honor their parents, their communities, their country, and each other.

The findings presented here are based solely on my research, primarily over the past three years. The discovery of additional sources or interpretations may affect the conclusions.

The Format

The National Genealogical Society Quarterly (NGSQ) generation numbering system format is used in this book in order of descent from the oldest paternal ancestor (Antonio Guerra-Cañamal Sr., 1570) to the fourteenth generation (Cooper Kehlet Guerra, 2019). I only show the direct lineage for each of the descendants of Antonio. I list all of the children for each descendant, but only the direct ancestors of José Antonio Guerra are listed in the next generation. Details of ancestors' lives are mentioned when available. I included all the ancestors of José Antonio Guerra that I found. As this book goes back fourteen generations to include female ancestral lines, it has been a challenge as there are more than 257 descendants of only Antonio Guerra-Cañamal Sr. and the number continues to increase.

Although this book is written in English, our Spanish ancestors' names and locations were originally written in Spanish. For the convenience of the reader I have minimized the use of Spanish terms and use present-day place names to avoid confusion. Spanish terms appear in italics on the first occasion of their use. However, Spanish place names that have been incorporated into modern American usage such as Rio Grande, Mexico, and San Antonio, as well as person names, are not italicized. Also, I use the term *tejano* for Texans who are ethnically Mexicans as per (Weber, 1982, p. xxii).

The Spanish Inquisition, established in 1478 by Catholic Monarchs Ferdinand II of Aragon and Isabelle I of Castile banned all other religions in order to use the Church to consolidate their power over the newly unified kingdom of Spain. So it is understandable that most immigrants to the New World spoke Spanish as well as adopting Spanish names or at least Spanish pronunciation and spelling of their names if their ancestors were either not Spaniards or not Catholic.

Spanish Names: Spanish naming customs are used not only in Spain, but also in the many Spanish-speaking regions of Latin America (BYU, 2018). Most people have one or two given names followed by two surnames that are passed from one generation to the next. The first (primary) surname is inherited from the father's paternal surname, the second is inherited from the mother's paternal surname. Women usually keep their names when they marry, unlike Anglo culture where a woman's surname is given up upon marriage. For example, if José Lopez Garcia marries María Reyes Cruz, both will keep their surnames unchanged. If they have a child named Tomás, his full name will be Tomás Lopez Reyes. Sometimes when there are two or more given names I have hyphenated the surnames (i.e. Lopez-Reyes) to help identify them, which is a bit more modern as well. Also, those living in or near the US border often adopt the Anglo custom of using only the father's surname (i.e. Guerra), or sometimes use the mother's surname as a middle name.

If that isn't confusing enough, poor spelling and not hearing the name spoken correctly by immigration, census, and other government officials can make the name of a person or location almost incomprehensible. It is not hard to see why some family members adopted English pronunciation and spelling of their names, soon after they began attending schools in the USA (i.e. Jorge Javier Guerra changed his name to George Xavier Guerra). In this book I have repeated the variations of the Guerra surname (i.e. Guerra-Cañamal, Guerra-Cañamar) based on the most common usage for that individual or generation.

Chapter 1 is about the Guerra ancestors. Practically all the information about José Antonio's ancestors was obtained from published sources describing Spain, Northern Mexico, and its ethnic history due to the lack of both written and oral sources from family ancestors themselves.

Chapter 2 is about the lives of José Antonio Guerra and Tecla Guerra. They are the focus of this book, and the parents of Guadalupe Guerra, my father-in-law.

The remaining chapters focus on the descendants of José Antonio Guerra and Tecla Guerra with a separate chapter for each of José Antonio Guerra's and Tecla Guerra's children who lived to be adults, beginning with the oldest, Teresa (Chapter 3) to the youngest, Evangelina (Chapter 10).

Each descendant is assigned a number. Also, for both ancestors and descendants, a small number appears after their first name, or after their middle name if they have a middle name. This number indicates what generation of descendant this person is relative to the person listed at the beginning of the chapter. For example, in Chapter 6 the "4" after Isabelle signifies that she is the 4th generation descending from Guadalupe Guerra who is listed at the beginning of Chapter 6 as person number 1. This is true except for Chapter 2 where the "10" after Antonio

Guerra signifies that he is the 10th generation descending from Antonio Guerra-Cañamal who is listed in Chapter 1 as person number 1.

Each of José Antonio's ancestors' names appears in parentheses after his name. First, his 6th great grandfather Antonio Guerra-Cañamal Sr. is followed by "1" indicating that Antonio Guerra-Cañamal Sr. is the 1st generation that I have any information on. If we someday find Antonio's father, he would become the 1st generation, and so on.

For descendants that married a person that already had children, I have included these children and their families in the book. Although they are not descendants by blood line, they are part of the Guerra family through marriage. Similarly, adopted children are included when their information was provided.

The book was developed with the "Family Tree Maker" computer application (MacKiev, 2019). Each of the chapters of the descendants of José Antonio Guerra and Tecla Guerra was developed from a separate "Descendant" genealogy report file built with Family Tree Maker. Each file has a number for each descendant of the primary person starting with "2." When there is a plus sign in front of the number, it indicates that the descendant also had children and will be listed again under the next generation farther along in the book.

This methodology is used to keep all of the descendants of each of José Antonio's children in one chapter. If we had just used one file for all the descendants, the family members would appear mixed throughout this section of the book, because the report file lists all descendants by generation. You can also use the index to find the name and page with information for that individual. José Antonio's ancestors are also listed by name in the index.

Guerra Family Movement

The Guerra name originated in the provinces of Asturias and Cantabria on the northern coast of Spain before spreading across the Iberian Peninsula and on to the new world (Arteaga & Guerra Jr., 1996, pp. 1, 47). In fact, humans have been living on this part of the Iberian Peninsula for more than 18,000 years as evidenced by the famous prehistoric paintings in the caves of Altamira (Inman, 1997, p. 108).

The first surname, originally De la Guerra, refers to war, hostility, or the profession of arms and is derived from the German-Frankish word "werra." During the early Middle Ages people were referred to by a single given name unless they were part of the aristocracy or needed to be distinguished by place of birth (i.e. Juana De Cordoba), distinguishing features, or occupation. Guerra could also be a misinterpretation of the Basque word ezquerra from esker meaning "left-handed." Or it could be a Castilianized Basque word for someone who lived in a break in the hills from the word gerri meaning "waist." So it is not uncommon that before about 1450 there were few fixed hereditary surnames, making tracking the family's past all the more difficult.

According to Guerra genealogist Raul Guerra Jr., the second surname, "Cañamal," was derived from a nearby location once occupied by a hospital. Apparently during the middle ages there were a series of hospitals established for the pilgrims who were coming from all parts of Europe to the shrine of Santiago de Compostela, in Galicia. There was one such hospital established near Llanes (say Ya-ness), and it was named San Lazaro Cañamal. The hospital ceased to exist about the late 17th or early 18th century, but for some time afterwards the area where the hospital was located was still called Cañamal and was part of the parish of Llanes, Asturias. Reportedly some of the hospital's remains are still visible in the tiny village of San Roque de Acabal, about two and a half miles from Llanes. Later, double surnames such as Guerra-Cañamal became one of the many Spanish customs that lost favor after Mexico's independence from Spain in 1821 (Arteaga & Guerra Jr., 1996, pp. 6, 12).

Spain's provinces with inset showing Asturias province on the northern coast of Spain and the Guerra ancestors' village of Llanes. –from freeworldmaps.net.

Nevertheless, the history of the Guerra family that we can trace are the movements of Antonio Guerra-Cañamal Sr.'s descendants. The background for this begins in Spain in the 1500's during the "Age of Discovery" and the Spanish Inquisition set up by the Monarchs Ferdinand II and Isabelle I to create a single, monolithic Catholic ideology in recently unified Spain. Jews, Protestants, Muslims and "false converts" to Catholicism were expelled or tried in special courts. By 1609 the last of the Moors were expelled despite their conversion to Christianity. The 1600's became Spain's "Golden Age" but also saw ruinous wars, economic decline, and loss of influence in Europe.

Antonio Guerra-Cañamal Sr.'s village of Llanes, Asturia on the rocky North Atlantic coast of Spain was not immune to these forces. By 1622 they may have caused at least one of his children, Antonio Guerra-Cañamal-II, after the death of his first wife, to emigrate to the new world, either from the Port of Llanes, or by way of southern Spain, down the Rio Guadalquivir to Cadiz, into the Mediterranean, and across the Atlantic to seek his destiny in *Nueva Espana*, which became Mexico. If the younger Antonio was like every young man in Spain at the time, he recognized that a new world had been discovered by Columbus and heard of the explorations of Cabeza De Vaca, Coronado, De Soto, Pineda, and Cortes. So he pursued service in the King's Army that allowed him to see this new world across the Atlantic. Sources show that Antonio was a Captain in the Spanish Army when he landed in the port of Veracruz, Mexico with the annual fleet from Spain in August, 1622 (Figueroa, Tejanos: Where We Came From, 2009). This was the time of year that about forty Spanish galleons usually arrived in the harbor to deliver goods and passengers to New Spain.

Left: The Cathedral of Mexico City in 1690 where Antonio Guerra-Cañamal-II married Maria Luisa Fernandez de Rio Frio in 1624 – from Salinas, 2018.

Antonio Guerra-Cañamal-II soon made his way to Mexico City where in 1624 he married his second wife at the Metropolitan Cathedral and by some accounts had at least seven children (Arteaga & Guerra Jr., 1996, p. 3). He served as the Royal Public Notary in Mexico City, the Puebla de Zaragoza, and later Salvatierra in the province of Guanajuato (See his signature and notary seal on page 6). By 1655 he had moved to Monterrey in the northeast of New Spain where he died. His oldest son Vicente, born in Spain, also came to New Spain and his grandson Captain Vicente Guerra-Cañamar in 1750 became the founder of Revilla (Old Guerrero) on the south side of the Rio Bravo (now called the Rio Grande) River in the new colony of Nuevo Santander.

Another son, Ignacio Guerra-Cañamar, born in Mexico City, meanwhile had become Captain of the town of Cerralvo north of Monterrey and also the public notary for the city of Monterrey in northeastern New Spain. Ignacio died in Cerralvo in 1701 leaving a widow, a will, and by all accounts 16 children from two marriages who expanded the Guerra line in New Spain (Guerra J. O., 1997).

Antonio Guerra-Cañamal-II Signature and Notary Seal
–from Arteaga & Guerra Jr., 1996.

Ignacio's grandson from his second marriage, Joseph Ramon Guerra, signed up as a colonist when the new colony of Nuevo Santander was established in 1746 and received a Spanish Land Grant (*Porción M-6*) of two square leagues (*sitios*) of grazing land (about 8,856 acres) known as Rancho San Lorenzo, near the village of Mier on the south side of the Rio Grande River. By 1753 one of Ignacio's grandsons, José Francisco Antonio Guerra, and his wife Maria Ana Josefa De la Garza had also moved north from Monterrey to the Rio Grande River to become one of the nineteen original founders of Mier. In 1767 he received a Spanish Land Grant of one sitio (*Porción M-66*) of grazing land near Mier on the north side of the Rio Grande River in what later became part of the state of Texas.

Thus the Guerra ancestors became a part of Spain's incredible conquest of a land much larger than its homeland, replacing entire civilizations with Spanish language, religion and customs. These conquistadors pushed north into the deserts and mountains of New Spain, bringing livestock, settlers, missions and presidios in their search for silver, souls, and slaves. By the mid-1700's Guerras were *pobladores* (settlers) and *vecinos* (residents) of Monterrey as well as the *villas del norte* settlements of Camargo, Cerralvo, Revilla, and Mier and owned *ranchos* on both sides of the Rio Grande in the province of Nuevo Santander (1747) which later became Tamaulipas (1824) under Mexico (Alonzo, 1998, p. 3).

Throughout the eighteenth century, New Spain's *pobladores*, like Spain's subjects everywhere, lived under the paternal despotism of Spanish monarchs who did not encumber themselves with constitutions or participation in government. Outsiders appointed by the Viceroy occupied every key post, and trade was forbidden with foreigners including Americans (Weber, 1982, p. 15). Ignoring the basic needs of this frontier economy led to a number of revolts which resulted in Mexico's independence from Spain in 1821. So in the village of Mier,

Ramon's descendants, José Antonio Albino Hinojosa Guerra and his son José Manuel Guerra, as well as all the other Guerra *pobladores*, who were Spanish (*espanoles*), without moving an inch, now became Mexicans (*Mejicanos*).

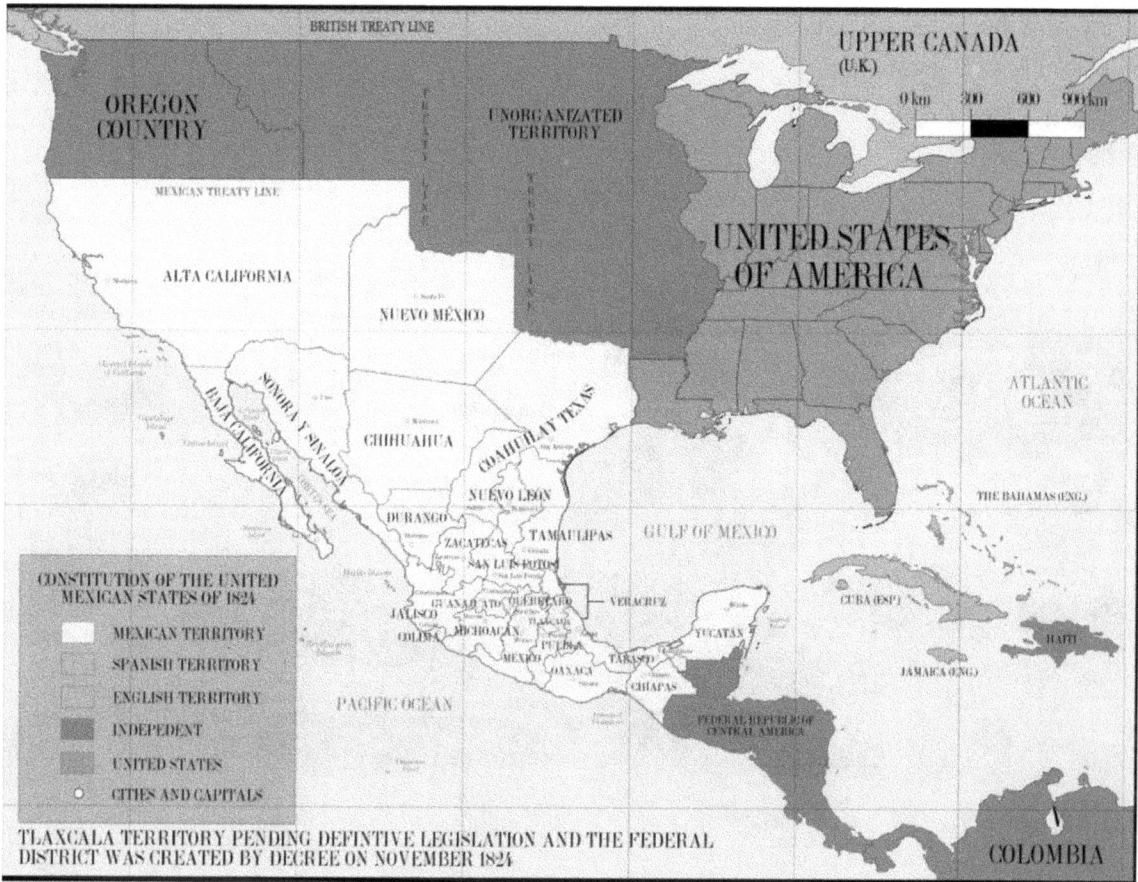

1824 Map of the United Mexican States

Unfortunately, the Federal Republic of Mexico adopted policies that made it difficult to control its northern borderlands. In 1827 the government ordered all Spanish-born residents of the republic to leave, thus emptying towns, missions and churches of businessmen and clergy (Weber, 1982, p. 45). Similarly, the constitution required all citizens and resident foreigners to become Catholics. Luckily José Manuel Guerra and his son Jesus of Mier, born in 1827, and the other Guerra *pobladores* were by now all Mexican-born Catholics. But Mexico was not able to populate the rangelands of its northern frontier and by 1836, *Americano* immigrants moving west into Texas outnumbered *tejanos* (Mexicans born in Texas) by ten to one (Weber, 1982, p. 177). Their lack of representation in Mexico's highly centralized government threw Texas into revolt breaking away to become the Republic of Texas in 1836. Once again, the Guerra *pobladores* changed citizenship (at least those north of the Rio Grande River) without moving an inch, now becoming citizens of Texas.

However, by March 1845 Mexico had broken relations with the United States over the annexation of Texas as a state. In the ensuing Mexican War of 1848 Mexico lost half of its territory to the United States. Twenty years later, after cattle raids and fighting during the U.S.

Civil War was over, the Guerra *pobladores* needed to prevent *Americano* claim jumpers from occupying their Spanish land grants on the north side of the Rio Grande River after it became the new international border. So about 1868, Jesus Maria Guerra moved his family and six year old son José Antonio from Mier Mexico to Rancho Colorado north of Roma Texas. By doing so they now became U.S. citizens.

View of Roma, Texas from the south side of the Rio Grande River –from "W.H. Emory's 1857 Report on the United States and Mexican Boundary Survey for the Secretary of the Interior."

Possibly all of Jesus' son José Antonio Guerra's descendants would have remained in the lower Rio Grande River Valley with its large Hispanic population if it had not been for world events. The first was the beginning of the Mexican Revolution in the fall of 1910 followed by the outbreak of World War I in 1914. As required, José Antonio's eligible son Abel registered for the draft when he was 21 years old in June 1917. But one story says his uncle on the Texas draft board was planning to use Abel to exempt his own son. Rather than being forced into conscription, Abel crossed the border and fought in the Mexican revolution instead. During the fighting he was forced to flee Mexico and ended up in Cuba where he met his future wife. He later returned to Mexico where he established a successful pharmaceutical business and lived the rest of his life. Many of Abel's descendants still live in Mexico.

José Antonio Guerra and his wife Tecla died during the 1918 influenza epidemic, leaving eight orphan children. Since Abel was fighting in Mexico, it was left up to the next oldest son, 18 year old Guadalupe, to raise his sisters and younger brother, which he did for the next fifteen years. Then during World War II, at age 41, Guadalupe enlisted in the U.S. Army Air Corps, and was sent first to Fort Sam Houston Texas, then to Gowan Army Air Field Idaho where in

1945 he married and lived the rest of his life. Another of José Antonio's sons, Fidencio, became a lawyer and worked in the State Department in both Spain and Columbia during World War II, then became a district court judge in Texas. Two of his sons also became lawyers and one left Texas and became an attorney in Arizona.

Female Ancestors Family Movement

Although the Guerra family name came from Spain, the familial DNA comes from female ancestors as well as male. As the Guerras married, their spouses passed on their ancestry to Guerra descendants as well. For example, DNA results (see Appendix 3. DNA Ethnicity Reports) for four cousins from this branch of the Guerra family living today show anywhere from 6% to 24% Native American ethnicity. One source may have come from Maria Luisa Fernandez de Rio Frio who in 1624 married the 2nd generation descendant of Antonio Sr., Antonio Guerra-Cañamal-II. She was reported to be a *Mestiza* (mixed-blood of Native American and Spanish descent). Born in Mexico City, her linage could have been Olmec, Aztec, Tlascalan, Huastec, Mixtec or a combination of tribes (Figueroa, Tejanos: Where We Came From, 2009).

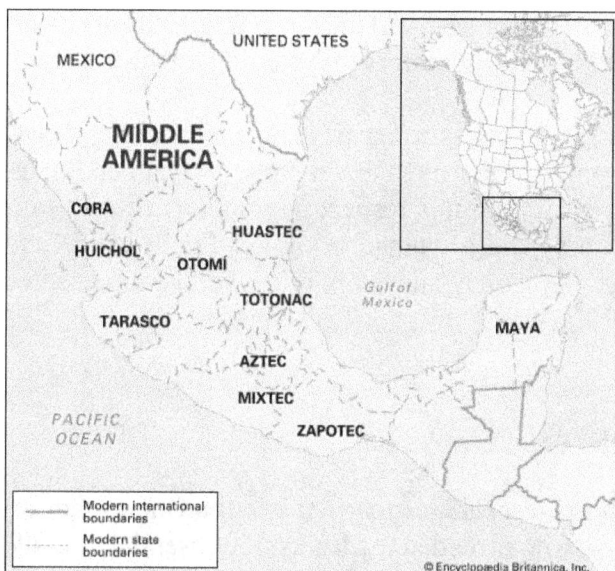

Left: Tribal Map of Middle America, ca. 1500 –from Encyclopedia Britannica.

Similarly, DNA results for the same four cousins show anywhere from 1% to 3% African ethnicity. One source may have been Dominga, a slave girl owned by Vicente Guerra-Cañamar, the 3rd generation descendant of Antonio Sr. She reportedly gave birth to his son Captain Juan Guerra-Cañamar in Mexico in 1662 (Somos, 2010). Dominga or her ancestors may have been brought to Mexico by the Spanish, or to Spain by the Moors.

José Lino de Jesus Guerra, the 8th generation descendant of Antonio Sr., married Maria del Rosario Peña-Ramirez in 1824. Her 3rd great grandfather was Juan Bautista Chapa, an immigrant to New Spain from Genoa, Italy. He was Secretary to nine governors of Nuevo Santander and wrote the first official history of the area now known as Texas (Chapa, 1997, p. 6).

Also, DNA results for the same four cousins show anywhere from 1% to 5% Jewish ethnicity. One source may have been Maria Andrea Peña, who married Jesus Maria Guerra, the son of José Lino de Jesus, in 1851. Her 6th great grandfather was the Spanish nobleman Marcos Alonso de la Garza Arcón from Lepe in the province of Huelva. He married Juana Quintanilla Treviño, whose family was also known to be converts from Jews to Christians. He settled with his family in Monterrey where many other families with Jewish roots had settled.

Due to the persecution of Jews in Spain by the Inquisition, his original surname of Alonso was dropped by his descendants. Apparently a well-known Jew in the New World named Hernando Alonzo financed and aided Conquistador Hernan Cortes. After the conquest of Mexico City, some feared that Alonzo was becoming too wealthy and powerful, and thus a threat. He was burned alive under orders of the Inquisition (Hordes, 2005, pp. 30-32). While no link has been established between Hernando Alonzo and Marcos Alonso, the name may have been dropped for protection (Monitor, 2001, p. 8E).

José Antonio Guerra's son Guadalupe, the 11th generation descendant of Antonio Sr., married Nettie Taylor who was from Oklahoma. Her parents were born in Georgia and her ancestors immigrated to America from Ireland and England before the American Revolution--see Taylor Family Movement in (Conklin D. G., 2020). Antonio's younger son Fidencio married Estela Margo who was born in Texas. Her paternal ancestors emigrated from France in the 1850s, and her maternal ancestors, the Clarkes, emigrated from Ireland.

Finally, it was not uncommon for settlers on the northern frontier of New Spain to receive dispensation from the Catholic Church to marry first and second cousins. As settlements were separated by vast and dangerous country, villages such as Mier, on the Rio Grande River, were settled by less than two dozen related families (Garza M. , 2018). So in many cases Guerra family lineages can be traced by female as well as male ancestors to Antonio Guerra-Cañamal.

The main role of women in this Hispanic society was as a marriage partner for the social-economic alliances by which the Spanish organized their lives. Each party (woman and man) represented a family, its status, and its property, and in this respect they met as equals, so it was vital that the right match be made. Not only did a woman bring her family name and prestige to secure an acceptable mate, but also the money and economic leverage represented by her dowry (Altman & Lockhart, 1976, p. 150).

Famous Guerra Ancestors and Relatives

Several Guerra ancestors (including those whose descendants married into the Guerra family) in New Spain were town founders or *capitanes*, who provided the leadership essential to guide the exploration, settlement and growth of Mexico and Texas. Mary Guerra's 9th great grandfather, *Capitan* **Marcos Alonso de la Garza Arcón**, was a Spanish nobleman who emigrated from Lepe in the Huelva district of the Province of Castilla. He was the originator of the uncommon Spanish surname *de la Garza*, which means "of the Herons." He founded the Garza family, many of whom married Guerra ancestors, and were military men and governors of New Spain (Alonzo, 1998, p. 32). There is debate that de la Garza Arcón's great grandfather, **Alonso de Estrada**, who arrived in Mexico City in 1524 and served with Cortes, was a natural son of **King Ferdinand II of Aragon** and one of his mistresses, Aldonza Ruiz de Ivorra.

True or not, Marcos Alonso de la Garza Arcón was among the first immigrants to New Spain in 1550 and became a miner in Durango. By 1603 Arcón owned the *estancia*, or stock farm, of San Fernando near Monterrey. One of his sons, Blas Maria de la Garza Falcón (now using the more modern word for "Falcón" than *Arcón)*, became a leading settler in the province, not only leading and furnishing armies to fight the nomadic Indians, but practically populating the land single-handedly. He noted with pride that by 1653 he had more than thirty-six grandchildren. His son, *Capitan* Miguel Gonzalez de la Garza Falcón, Mary Guerra's 7th great grandfather, was by 1740 commander of Presidio Santa Rosa near the Sabinas River in Nuevo León (Alonzo, 1998, p. 32).

Juan Bautista Chapa, Mary Guerra's other 7th great grandfather, emigrated from Italy in 1647 to New Spain. Chapa lived in Mexico City at first, then in 1652 moved to Cadereyto to become Secretary to the village, serving for ten years. Then in 1662 he moved to Monterrey and served as secretary to nine governors of Nuevo Santander and accompanied Governor Alonso De Leon on several expeditions north of the Rio Grande. As a result, in 1691 he wrote *"Historia del Nuevo Reino de Leon."* The book became the first official history of the area now known as Texas (Chapa, 1997, p. 6).

Drawing and signature of
Juan Bautista Chapa.

Capitan Blas Maria de la Garza Falcón III,
Colonizer of South Texas –from (Garcia, 1984).

Capitan Miguel's grandson (Mary Guerra's 5th great grandfather) was *Capitan* **Blas Maria de la Garza Falcón III**, known as "the colonizer of South Texas." Most sources say he was born in Cerralvo in 1712. He married in 1731 and by 1734 he was a captain at Presidio de San Gregorio de Cerralvo in Nuevo León.

In 1747 José de Escandón, the colonizer of Nuevo Santander, chose Garza Falcón to explore the south bank of the Rio Grande. Garza Falcón led a contingent of fifty men from the presidio of Cerralvo to the mouth of the river. Escandón's plan, as implemented by Garza Falcón, was to establish seven settlements along the river: Revilla, Camargo, Mier, Dolores, Reynosa,

Laredo, and Vedoya. On March 5, 1749, Garza Falcón arranged for forty families from Nuevo León to settle at Camargo on the banks of the Rio Grande. He founded the villa of Camargo, a presidio for the military squadron, and a mission, San Agustín de Laredo, for the Indians. Escandón named him captain and chief justice of Camargo, the first settlement founded on the Rio Grande. In 1752 Garza Falcón established a ranch, Carnestolendas, now the site of Rio Grande City, Texas, on the north side of the river.

After two unsuccessful attempts to settle and colonize land near the Nueces River, Escandón gave the assignment to Garza Falcón. By 1766 Garza Falcón had established a ranching outpost named Santa Petronila in what is now Nueces County, Texas. He took his family and his workers there. The rancho, eight miles east of the Nueces River, served as an outpost, way station, and camp for the soldiers from Presidio Nuestra Señora de Loreto who explored the vicinity while patrolling in 1767.

In 1767 Garza Falcón returned to Camargo, where he died and was buried in his private chapel, Nuestra Señora de Guadalupe. After his death land grants were distributed to the settlers. His family received land extending from the Rio Grande to the Nueces River in South Texas (Garcia, 1984, p. 8). There is a statue of him mounted on his horse in downtown Corpus Christi, Texas.

A selection of noteworthy Guerras throughout the world are discussed below alphabetically by their given name (Wikipedia, 2019):

Aureliano Fernández Guerra y Orbe (1816-1894) was a Spanish historian, epigrapher and antiquarian, also remembered as a poet and playwright.

César Guerra-Peixe (18 Mar 1914 – 26 Nov 1993) was a Brazilian violinist, composer, and conductor. Guerra-Peixe was born in Petrópolis, son of Portuguese immigrants with Romani origins. His music can be heard in many Brazilian films, such as Terra é Sempre Terra, O Canto do Mar, Quero Essa Mulher Tanto Assim, Riacho de Sangue, Meu Nome é Lampião, and Soledade. As an ethnomusicologist, he wrote an important book on maracatu "Os Maracatus do Recife" (1955, second edition 1980). He died in Rio de Janeiro.

General Donato Guerra (1832-1876) was the leader of the Mexican Army during the time of La Reforma. Born in Jalisco, he participated in the Reform War and in the French intervention. He joined the Plan de la Noria and Tuxtepec. Guerra was an ally of Ángel Trías, during his anti-government campaign of June 1875, but was captured on 18 September of the same year, and incarcerated in Ávalos, a suburb of Chihuahua City. He was assassinated in Ávalos by Lerdistas in 1876, and interred in the Panteón de Dolores on 27 May 1896. The town of Donato Guerra in the State of Mexico is named for him.

1756 Map of the Spanish colony of Nuevo Santander showing the settlements established by Blas Maria de la Garza Falcón III along the Rio Grande, known then as the Rio Bravo del Norte (Wild River of the North) –from (Santos, 2010).

José Manuel Gutiérrez Guerra, known as "the last Oligarch," (Sucre, Bolivia, 5 Sep 1869 – Antofagasta, Chile, 3 Feb 1929) was an economist and statesman, President of Bolivia between 1917 and 1920. He was the grandson of 1879 President Pedro José Domingo de Guerra, a man of high integrity and chief justice of the Supreme Court, who had died in office. By 1920, Twenty-plus years of unbroken Liberal control of the government (the longest by one party in the history of Bolivia) had fatigued most Bolivians, and turned them against the ruling elites and their methods. This earned the red-bearded, green-eyed head of state of this Andean nation, where the majority of people are Indian, the nickname "the last Oligarch."

All of this culminated in the 1920 coup d'état which, with military help, brought to power the opposition Republican Party under the leadership of Bautista Saavedra. Gutierrez-Guerra sought refuge in the United States legation at La Paz and went on to take a banking position at New York-based Chase National. He lived the rest of his days in exile, dying in Chile.

Juan Luis Guerra-Seijas (b. 7 Jun 1957), is a Dominican musician, singer, composer, and record producer. He has sold over 70 million records, and has won numerous awards including 21 Latin Grammy Awards, two Grammy Awards, and two Latin Billboard Music Awards. Guerra won 3 Latin Grammy Awards in 2010, including Album of the Year. In 2012, he won the Latin Grammy Award for Producer of the Year.

Guerra is one of the most internationally recognized Latin artists of recent decades. His popular style of merengue and Afro-Latin fusion has garnered him considerable success throughout Latin America. He is also credited for popularizing bachata music on a global level and is often associated with the genre. His distinct style of bachata however, features a more traditional bolero rhythm and aesthetic mixed with bossa-nova influenced melodies and harmony in some of his songs. He does not limit himself to one style of music; instead, he incorporates diverse rhythms like merengue, bachata-fusion, balada, salsa, rock and roll, and even gospel. "Ojalá Que Llueva Café" ("I Hope it Rains Coffee") is one of his most critically acclaimed pieces.

Juan Nepomuceno Guerra-Cárdenas (18 Jul 1915 – 12 Jul 2001) was a Mexican crime lord, bootlegger, businessman and smuggler who founded the Gulf Cartel, a drug trafficking organization. He is often considered the "godfather" of U.S-Mexico border cartels. He began his criminal career in the 1930s by smuggling alcohol from Mexico during Prohibition in the United States. He later diversified to other cross-border smuggling activities. He is the uncle of Juan García Ábrego, once Mexico's most-wanted man.

Rafael Guerra-Bejarano "Guerrita" (Jan 1862 – 6 Feb 1941) was born in Cordoba, in the household of an employee of the slaughterhouse, one and half months before his side-whiskered uncle José "El Pepote" was killed in Madrid by "Jocinero" on March 6, 1862. In 1878 he started a long apprenticeship as a *banderillero* (banderilla man) and second swordsman. He became a full bullfighter on 29 Sep 1887, in Madrid. His sponsor (*apoderado*) was "Lagartijo" (matador Rafael Molina). On this occasion "Guerrita" announced "I trust rather the benevolence of the public than my own merits and will try to fulfill my task by doing my best."

A Spanish hand fan commemorating the 1887 event—Rafael Guerra's "*alternativa*"—survives in the collection of the Staten Island Historical Society at Historic Richmond Town in New York. It features a depiction of "Guerrita" receiving the sword of "Lagartijo." This ceremony marked the elevation of Rafael Guerra Bejarano from an apprentice to a professional matador.

On May 19, 1895, at six o'clock in the morning, he got dressed (he wore a gold and green costume that he would not take off until nightfall) to kill three of Saltillo's bulls at 7:00 A.M. in San Fernando, three more of Cámara's at 10:30 A.M. in Jerez, and three more of Murube's at 5:30 P.M. in Seville.

For ten years, he maintained his superiority and stature. Especially from 1890 to 1899 this Cordovan bullfighter was in open battle with anybody that was not him. By 15 Oct 1899 he was still unvanquished, but crestfallen. He surrendered unconditionally in a hotel in Zaragoza, saying, "I quit bullfighting, but not of my own accord, I'm spelled." "Guerrita" took part in 891 bullfights, killed 2,547 bulls and never had three rules warnings.

Reynaldo Guerra-Garza (7 Jul 1915 - 14 Sep 2004) was a United States Circuit Judge of the United States Court of Appeals for the Fifth Circuit. He was the first Mexican-American appointed to a federal court when he was appointed as a United States District Judge of the United States District Court for the Southern District of Texas and would later become the first Mexican-American, as well as the first Latin American, appointed to any circuit of the United States Court of Appeals.

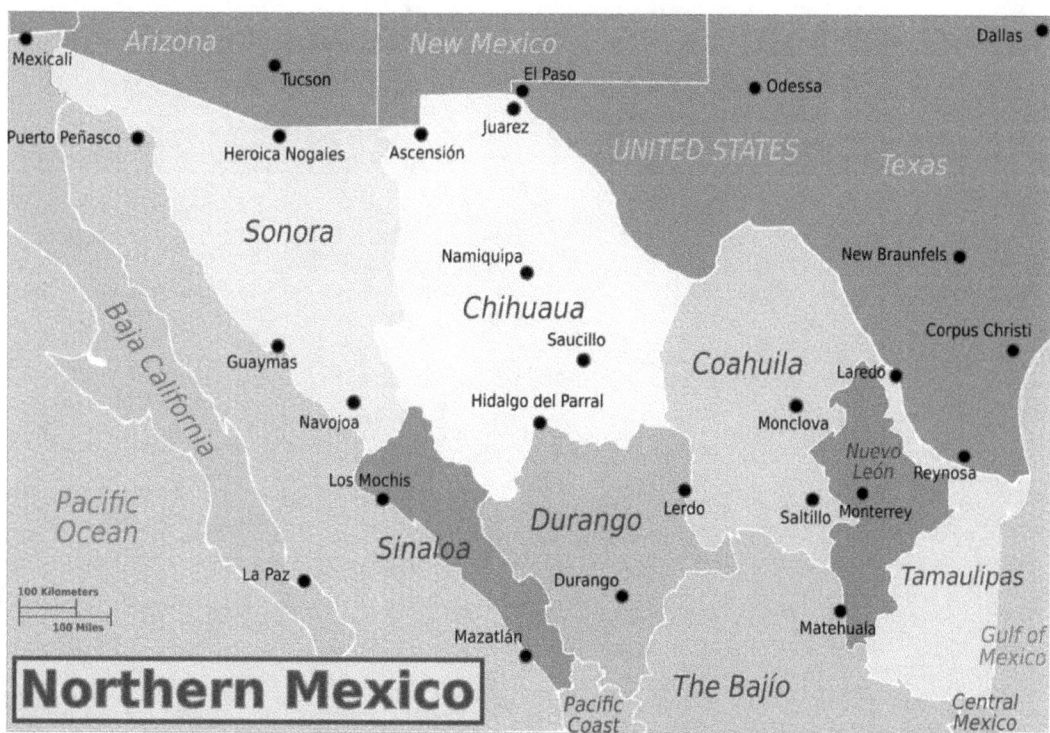

Map of the major cities and current states of Northern Mexico.

Chapter 1. Ancestors of José Antonio Guerra

This chapter presents the ancestors of José Antonio Guerra beginning with Antonio Guerra-Cañamal who was born in 1570. For more information about the context of the Guerra ancestors' life and times see *"Thirteen Generations of Guerra in the New World."* (Arteaga, Martha and Raul J. Guerra Jr. 1996).

Generation 1

1. ANTONIO*[1]* **G**UERRA-CAÑAMAL was born in 1570 in Llanes, Asturias, Asturias, Spain. He died on 06 Sep 1672 in Spain. He married Maria Porras, daughter of José Porras Molinas and Fernanda Muñoz, about 1588. She was born in 1570 in Llanes, Asturias, Asturias, Spain. She died in 1604 in Llanes, Asturias, Asturias, Spain.

It is believed that the Guerra line originated in the *concejo* (a district composed of several parishes with one common jurisdiction) of Ibio in the valley of Cabezon de la Sal, in the jurisdiction of Cabueraiga (Santander) Spain. One branch took up residence in the eastern part of Asturias, in the village of Alles, under the government of Peñamellera and the district of Llanes, later proving its nobility in the orders of Alcantara and Santiago (Arteaga & Guerra Jr., 1996, p. vi).

Guerra family Coat of Arms:
On a field of gold, a brown tower with flames coming out of the windows and openings in the parapet, and with the motto "Ave Maria Gratia Plena" (Hail Mary Full of Grace) on the sides of the tower flanking the shield –from (Arteaga & Guerra Jr., 1996).

Antonio Guerra-Cañamal is the earliest ancestor that I have been able to trace so far. We cannot be certain of his profession but Llanes was the cradle of Asturian nobility. Rodrigo Alvarez de Asturias, grandfather of the famous Spanish warrior Rodrigo Diaz de Vivar "El Cid" was born here in the tenth century. We can only speculate whether Antonio Guerra-Cañamal was himself a nobleman, soldier, tradesman, or farmer. But according to family tradition, he declared in 1607 that he was a soldier who had "served his majesty since he has been able to bear arms"

(Alonzo, 1998, p. 33).

Antonio Guerra-Cañamal and Maria Porras had the following children:

2.   i.   MARIA² GUERRA-CAÑAMAL was born on 01 Jan 1589/90 in Llanes, Asturias, Asturias, Spain.
3.   ii.   ANTONIA GUERRA-CAÑAMAL was born in 1592 in Llanes, Asturias, Asturias, Spain.
4.   iii. JUAN GUERRA-CAÑAMAL was born in 1594 in Llanes, Asturias, Asturias, Spain.
5.   iv.   JUAN GUERRA-CAÑAMAL II was born in 1595 in Llanes, Asturias, Asturias, Spain.
6.   v.   PASQUALA GUERRA-CAÑAMAL was born in 1598 in Llanes, Asturias, Asturias, Spain.
7.   vi.   DOMINGO GUERRA-CAÑAMAL was born in 1601 in Llanes, Asturias, Asturias, Spain.
+8. vii. ANTONIO GUERRA-CAÑAMAL-II was born on 26 Jun 1603 in Llanes, Asturias, Asturias, Spain (Montanas de Castilla). He died in 1655 in Monterrey, Nuevo León, Mexico.

Generation 2

8. ANTONIO² GUERRA-CAÑAMAL II (Antonio¹) was born on 26 Jun 1603 in Llanes, Asturias, Asturias, Spain (Montanas de Castilla). He died in 1655 in Monterrey, Nuevo León, Mexico. He married (1) **CATALINA DE VELA** about 1618. She was born about 1600 in Castilla, Spain (Montanas de Castilla). She died about 1620 in Burgos, Castilla-Leon, Spain. He married (2) **MARIA LUISA FERNANDEZ DE RIO FRIO**, daughter of Alonso Lopez de Rio Frio and Maria de Valencia, on 22 Dec 1624 in Mexico City, Distrito Federal, Mexico (Mexico City Cathedral). She was born on 22 Dec 1604 in in the mountains above Castilla, Spain. She died on 11 May 1658 in Monterrey, Nuevo León, Mexico.

The youngest of seven children, Antonio Guerra-Cañamal II was also born in Llanes and followed in the footsteps of his ancestors by becoming a soldier as well. According to his 6th great grandson, Guadalupe Guerra, "They claim they came from the northern part of Spain which at that time was Castilla La Vieja." (Guerra G. , 1978). Sources say his first marriage was to Catalina de Vela of Castilla, Spain who gave him his oldest son Vicente in about 1618, dying in childbirth or not long after. After the death of his wife, if the younger Antonio was like every young man in Spain at the time, he recognized that a new world had been discovered by Columbus and heard of the explorations of Cabeza De Vaca, Coronado, De Soto, Piñeda, and Cortez. So he pursued service in the King's Army that allowed him to see this new world across the Atlantic. Sources show that Antonio was a Captain in the Spanish Army when he arrived in the port of Veracruz, Mexico with the annual fleet from Spain in August 1622 (Figueroa, Tejanos: Where We Came From, 2009). This was the time of year that about forty Spanish galleons usually arrived in the harbor to deliver goods and passengers to New Spain.

Left: Spanish galleons unloaded goods and passengers at the port of Veracruz in New Spain in the 1600s.

Antonio Guerra-Cañamal-II marched with the Spanish Army to Mexico City, where he would serve as the Royal Public Notary. By then Mexico City was the bustling hub of commerce and government for New Spain, with a university, hospitals and the first printing press in the New World (Figueroa, Antiguos Pobladores: Ancient Colonizers de la Nueva Espana, Nuevo Reyno De Leon, and Nuevo Santander, The Guerra Canamar History, 2004, p. 79). In 1624, about two years after his arrival in Mexico City, Antonio married Maria Luisa Fernandez de Rio Frio at the Metropolitan Cathedral. She was reported to be a Mestiza of Native American and Spanish descent. Her Native American Lineage could have been Olmec, Aztec, Tlascalan, Haustec, Mixtec or a combination of tribes (Figueroa, Tejanos: Where We Came From, 2009). By some accounts Antonio and Maria had as many as seven children.

By 1629 Antonio was serving as the Public and Town Notary for Puebla de los Angeles (now Zaragoza) where his son Antonio III was born. Then in 1633 he again was serving as the Royal Public Notary back in Mexico City where his son Ignacio was born. Sometime after 1646 when his last child was born, he left Mexico City for Salvatierra in the province of Guanajuato where he was the Public and Town Notary from at least 1650 to 1653 (Arteaga & Guerra Jr., 1996, p. 3). Some sources say that he then moved to Monterrey in northeast New Spain where he died in 1655 (See his signature and notary seal on page 6 of the Introduction).

Antonio Guerra-Cañamal-II and Catalina de Vela had the following child:

+9. i. VICENTE³ GUERRA-CAÑAMAR was born about 1618 in Villa de Llanes de las Asturias y Montañas de Burgos, Castilla-Leon, Spain. He died on 25 Nov 1670 in Coahuila, San Luis Potosi, Mexico. He married (1) DOMINGA about 1660. She was born in Llanes, Asturias, Asturias, Spain (reported to be a slave girl of African descent). He married (2) LEONOR DE MORALES.

Antonio Guerra-Cañamal-II and Maria Luisa Fernandez de Rio Frio had the following children:

10. i. ANTONIO³ GUERRA-CAÑAMAR III was born on 25 Jun 1629 in Puebla de Zaragoza, Puebla, Mexico. He died in Mexico.

+11. ii. IGNACIO GUERRA-CAÑAMAR was born on 06 Nov 1633 in Mexico City, Mexico. He died on 07 Dec 1701 in Monterrey, Nuevo León, Mexico. He married (1) MARIA DE LA GARZA CAVAZOS, daughter of Capitan Juan Cavazos del Campo and Elena De la Garza Rodriguez, in 1660 in Monterrey, Mexico. She was born in 1640 in Monterrey, Nuevo León, Mexico. She died on 17 Dec 1675 in Monterrey, Nuevo León, Mexico.

He married (2) CATALINA FERNANDEZ DE TIJERINA, daughter of Gregorio Fernandez De Tijerina and Beatriz Gonzalez Hidalgo, on 04 Aug 1676 in the Metropolitan Cathedral, Monterrey, Nuevo León, Mexico. She was born in 1656 in Monterrey, Nuevo León, Mexico. She died on 03 Apr 1752 in Monterrey, Nuevo León, Mexico.

12. iii. JOSEPH GUERRA-CAÑAMAR was born in 1638.
13. iv. MARIA GUERRA DE VALENCIA RIO FRIO was born in 1643 in Mexico City, Mexico. She married on 11 May 1658 in Celaya, Guanajuato, Mexico.
14. v. JOSEPH VICENTE GUERRA was born in 1643 in Mexico City, Mexico. He married Ildefonsa de Vidaurri on 16 Apr 1655 in Selaya, Michoacan, Mexico. She was born about 1635.

Generation 3

9. VICENTE[3] GUERRA-CAÑAMAR (Antonio[2] Guerra-Cañamal II, Antonio[1] Guerra-Cañamal) was born about 1618 in Villa de Llanes de las Asturias y Montanas de, Burgos, Castilla-Leon, Spain. He died on 25 Nov 1670 in Coahuila, San Luis Potosi, Mexico. He married (1) **DOMINGA** (reportedly son Juan's mother was the slave girl Dominga). She was born in Llanes, Asturias, Asturias, Spain. He married (2) **LEONOR DE MORALES**.

This generation was the first to begin using Guerra-Cañamar as a surname led by Vicente and Ignacio Guerra-Cañamar. So far I have found very little information about Vicente, except that he was born in Llanes, Asturias, Spain like his father and at some point followed his father Antonio Guerra-Cañamar II to New Spain. Sources say that he brought the slave girl Dominga to New Spain with him where she reportedly gave birth to his son Captain Juan Guerra-Cañamar in 1662 (Somos Primos, 2010). Ancestral DNA suggests that her ancestors may have been from the Cameroon, Congo, or Southern Bantu and may have been bought by the Spanish or the Moors.

Vicente Guerra-Cañamar and Dominga had the following child that we know of:
+15. i. CAPITAN JUAN[4] GUERRA-CAÑAMAR was born on 19 Mar 1662/63 in Jalisco, Mexico. He died in Dec 1718 in Nuevo León, Mexico. He married (1) ELENA CAVAZOS MONTEMAYOR in Sep 1694 in Monterrey, Nuevo León, Mexico (the Metropolitan Cathedral). She was born on 07 Mar 1675/76 in Monterrey, Nuevo León, Mexico. She died in 1710. He married (2) CATALINA DE LA GARZA RENTERIA on 10 Jan 1710/11.

11. IGNACIO[3] GUERRA-CAÑAMAR (Antonio[2] Guerra-Cañamal II, Antonio[1] Guerra-Cañamal) was born on 06 Nov 1633 in Mexico City, Mexico. He died on 07 Dec 1701 in Monterrey, Nuevo León, Mexico. He married (1) **MARIA DE LA GARZA CAVAZOS**, daughter of Capitan Juan Cavazos del Campo and Elena De La Garza Rodriguez, in 1660 in Monterrey, Mexico. She was born in 1640 in Monterrey, Nuevo León, Mexico. She died on 17 Dec 1675 in Monterrey, Nuevo León, Mexico. He married (2) **CATALINA FERNANDEZ DE TIJERINA**, daughter of Gregorio Fernandez De Tijerina and Beatriz Gonzalez Hidalgo, on 04 Aug 1676 in the Metropolitan Cathedral, Monterrey, Nuevo León, Mexico. She was born in 1656 in Monterrey, Nuevo León, Mexico. She died on 03 Apr 1752 in Monterrey, Nuevo León, Mexico.

Ignacio was Antonio Guerra-Cañamal-II and Maria Luisa Fernandez de Rio Frio's second son, born while they were tithe-paying *vecinos* of Mexico City. When he was age fourteen he moved with his parents to Salvatierra in the province of Guanajuato. He was given some amount of formal education as he could read and write and later became a public notary. As a young man he served as a sergeant in the Armada de Barlovento, the fleet that protected the Spanish galleons from piracy in the windward islands of the Caribbean. But by 1658 he was again a citizen of Mexico City. In 1659 he went north to Monterrey where he married his first wife, Maria de la Garza Cavazos, became the Public Notary, and raised eight children (Arteaga & Guerra Jr., 1996, p. 5).

Ignacio Guerra-Cañamar Signature and Notary Seal
–from (Arteaga & Guerra Jr., 1996).

Public Notaries were very important in those times when most people did not have a formal education. Many could not even write their own names, so educated scribes prepared and entered legal documents for them into the records. For example, records dealing with mines, land transactions, debts and wills were very important and Ignacio's signature appeared on many documents. It was recorded that Ignacio was on the city council government of Monterrey during his time there (Guerra J. O., 1997). He also held many other important positions including adjutant to the Sergeant Major of Nuevo León; Captain of the Garrison at San Gregorio de Cerralvo; Alderman of Monterrey (1661, 1676 and 1678); Justice (1662 and 1666); *Alcalde* (Mayor) (1671); Major and Captain of War (1683); and Chief Justice (1688, 1689, 1691-1699) (Salinas, 2018, p. 8).

A year after the death of his first wife in 1675 and most likely after consultation with his son Domingo, who was now a priest, Ignacio married Catalina Fernandez De Tijerina and raised eight more children. Ignacio died on 7 Dec 1701 at the age of 68 in the village of Cerralvo, but not before writing and recording his will on 20 Nov 1701 which is still a public record. In it he stated that he wanted to be buried in a humble place in the Convent of San Francisco in Monterrey; that his first marriage to Maria de la Garza produced a dowry of 2000 pesos made up partially of grains, corn, and other products produced from the soil; that he has a home which he was still living in at the time of the writing of the will; and that his second marriage had a dowry of 500 pesos that his father-in-law, Gregorio Fernandez, pledged to him but never produced (Guerra J. O., 1997).

Ignacio Guerra-Cañamar and Maria de la Garza Cavazos had the following children:

16. i.   ELENA[4] GUERRA-CAÑAMAR was born about 1660.

+17. ii.   JUAN GUERRA-CAÑAMAR II was born about 1666. He died in Jun 1745 in Monterrey, Nuevo León, Mexico. He married JUANA FLORES DE ABREGO. She was born in 1680. She died before 1741.

18. iii. DOMINGO GUERRA-CAÑAMAR was born in 1668.

19. iv. JOSÉ GUERRA-CAÑAMAR was born in 1670. He married (1) MARIA PERALES. He married (2) MARIA DE LA GARZA.

+20. v.   ANTONIO GUERRA-CANAMAR was born in 1672 in Monterrey, Nuevo León, Mexico. He died on 09 Apr 1741 in Monterrey, Nuevo León, Mexico. He married Antonia Josefa De La Garza Treviño on 18 Jul 1695 in Monterrey, Nuevo León, Mexico (the Metropolitan Cathedral). She was born in 1680 in Monterrey, Nuevo León, Mexico. She died in 1711 in Monterrey, Nuevo León, Mexico.

21. vi. IGNACIO GUERRA-CAÑAMAR II was born on 06 Nov 1673 in Monterrey, Nuevo León, Mexico. He died in Jul 1757 in Monterrey, Nuevo León, Mexico. He married MARIA DEL BOSQUE.

22. vii. ANDRES GUERRA-CAÑAMAR was born in 1675.

23. viii. CLARA GUERRA-CAÑAMAR.

Ignacio Guerra-Cañamar and Catalina Fernandez De Tijerina had the following children:

+24. i.   CAPITAN CRISTÓBAL[4] GUERRA-CAÑAMAR was born in 1677 in Monterrey, Nuevo León, Mexico. He died on 26 Apr 1759 in Monterrey, Nuevo León, Mexico. He married Nicolasa Baez De Treviño, daughter of Francisco Baez De Treviño and Catalina De Maya, on 26 Feb 1702 in Monterrey, Nuevo León, Mexico (the Metropolitan Cathedral). She was born on 10 Sep 1687 in Monterrey, Nuevo León, Mexico. She died on 10 Apr 1760 in Monterrey, Nuevo León, Mexico.

25. ii. MARIA GUERRA-CAÑAMAR was born on 20 Apr 1680 in Monterrey, Nuevo León, Mexico. She died on 07 Jun 1700 in Monterrey, Nuevo León, Mexico.

26. iii. FRANCISCA GUERRA-CAÑAMAR was born in 1682 in Monterrey, Nuevo León, Mexico. She died in 1682, as an infant.

27. iv. MANUELA GUERRA-CAÑAMAR was born in 1683 in Monterrey, Nuevo León, Mexico. She died in 1735 in Monterrey, Nuevo León, Mexico.

28. v.   LUISA GUERRA-CAÑAMAR was born in 1684 in Monterrey, Nuevo León, Mexico. She died in Monterrey, Nuevo León, Mexico.

29. vi. CLARA GUERRA-CAÑAMAR II was born in 1686 (Twin of Catalina).

30. vii. CATALINA GUERRA-CAÑAMAR was born in 1686 (Twin of Clara).

31. viii. GREGORIA GUERRA-CAÑAMAR was born in 1690.

Generation 4

15. CAPITAN JUAN[4] GUERRA-CAÑAMAR (Vicente[3], Antonio[2] Guerra-Cañamal II, Antonio[1] Guerra-Cañamal) was born on 19 Mar 1662/63 in Jalisco, Mexico. He died in Dec 1718 in Nuevo León, Mexico. He married (1) **ELENA CAVAZOS MONTEMAYOR** in Sep 1694 in Monterrey, Nuevo León, Mexico (the Metropolitan Cathedral). She was born on 07 Mar

1675/76 in Monterrey, Nuevo León, Mexico. She died in 1710. He married (2) CATALINA DE LA GARZA RENTERIA on 10 Jan 1710/11.

Capitan Juan Guerra-Cañamar and Elena Cavazos Montemayor had the following children:

32.   i.   MARIA JOSEFA[5] GUERRA-CAÑAMAR was born in 1698. She died on 25 Dec 1770 in Revilla, Tamaulipas, Mexico.

33.   ii.   MARGARITA GUERRA-CAÑAMAR was born in 1702 in Monterrey, Nuevo León, Mexico. She died in 1770. She married an unknown spouse on 16 Jun 1720 in Villa de Garcia, Nuevo León, Mexico.

34.   iii.   JUAN AMADOR GUERRA-CAÑAMAR was born in 1703 in Monterrey, Nuevo León, Mexico. He died in 1752. He married an unknown spouse on 17 Jul 1732.

35.   iv.   JOSÉ GUERRA-CAÑAMAR II was born in 1705 in De Leon, Comanche, Texas.

36.   v.   CAPITAN VICENTE GUERRA-CAÑAMAR II was born on 02 Aug 1705 in Monterrey, Nuevo León, Mexico. He died in 1753 in Revilla, Tamaulipas, Mexico. He married Micaela Geronima de la Garza Falcón about 1730. She was born in 1710. She died on 01 Jun 1780.

17. JUAN[4] GUERRA-CAÑAMAR II (Ignacio[3], Antonio[2] Guerra-Cañamal II, Antonio[1] Guerra-Cañamal) was born about 1666. He died in Jun 1745 in Monterrey, Nuevo León, Mexico. He married **JUANA FLORES DE ABREGO**. She was born in 1680. She died before 1741.

We know little about Juan other than he and his wife Juana were *vecinos* of Cerralvo in 1718 and their son Vicente, one of 5 children, was a Captain who had engaged in stockraising and mining near Cerralvo and married a sister of Captain Blas Maria de la Garza Falcón (Alonzo, 1998, p. 33).

Juan Guerra-Cañamar-II and Juana Flores de Abrego had 5 children of which I only have the name of one:

37.   i.   CAPITAN VICENTE[5] GUERRA.

20. ANTONIO[4] GUERRA-CAÑAMAR (Ignacio[3], Antonio[2] Guerra-Cañamal II, Antonio[1] Guerra-Cañamal) was born in 1672 in Monterrey, Nuevo León, Mexico. He died on 9 Apr 1741 in Monterrey, Nuevo León, Mexico. He married Antonia Josefa de la Garza Treviño on 18 Jul 1695 in Monterrey, Nuevo León, Mexico (the Metropolitan Cathedral). She was born in 1680 in Monterrey, Nuevo León, Mexico. She died in 1711 in Monterrey, Nuevo León, Mexico.

The Metropolitan Cathedral in Monterrey, Mexico.

Antonio Guerra-Cañamar and Antonia Josefa de la Garza Treviño had the following children:

38. i.   JOSEFA MANUELA[5] GUERRA was born in 1698 in Monterrey, Nuevo León, Mexico.

+39. ii.   JOSÉ FRANCISCO ANTONIO GUERRA was born on 24 Mar 1708 in Cerralvo, Nuevo León, Mexico. He died on 22 Jan 1783 in Ciudad Mier, Tamaulipas, Mexico. He married Maria Ana Josefa De la Garza, daughter of José Clemente Falcón De la Garza Renteria and María Josefa De la Garza, on 29 Oct 1735 in Cerralvo, Nuevo León, Mexico. She was born on 29 Jun 1713 in Monterrey, Nuevo León, Mexico. She died on 10 Dec 1805 in Mier, Nuevo Santander, Mexico.

40. iii.   GERBACIO GUERRA was born in 1732 in Mier, Tamaulipas, Mexico.

+41. iv.   MARIA CANDIDA FRANCISCA GUERRA was born on 18 Oct 1742 in Mier, Tamaulipas, Mexico. She died on 20 Dec 1808 in Mier, Tamaulipas, Mexico. She married Juan José De la Garza Falcón, son of Blas Maria de la Garza Falcón III and Catarina Gomez de Castro, on 02 Apr 1770 in Camargo, Tamaulipas, Mexico. He was born in 1740 in Cerralvo, Nuevo León, Mexico. He died on 02 Aug 1796 in Mier, Tamaulipas, Mexico (Death record under Juan José de la Garza).

42. v.   MARIA MAGDALENA GUERRA.

43. vi.   ANTONIA IGNACIA GUERRA.

44. vii.   MARIA ISABEL GUERRA.

45. viii. MARIA LEONOR GUERRA.

46. ix.   MARIA ROSA GUERRA.

47. x.   MARIA DE LOS SANTOS GUERRA.

48. xi.   JOSÉ TOMAS GUERRA.

49. xii.   JOSÉ SILVERIO GUERRA.

24. CAPITAN CRISTÓBAL*⁴* GUERRA-CAÑAMAR (Ignacio*³*, Antonio*²* Guerra-Cañamal II, Antonio*¹* Guerra-Cañamal) was born in 1677 in Monterrey, Nuevo León, Mexico. He died on 26 Apr 1759 in Cerralvo, Nuevo León, Mexico. He married **Nicolasa Baez De Treviño**, daughter of Francisco Baez De Treviño and Catalina De Maya, on 26 Feb 1702 in Monterrey, Nuevo León, Mexico (the Metropolitan Cathedral). She was born on 10 Sep 1687 in Monterrey, Nuevo León, Mexico. She died on 10 Apr 1760 in Monterrey, Nuevo León, Mexico.

Cristóbal Guerra-Cañamar was the oldest of Ignacio Guerra-Cañamar and his second wife Catalina Fernandez De Tijerina's eight children and a direct paternal ancestor of José Antonio Guerra. It is believed that Cristóbal was born in Cerralvo during the period that his father Ignacio was Captain of the Presidio there. He married Nicolasa Baez De Treviño, his third cousin, which as mentioned in the introduction, was not uncommon on the frontier of New Spain (Arteaga & Guerra Jr., 1996, p. 7).

Nicolasa Baez De Treviño's signature from her joint will of 23 April 1749.
–from (Arteaga & Guerra Jr., 1996).

Nicolasa's father was General Francisco Baez De Treviño, the first native-born Governor of Nuevo León in 1703. She was one of the few women in that age that knew how to write and sign her name. Many of the first settlers could read and write, most probably learned from a parish priest or a family member. Sources say that Cristóbal could not write, and had to sign his name with an "X." They had 15 children of which the ninth was Joseph Ramon Guerra, the direct paternal ancestor of José Antonio Guerra (Guerra J. O., 1997).

Capitan Cristóbal Guerra-Cañamar and Nicolasa Baez De Treviño's 9th child was:
+50. i. JOSEPH RAMON*⁵* GUERRA was born on 23 Apr 1715 in Monterrey, Nuevo León, Mexico. He died on 23 Jun 1798 in Cerralvo, Nuevo León, Mexico. He married Maria Rosalia Chapa Hinojosa, daughter of José Manuel Hinojosa de la Garza and Maria Inez Chapa-Benavidez, on 16 Feb 1752 in Cerralvo, Nuevo León, Mexico. She was born in 1735 in Saltillo, Coahuila de Zaragoza, Mexico. She died on 14 Jun 1773 in Mier, Tamaulipas, Mexico.

1759 Death Record of Cristóbal Guerra-Cañamar from the Monterrey Cathedral —from Family Search.

Generation 5

39. JOSÉ FRANCISCO ANTONIO^5 GUERRA (Antonio^4 Guerra-Cañamar, Ignacio^3 Guerra-Cañamar, Antonio^2 Guerra-Cañamal II, Antonio^1 Guerra-Cañamal) was born on 24 Mar 1708 in Cerralvo, Nuevo León, Mexico. He died on 22 Jan 1783 in Ciudad Mier, Tamaulipas, Mexico. He married **Maria Ana Josefa De la Garza**, daughter of José Clemente Falcón de la Garza Renteria and María Josefa De la Garza, on 29 Oct 1735 in Cerralvo, Nuevo León, Mexico. She was born on 29 Jun 1713 in Monterrey, Nuevo León, Mexico. She died on 10 Dec 1805 in Mier, Nuevo Santander, Mexico.

Commonly known as Francisco Guerra, Mary Guerra's 5th great-uncle was the first generation to drop the Cañamar name, using only Guerra for the most part in following generations. Francisco and his wife Josefa were also among the 19 original founding families of Mier in 1753 (Garza M. , 2018). When the Spanish land grants were to be partitioned in 1767, Francisco and his half-cousin Joseph Ramon Guerra (Mary Guerra's 5th great-grandfather) were selected by the Spanish Royal Commission to assist with surveying and establishing the *porciónes* (tracts) for each Mier settler, the townsite, and the lands for the mission. When finally accomplished for each settlement, this resulted in the establishment of private ownership throughout the Colony of Nuevo Santander, which is still recognized in the state of Texas today.

In this arid region most of the *porciónes* were intended for livestock grazing and were surveyed into long, thin strips of land, each with a frontage on a permanent water course such as the Rio Grande. Each *porción* measured nine-thirteenths of a mile of river frontage (width) by eleven to fourteen miles deep (length), and consisted of 2 *sitios*, or leagues, of land totaling about 8,856 acres (Alonzo, 1998, p. 40). Francisco received Mier *Porción 66* (M-66) consisting of one league (4,429 acres) on the north side of the Rio Grande River across from Mier which later became part of Texas.

1936 Starr County Texas Land Map showing on left Francisco Guerra's Spanish Land Grant Porción M-66 and subsequent subdivisions west of Roma –from Starr County Clerk & Recorder Office, 14 Jan 2019.

José Francisco Antonio Guerra and Maria Ana Josefa De la Garza had the following children:

51. i.   JOSÉ PEDRO REGALADO[6] GUERRA was born in 1740 in Mier, Tamaulipas, Mexico. He died on 08 Oct 1784 in Mier, Tamaulipas, Mexico.

+52. ii. JUAN MANUEL GUERRA was born on 26 Jan 1742 in Cerralvo, Nuevo León, Mexico. He died on 26 Jan 1823 in Mier, Tamaulipas, Mexico. He married Isabel Maria Treviño-Garcia, daughter of Capitan Bartolome de Treviño-Leal and Ana Maria Garcia-Guajardo, on 14 Jul 1773 in Camargo. She was born in 1756 in Mier, Tamaulipas, Mexico. She died on 08 Nov 1802 in Mier, Tamaulipas, Mexico.

53. iii. JOSEPH ANTONIO GUERRA was born in 1754 in Mier, Tamaulipas, Mexico. He died in 1820 in Mier, Tamaulipas, Mexico. He married Maria Luisa Chapa on 13 Jan 1776 in Inmaculada Concepción, Mier, Tamaulipas, Mexico. She was born in 1758 in Mier, Tamaulipas, Mexico. She died on 27 Apr 1820 in Mier, Tamaulipas, Mexico.

41. Maria Candida Francisca[5] Guerra (Antonio[4] Guerra-Cañamar, Ignacio[3] Guerra-Cañamar, Antonio[2] Guerra-Cañamal II, Antonio[1] Guerra-Cañamal) was born on 18 Oct 1742 in Mier, Tamaulipas, Mexico. She died on 20 Dec 1808 in Mier, Tamaulipas, Mexico. She married **Juan José de la Garza Falcón**, son of Blas Maria de la Garza Falcón III and Catarina Gomez de Castro, on 02 Apr 1770 in Camargo, Tamaulipas, Mexico. He was born in 1740 in Cerralvo, Nuevo León, Mexico. He died on 02 Aug 1796 in Mier, Tamaulipas, Mexico (Death record under Juan José de la Garza).

Maria Candida Guerra was Francisco Guerra's younger sister and Mary Guerra's maternal 4th great grandmother. Her children below are the grandchildren of Blas Maria de la Garza Falcón III, the famous "Colonizer of South Texas." Maria's husband, Juan José de la Garza Falcón, was the original grantee of Camargo *Porción C-81* in about 1767 in Camargo, Mexico.

Juan José de la Garza Falcón and Maria Candida Francisca Guerra had the following children:

54.   i.   Maria Gertrudis[6] De La Garza Falcón was born on 12 Mar 1765 in Camargo, Tamaulipas, Mexico. Maria Gertrudis died in Camargo, Tamaulipas, Mexico.

55.   ii. Juan José Manuel De La Garza Falcón was born on 17 Aug 1766 in Mier, Tamaulipas, Mexico. He died on 26 Aug 1836 in Mier, Tamaulipas, Mexico.

56.   iii. Francisco Antonio De La Garza Falcón was born on 04 Apr 1771 in Mier, Nuevo Santander. He died on 10 Jul 1816 in Mier, Tamaulipas, Mexico.

57.   iv. Blas Maria De La Garza Falcón VI was born in 1772 in Mier, Nuevo Santander, Mexico. He died in 1820.

58.   v.   José Nepomuceno Falcón was born on 25 May 1773 in Mier, Tamaulipas, Mexico. He died on 26 Aug 1833.

+59. vi. Maria Rita De La Garza Falcón was born on 31 May 1782 in Mier, Tamaulipas, Mexico. She died in 1825 in Eagle Pass, Maverick, Texas. She married José Eugenio Ramirez, son of José Cristóbal Ramirez and Maria Matiana Hinojosa de Chapa, on 28 Jan 1800 in Mier, Tamaulipas, Mexico. He was born on 17 Dec 1757 in Mier, Tamaulipas, Mexico. He died on 30 Apr 1825 in Mier, Tamaulipas, Mexico.

50. Joseph Ramon[5] Guerra (Capitan Cristóbal[4] Guerra-Cañamar, Ignacio[3] Guerra-Cañamar, Antonio[2] Guerra-Cañamal II, Antonio[1] Guerra-Cañamal) was born on 23 Apr 1715 in Monterrey, Nuevo León, Mexico. He died on 23 Jun 1798 in Cerralvo, Nuevo León, Mexico. He married **Maria Rosalia Chapa Hinojosa**, daughter of José Manuel Hinojosa de la Garza and Maria Inez Chapa-Benavidez, on 16 Feb 1752 in Cerralvo, Nuevo León, Mexico. She was born in 1735 in Saltillo, Coahuila, Mexico. She died on 14 Jun 1773 in Mier, Tamaulipas, Mexico.

Joseph Ramon Guerra, Mary Guerra's paternal 4th great grandfather, was baptized on 01 May 1715 in Monterrey, Nuevo León, Mexico in the Chapel of San Francisco Xavier. In 1752 he was granted church dispensation to marry his third cousin, Maria Rosalia Chapa Hinojosa. Ramon, as he was called, became a *ranchero* (rancher) in the Cerralvo area, most likely raising cattle, sheep and goats. By 1757 he and his wife and children were living in Mier, Tamaulipas, Mexico where the census listed him with his wife, children, arms, four horses, and three burros (Salinas, 2018, p. 11). The settlers faced the constant threat of drought, famine and raids by hostile natives, but Mier prospered in spite of these dangerous conditions along the Rio Grande.

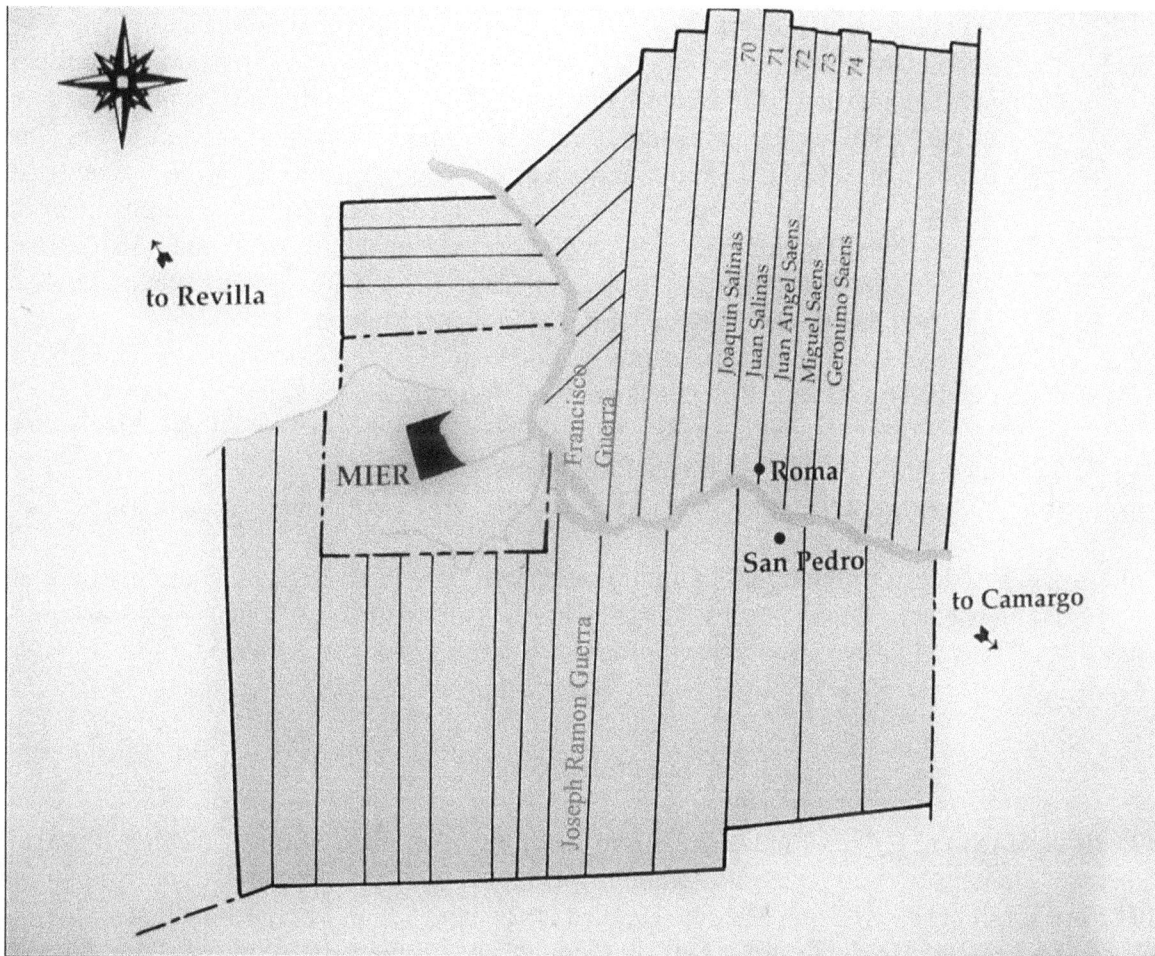

Map of the townsite of Mier and surrounding pasturelands divided into porciónes (tracts) for allocation to farmers and ranchers –Courtesy Roma Historical Museum.

Since he was one of the colonizers of Nuevo Santander when it was established in 1746, Ramon and his half-cousin Francisco (39) were selected in 1767 by the Spanish Royal Commission to assist with surveying and establishing the porciónes for Mier settlers. In 1790 he finally received a land patent (*Porción M-6*) for 8,800 acres of his Rancho San Lorenzo, directly south of the Rio Grande from his half-cousin Francisco's land on the north bank (see map). Census records show he was living at his ranch in Mier, Tamaulipas, Mexico in 1782 (Rancho San Lorenzo de Ramon Guerra) and 1790 (Rancho San Lorenzo), dying at the ripe old age of 83.

Joseph Ramon Guerra and Maria Rosalia Chapa Hinojosa had at least ten children which two (61) (63) are direct ancestors of the **José Manuel Guerra branch** of the Guerra family:

 60. i.   MARIA CATARINA GUERRA was born in 1755 in Mier, Tamaulipas, Mexico. She died in Mier, Tamaulipas, Mexico.

+61. ii. JOSÉ ANTONIO ALBINO HINOJOSA[6] GUERRA was born about 1756 in Mier, Tamaulipas, Mexico. He died on 26 Aug 1833 in Mier, Tamaulipas, Mexico. He married Maria Rosalia Garcia Salinas, daughter of José Joaquin Salinas and Maria de los

Santos Garcia, on 17 Aug 1774 in Mier, Tamaulipas, Mexico. She was born in 1758. She died on 27 Oct 1840 in Mier, Tamaulipas, Mexico.

62. iii. MARIA IGNACIA GUERRA was born about 1760 in Mier, Tamaulipas, Mexico.

+63. iv. JOSÉ ALEJANDRO HINOJOSA GUERRA was born on 03 Mar 1763 in Mier, Tamaulipas, Mexico. He died on 19 Nov 1833 in Mier, Tamaulipas, Mexico. He married Maria Lugarda Salinas Garcia, daughter of José Joaquin Garcia and Maria Rosalia Peña Salinas, on 03 Mar 1783 (Immaculate Conception Church), Mier, Tamaulipas, Mexico. She was born on 26 Aug 1767 in Rancho San Lorenzo, Mier, Tamaulipas, Mexico. She died on 02 Sep 1813 in Mier, Tamaulipas, Mexico.

64. v. MARIA JUANA FRANCISCA GUERRA was born in 1764 in Mier, Tamaulipas, Mexico. She died on 14 Nov 1844 in Mier, Tamaulipas, Mexico.

65. vi. JOSÉ ANTONIO HINOJOSA GUERRA was born in 1765 in Mier, Tamaulipas, Mexico. He died on 02 Jan 1805 in Matamoros, Tamaulipas, Mexico.

66. vii. JOSÉ VICENTE GUERRA was born on 10 Feb 1768 in Mier, Tamaulipas, Mexico. He died on 13 Jul 1799 in Mier, Tamaulipas, Mexico.

67. viii. JOSÉ IGNACIO HIGNINIO GUERRA was born in 1770 in Mier, Tamaulipas, Mexico. He died probably as an infant.

68. ix. JOSÉ IGNACIO POLICARPIO GUERRA was born on 09 Feb 1772 in Mier, Tamaulipas, Mexico. He died on 15 Feb 1836 in Mier, Tamaulipas, Mexico.

69. x. MARIA LEANDRA GUERRA was born in Mier, Tamaulipas, Mexico.

Generation 6

52. JUAN MANUEL^6 GUERRA (José Francisco Antonio^5, Antonio^4 Guerra-Cañamar, Ignacio^3 Guerra-Cañamar, Antonio^2 Guerra-Cañamal II, Antonio^1 Guerra-Cañamal) was born on 26 Jan 1742 in Cerralvo, Nuevo León, Mexico. He died on 26 Jan 1823 in Mier, Tamaulipas, Mexico. He married **Isabel Maria Treviño-Garcia**, daughter of Capitan Bartolome de Treviño-Leal and Ana Maria Garcia-Guajardo, on 14 Jul 1773 in Camargo. She was born in 1756 in Mier, Tamaulipas, Mexico. She died on 08 Nov 1802 in Mier, Tamaulipas, Mexico.

Juan Manuel Guerra and Isabel Maria Treviño-Garcia had the following children:

70. i. LUCIANO TREVINO^7 GUERRA was born in 1774 in Mier, Tamaulipas, Mexico. He died in 1849 in Mier, Tamaulipas, Mexico.

71. ii. FRANCISCO TREVINO GUERRA was born on 17 Mar 1775 in Mier, Nuevo Santander, Mexico. He died on 04 Dec 1846 in Mier, Tamaulipas, Mexico.

72. iii. ANTONIO MARIA TREVINO GUERRA was born on 24 Dec 1777 in Mier, Nuevo Santander, Mexico. He died on 29 Jan 1850 in Mier, Tamaulipas, Mexico.

+73. iv. **MARIA TOMASA GUERRA** was born on 05 Mar 1780 in Mier, Tamaulipas, Mexico. She died on 02 Jan 1856. She married José Manuel Guerra, son of José Antonio Albino Hinojosa Guerra and Maria Rosalia Garcia Salinas, on 26 Jan 1802 in Mier, Tamaulipas, Mexico (Immaculate Conception Church). He was born on 12 Oct 1784 in Mier, Tamaulipas, Mexico. He died on 24 Jun 1833 in Mier, Tamaulipas, Mexico (reportedly killed by Indians).

74. v. MARIA JULIA GUERRA was born about 1786. She married José de los Angeles Guerra-Cañamar, son of José Antonio Albino Hinojosa Guerra and Maria Rosalia

Garcia Salinas, on 17 Jun 1826 in Mier, Tamaulipas, Mexico (Immaculate Conception Church). He was born in 1784 in Mier, Tamaulipas, Mexico. He died on 8 Apr 1849 in Mier, Tamaulipas, Mexico

75. vi. JUAN JOSÉ FELIPE GUERRA was born in 1788 in Mier, Tamaulipas, Mexico. He died on 03 Nov 1809 in Texas.

76. vii. FRANCISCA GUERRA-TREVINO was born on 18 Sep 1800 in Mier, Tamaulipas, Mexico. She died on 18 Sep 1800 in Mier, Tamaulipas, Mexico. She married JOSÉ GREGORIO RAMIREZ. He was born in 1774. He died in 1821.

59. MARIA RITA DE LA^6 GARZA FALCÓN (Maria Candida Francisca^5 Guerra, Antonio^4 Guerra-Cañamar, Ignacio^3 Guerra-Cañamar, Antonio^2 Guerra-Cañamal II, Antonio^1 Guerra-Cañamal) was born on 31 May 1782 in Mier, Tamaulipas, Mexico. She died in 1825 in Eagle Pass, Maverick, Texas. She married **José Eugenio Ramirez**, son of José Cristóbal Ramirez and Maria Matiana Hinojosa de Chapa, on 28 Jan 1800 in Mier, Tamaulipas, Mexico. He was born on 17 Dec 1757 in Mier, Tamaulipas, Mexico. He died on 30 Apr 1825 in Mier, Tamaulipas, Mexico.

José Eugenio Ramirez and Maria Rita de la Garza Falcón had the following children:

77. i. JOSÉ JULIAN ILDEFONSO^7 RAMIREZ was born in 1801 in Mier, Tamaulipas, Mexico. He died on 10 Feb 1852 in Mier, Tamaulipas, Mexico.

78. ii. MARIA DOMINGA RAMIREZ was born in 1810 in Mier, Tamaulipas, Mexico. She died on 11 Mar 1857 in Mier, Tamaulipas, Mexico.

+79. iii. MARIA PAULA GUADALUPE RAMIREZ was born in 1811 in Mier, Tamaulipas, Mexico. She died on 07 Oct 1842 in Mier, Tamaulipas, Mexico. She married José Francisco De la Peña, son of José Antonio De la Peña and Maria Petra Garcia-Barrera, on 22 Nov 1824 in Mier, Tamaulipas, Mexico (Immaculate Conception Church). He was born on 09 Jun 1805 in Mier, Tamaulipas, Mexico. He died before 01 Jan 1851 in Nuevo Santander, Mexico.

80. iv. JOSÉ JUAN MANUEL RAMIREZ was born in 1817 in Mier, Tamaulipas. He died after 1910 in Texas.

61. JOSÉ ANTONIO ALBINO HINOJOSA^6 GUERRA (Joseph Ramon^5, Capitan Cristóbal^4 Guerra-Cañamar, Ignacio^3 Guerra-Cañamar, Antonio^2 Guerra-Cañamal II, Antonio^1 Guerra-Cañamal) was born about 1754 in Mier, Tamaulipas, Mexico. He died on 26 Aug 1833 in Mier, Tamaulipas, Mexico. He married **Maria Rosalia Garcia Salinas**, daughter of José Joaquin Salinas and Maria de los Santos Garcia, on 17 Aug 1774 in Mier, Tamaulipas, Mexico. She was born in 1758. She died on 27 Oct 1840 in Mier, Tamaulipas, Mexico.

José Antonio Albino Hinojosa Guerra was the second of Joseph Ramon's ten children. He married Maria Rosalia Garcia Salinas, the daughter of Joaquin Salinas and Maria de los Santos Garcia from Cerralvo and the original grantee of Mier Porcion M-70 on north bank of Rio Grande (see map of Mier and its surroundings on page 29). José and Maria had at least 12 children together. Diodoro Vidal's branch of the Guerra family is descended from their sixth child, **José de los Angeles Guerra-Cañamar;** while José Antonio's branch of the family (the one Mary Guerra belongs to) is descended from their third child, **José Manuel Guerra.**

Left: Rugged Spanish pobladores (settlers) followed the conquistadors to colonize the harsh lands of northeastern New Spain and defend their settlements from Indian attack with promises from the Crown of receiving land of their own – Courtesy Museum of South Texas History.

José Antonio Albino Hinojosa Guerra and Maria Rosalia Garcia Salinas had the following children:

81.   i.   MARIA GUADALUPE[7] GUERRA was born in 1774 in Mier, Tamaulipas, Mexico. She died on 09 Feb 1836 in Mier, Tamaulipas, Mexico. She married José de los Santos-Ramirez in 1797 in Mier, Tamaulipas, Mexico (Immaculate Conception Church).

82.   ii.   MARIA MANUELA GUERRA was born on 25 Aug 1776 in Mier, Tamaulipas, Mexico. She died on 29 Aug 1864. She married José Rafael Gonzalez in 1803 in Mier, Tamaulipas, Mexico.

+83.   iii.   JOSÉ MANUEL GUERRA was born in 1778 in Mier, Tamaulipas, Mexico. He died on 24 Jun 1833 in Mier, Tamaulipas, Mexico (reportedly killed by Indians). He married Maria Tomasa Guerra, daughter of Juan Manuel Guerra and Isabel Maria Treviño-Garcia, on 26 Jan 1802 in Mier, Tamaulipas, Mexico (Immaculate Conception Church). She was born on 05 Mar 1780 in Mier, Tamaulipas, Mexico. She died on 02 Jan 1856.

84.   iv.   JOSÉ LAUREANO DE JESUS GUERRA was born in 1780 in Mier, Tamaulipas, Mexico. He died on 07 Jan 1791.

85.   v.   JOSÉ HILARIO DE JESUS GUERRA was born in 1782 in Mier, Tamaulipas, Mexico. He died on 11 Jan 1847 in Mier, Tamaulipas, Mexico.

+86.   vi.   JOSÉ DE LOS ANGELES GUERRA-CANAMAR was born in 1784 in Mier, Tamaulipas, Mexico. He died on 08 Apr 1849 in Mier, Tamaulipas, Mexico. He married (1) MARIA ROSALIA TIMOTEA HINOJOSA, daughter of José Gervacio Hinojosa and Maria Teresa Treviño, on 11 Jan 1811 in Mier, Tamaulipas, Mexico (Immaculate Conception Church). She was born on 31 Aug 1788 in Mier, Tamaulipas, Mexico. She died on 29 Nov 1825 in Mier, Tamaulipas, Mexico. He married (2) MARIA JULIA GUERRA on 17 Jun 1826 in Mier, Tamaulipas, Mexico (Immaculate Conception Church).

87.   vii.   MARIA FRANCISCA GUERRA was born in 1786 in Mier, Tamaulipas, Mexico. She died on 10 Nov 1853.

88.   viii.   MARIA RITA GUERRA was born in 1788 in Mier, Tamaulipas, Mexico.

89.   ix.   JUAN CRISTÓBAL GUERRA was born in 1790 in Mier, Tamaulipas, Mexico. He died on 25 Feb 1790 in Mier, Tamaulipas, Mexico (died as an infant).

90.   x.   JOSÉ FELIPE GUERRA was born about 1792 in Mier, Tamaulipas, Mexico.

91.   xi.   MARIA DE LOS SANTOS GUERRA was born in 1794 in Mier, Tamaulipas, Mexico. She died on 08 Feb 1847 in Mier, Tamaulipas, Mexico.

92.   xii.   MARIA BRIGIDA GUERRA was born in 1796 in Mier, Tamaulipas, Mexico.

Sketch Map of Northern Nuevo Santander (South Texas) 1540-1765 –from (Garcia, 1984).

José Alejandro Hinojosa Guerra and Maria Lugarda Salinas Garcia had the following children:

93. i.   MARIA CASILDA GARCIA[7] GUERRA was born on 22 Apr 1786 in Inmaculada Concepción, Mier, Tamaulipas, Mexico. She died on 21 Nov 1825 in Mier, Tamaulipas, Mexico.

+94. ii.   JUAN JOSÉ HERMENEGILDO GUERRA was born on 22 Apr 1789 in Mier, Tamaulipas, Mexico. He died in 1834 in Texas. He married Maria Francisca Saenz Hinojosa, daughter of José Antonio Saenz and Maria Gregoria Hinojosa, on 30 Jan 1811 in Mier, Tamaulipas, Mexico (Immaculate Conception Church). She was born on 26 Jan 1794 in Mier, Tamaulipas, Mexico. She died after 1834 in Mier, Tamaulipas, Mexico.

95. iii.   MARIA ESPIRIDIONA GARCIA GUERRA was born on 25 Dec 1797 in Mier, Tamaulipas, Mexico.

96. iv.   MARIA LUISA GARCIA GUERRA was born on 26 Aug 1804 in Mier, Tamaulipas, Mexico. She died on 29 Nov 1855 in Mier, Tamaulipas, Mexico.

97. v.   JOSÉ CESARIO GARCIA GUERRA was born on 03 Mar 1816 in Mier, Tamaulipas, Mexico. He died before 11 Sep 1893.

Generation 7

79. MARIA PAULA GUADALUPE[7] RAMIREZ (Maria Rita de la[6] Garza Falcón, Maria Candida Francisca[5] Guerra, Antonio[4] Guerra-Cañamar, Ignacio[3] Guerra-Cañamar, Antonio[2] Guerra-

Cañamal II, Antonio[1] Guerra-Cañamal) was born in 1811 in Mier, Tamaulipas, Mexico. She died on 07 Oct 1842 in Mier, Tamaulipas, Mexico. She married **José Francisco De la Peña**, son of José Antonio De la Peña and Maria Petra Garcia-Barrera, on 22 Nov 1824 in Mier, Tamaulipas, Mexico (Immaculate Conception Church). He was born on 09 Jun 1805 in Mier, Tamaulipas, Mexico. He died before 01 Jan 1851 in Tamaulipas, Mexico.

José Francisco De la Peña and Maria Paula Guadalupe Ramirez had the following children:

99. i. JOSÉ ESEQUIEL[8] PEÑA was born in 1827 in Mier, Tamaulipas, Mexico. He died in 1896.

100. ii. MARIA DEL REFUGIO DE LA PEÑA RAMIREZ was born on 09 Nov 1828 in Mier, Tamaulipas, Mexico.

101. iii. MARIA ANTONIA PEÑA was born in 1832.

+102. iv. MARIA ANDREA PEÑA was born on 23 Jan 1833 in Mier, Tamaulipas, Mexico. She died in 1906 in Laredo, Webb, Texas. She married Jesus Maria Guerra, son of José Lino de Jesus Guerra and Maria del Rosario Peña-Ramirez, on 6 Feb 1851 in Mier, Tamaulipas, Mexico (Immaculate Conception Church). He was born on 7 May 1827 in Mier, Tamaulipas, Mexico. He died about 1899 in Roma, Starr, Texas before his grandson Guadalupe was born in 1900.

83. JOSÉ MANUEL[7] GUERRA (José Antonio Albino Hinojosa[6], Joseph Ramon[5], Capitan Cristóbal[4] Guerra-Cañamar, Ignacio[3] Guerra-Cañamar, Antonio[2] Guerra-Cañamal II, Antonio[1] Guerra-Cañamal) was born in 1778 in Mier, Tamaulipas, Mexico. He died on 24 Jun 1833 in Mier, Tamaulipas, Mexico (reportedly killed by Indians). He married **(+73.) MARIA TOMASA[7] GUERRA**, daughter of Juan Manuel Guerra and Isabel Maria Treviño-Garcia, on 26 Jan 1802 in Mier, Tamaulipas, Mexico (Immaculate Conception Church). She was born on 05 Mar 1780 in Mier, Tamaulipas, Mexico. She died on 02 Jan 1856.

Manuel Guerra, as he was commonly known, was the 3rd great grandfather of Mary Guerra. He was the son of José Antonio Albino Hinojosa Guerra and the beginning of the family line that produced José Antonio Guerra. Manuel's brother, **José de los Angeles Guerra-Cañamar**, was the beginning of the family line that produced José Antonio Guerra's wife, Tecla Guerra de Guerra, and the family line of her brother Diodoro Vidal Guerra.

Maria Tomasa Guerra (+73.) (Juan Manuel[6], José Francisco Antonio[5], Antonio[4] Guerra-Cañamar, Ignacio[3] Guerra-Cañamar, Antonio[2] Guerra-Cañamal II, Antonio[1] Guerra-Cañamal) was born on 05 Mar 1780 in Mier, Tamaulipas, Mexico. She died on 02 Jan 1856. She married **José Manuel Guerra**, son of José Antonio Albino Hinojosa Guerra and Maria Rosalia Garcia Salinas, on 26 Jan 1802 in Mier, Tamaulipas, Mexico (Immaculate Conception Church). He was born in 1778 in Mier, Tamaulipas, Mexico. He died on 24 Jun 1833 in Mier, Tamaulipas, Mexico (reportedly killed by Indians).

José Manuel Guerra and Maria Tomasa Guerra had the following child:

+98. i. JOSÉ LINO DE JESUS[8] GUERRA was born on 21 Sep 1802 in Mier, Tamaulipas, Mexico. He died on 23 Apr 1830 (he died before his son Jesus was 3 years old). He married María del Rosario Peña-Ramírez, daughter of José Dionicio Garcia De la Peña and Maria Leonarda Chapa Ramirez, on 20 Jan 1824 in Mier, Tamaulipas, Mexico

(Immaculate Conception Church). She was born on 16 Nov 1804 in Mier, Tamaulipas, Mexico. She died on 04 Dec 1877 in Mier, Tamps, Mexico.

86. JOSÉ DE LOS ANGELES[7] GUERRA-CAÑAMAR (José Antonio Albino Hinojosa[6] Guerra, Joseph Ramon[5] Guerra, Capitan Cristóbal[4] Guerra-Cañamar, Ignacio[3] Guerra-Cañamar, Antonio[2] Guerra-Cañamal II, Antonio[1] Guerra-Cañamal) was born in 1784 in Mier, Tamaulipas, Mexico. He died on 08 Apr 1849 in Mier, Tamaulipas, Mexico. He married (1) **MARIA ROSALIA TIMOTEA HINOJOSA**, daughter of José Gervacio Hinojosa and Maria Teresa Treviño, on 11 Jan 1811 in Mier, Tamaulipas, Mexico (Immaculate Conception Church). She was born on 31 Aug 1788 in Mier, Tamaulipas, Mexico. She died on 29 Nov 1825 in Mier, Tamaulipas, Mexico. He married (2) **MARIA JULIA GUERRA** on 17 Jun 1826 in Mier, Tamaulipas, Mexico (Immaculate Conception Church).

José Angel Guerra, as he was commonly known, was the sixth child of José Antonio Albino Hinojosa Guerra and Maria Rosalia Garcia Salinas, and was the last to use the Cañamar surname. After Mexico gained its independence from Spain in 1821, many Spanish customs, such as double surnames were not considered to be in good taste. (Arteaga & Guerra Jr., 1996, p. 12)

He was married twice, first to Maria Rosalia Timotea Hinojosa, the daughter of Gervacio Hinojosa (original grantee of Mier *Porción 8*) and Maria Teresa Treviño. His second marriage was to Maria Julia Guerra, daughter of Juan Manuel Guerra. Maria Julia was a first cousin to José Angel's first wife, since his wives' mothers, Teresa Maria Treviño and Isabel Maria Treviño, were sisters. They were daughters of Bartolome Treviño and Ana Maria Garcia of Camargo. They were the original grantees of Camargo *Porción C-97*. José de los Angeles had eight known children with his first wife Rosalia Timotea Hinojosa, and an additional seven children with his second wife Maria Julia Guerra.

José de los Angeles Guerra-Cañamar and Maria Rosalia Timotea Hinojosa' youngest child was:
+103.   i.   JOSÉ FELIPE[8] GUERRA-HINOJOSA was born on 09 May 1824 in Mier, Tamaulipas, Mexico. He died in Mar 1891 in Roma, Starr, Texas. He married Maria Josefa Gonzalez on 12 May 1845 in Mier, Tamaulipas, Mexico (Inmaculada Concepcion Church). She was born on 08 Nov 1829 in San Diego, Duval, Texas.

94. JUAN JOSÉ HERMENEGILDO[7] GUERRA (José Alejandro Hinojosa[6], Joseph Ramon[5], Capitan Cristóbal[4] Guerra-Cañamar, Ignacio[3] Guerra-Cañamar, Antonio[2] Guerra-Cañamal II, Antonio[1] Guerra-Cañamal) was born on 22 Apr 1789 in Mier, Tamaulipas, Mexico. He died in 1834 in Texas. He married **Maria Francisca Saenz Hinojosa**, daughter of José Antonio Saenz and Maria Gregoria Hinojosa, on 30 Jan 1811 in Mier, Tamaulipas, Mexico (Immaculate Conception Church). She was born on 26 Jan 1794 in Mier, Tamaulipas, Mexico. She died after 1834 in Mier.

Juan José Hermenegildo Guerra and Maria Francisca Saenz Hinojosa had the following children:
104. i.   ALBINO[8] GUERRA was born on 07 Apr 1815 in Mier, Tamaulipas, Mexico.

105. ii.   MARIA LORENZA GUERRA was born in 1817 in Mier, Tamaulipas, Mexico. She died in Mier, Tamaulipas, Mexico. She married José Jacinto Ramirez on 30 Jul 1834 in Mier, Tamaulipas, Mexico.

106. iii. MARIA DE SAN JUAN GUERRA-SAENZ was born on 18 Apr 1820 in Mier, Tamaulipas, Mexico. She died on 18 Jul 1820 in Mier, Tamaulipas, Mexico.

107. iv.   ISIDORO GUERRA was born in 1824. He died on 23 May 1889 in Mier, Tamaulipas, Mexico (Age 65).

108. v.   ANTONIO SAENZ GUERRA was born on 20 Apr 1824 in Mier, Tamaulipas, Mexico. He died on 11 Apr 1849 in Mier, Tamaulipas, Mexico.

109. vi.   GUILLERMO GUERRA was born on 15 Feb 1828 in Mier, Tamaulipas, Mexico. He died on 24 Jul 1899 in General Treviño, Nuevo León, Mexico. He married RAFAELA OSUNA.

+110. vii. JOSÉ HERCULANO GUERRA was born in Nov 1834 in Mier, Tamaulipas, Mexico. He died about 1921 in Hebbronville, Jim Hogg, Texas. He married Maria Teresa Longoria in 1868. She was born Aug 1852 in Mexico. She died in Nov 1937 in Hebbronville, Jim Hogg, Texas.

Generation 8a - *José Manuel Guerra Branch of Guerra Family*

98. JOSÉ LINO DE JESUS[8] GUERRA (José Manuel[7], José Antonio Albino Hinojosa[6], Joseph Ramon[5], Capitan Cristóbal[4] Guerra-Cañamar, Ignacio[3] Guerra-Cañamar, Antonio[2] Guerra-Cañamal II, Antonio[1] Guerra-Cañamal) was born on 21 Sep 1802 in Mier, Tamaulipas, Mexico. He died on 23 Apr 1830 (he died before his son Jesus was 3 years old). He married **Maria del Rosario Peña-Ramirez**, daughter of José Dionicio Garcia De la Peña and Maria Leonarda Chapa Ramirez, on 20 Jan 1824 in Mier, Tamaulipas, Mexico (Immaculate Conception Church). She was born on 16 Nov 1804 in Mier, Tamaulipas, Mexico. She died on 04 Dec 1877 in Mier, Tamaulipas, Mexico.

José Lino de Jesus Guerra and María del Rosario Peña-Ramírez had the following children:

111. i.   RAFAEL ANTONIO[9] GUERRA was born on 28 Nov 1824 in Mier, Tamaulipas, Mexico. He died on 26 Sep 1825 in Mier.

112. ii.   JUAN DE DIOS GUERRA was born on 25 Sep 1825 in Mier, Tamaulipas, Mexico. He died on 26 Sep 1825 in Mier, Tamaulipas, Mexico (died as an infant).

+113. iii. JESUS MARIA GUERRA was born on 07 May 1827 in Mier, Tamaulipas, Mexico. He died about 1899 in Roma, Starr, Texas (died before grandson Guadalupe born in 1900). He married Maria Andrea Peña, daughter of José Francisco De la Peña and Maria Paula Guadalupe Ramirez, on 06 Feb 1851 in Mier, Tamaulipas, Mexico (Immaculate Conception Church). She was born on 23 Jan 1833 in Mier, Tamaulipas, Mexico. She died in 1906 in Laredo, Webb, Texas.

114. iv.   JOSÉ ELIGIO GUERRA was born on 02 Dec 1829 in Mier, Tamaulipas, Mexico.

115. v.   MARIA DE JESUS GUERRA.

110. JOSÉ HERCULANO[8] GUERRA (Juan José Hermenegildo[7], José Alejandro Hinojosa[6], Joseph Ramon[5], Capitan Cristóbal[4] Guerra-Cañamar, Ignacio[3] Guerra-Cañamar, Antonio[2] Guerra-Cañamal II, Antonio[1] Guerra-Cañamal) was born in Nov 1834 in Mier, Tamaulipas, Mexico.

He died about 1921 in Hebbronville, Jim Hogg, Texas. He married **Maria Teresa Longoria** in 1868. She was born in Aug 1852 in in Mexico. She died in Nov 1937 in Hebbronville, Jim Hogg, Texas.

Right: Maria Teresa Longoria, wife of José Herculano Guerra –photo taken in late 1860s.

José Herculano Guerra and Maria Teresa Longoria had the following children:

128. i.   PAULA[9] GUERRA was born about 1870 in McAllen, Hidalgo, Texas.

129. ii. RAMONA GUERRA was born about 1871 in McAllen, Hidalgo, Texas.

130. iii. COSME GUERRA was born Aug 1873 in Texas.

+131. iv. TECLA GUERRA DE GUERRA was born on 23 Sep 1875 in Roma, Starr, Texas (Rancho Colorado). She died on 27 Oct 1918 in McAllen, Hidalgo, Texas. She married José Antonio Guerra, son of Jesus Maria Guerra and Maria Andrea Peña, on 15 Jun 1892 in Roma, Starr, Texas (Rancho San Antonio Viejo). He was born on 07 Nov 1862 in Mier, Tamaulipas, Mexico. He died on 07 Jan 1919 in McAllen, Hidalgo, Texas.

132. v.   EUGENIO GUERRA was born in Nov 1877 in Texas.

133. vi. MARIA D GUERRA was born on 17 Aug 1880. She died on 15 Jan 1968 in Weslaco, Hidalgo, Texas.

+134. vii. DONACIANO ERNESTO GUERRA was born on 24 May 1885 in Guerra, Jim Hogg, Texas. He died on 11 Aug 1962 in Hebbronville, Jim Hogg, Texas. He married RAFAELA HINOJOSA. She was born on 27 Nov 1889 in Mier, Tamaulipas, Mexico. She died in Mar 1976 in Hebbronville, Jim Hogg, Texas.

135. viii. AGUSTIN GUERRA was born Aug 1888 in Texas.

136. ix. DIONICIO GUERRA was born about 1890 in Texas.

Generation 8b – *José de los Angeles Guerra Branch of Guerra Family*

103. JOSÉ FELIPE[8] GUERRA-HINOJOSA (José de los Angeles[7] Guerra-Cañamar, José Antonio Albino Hinojosa[6] Guerra, Joseph Ramon[5] Guerra, Capitan Cristóbal[4] Guerra-Cañamar, Ignacio[3] Guerra-Cañamar, Antonio[2] Guerra-Cañamal II, Antonio[1] Guerra-Cañamal) was born on 09 May 1824 in Mier, Tamaulipas, Mexico. He died in Mar 1891 in Roma, Starr, Texas. He married **Maria Josefa Gonzalez** on 12 May 1845 in Mier, Tamaulipas, Mexico (Immaculate Conception Church). She was born on 08 Nov 1829 in San Diego, Duval, Texas.

Left: Pioneer Stockman José Felipe Guerra-Hinojosa and his wife María Josefa Gonzalez –from (Salinas, 2018).

José Felipe Guerra-Hinojosa, commonly known as Felipe, was born only three years after Mexican independence. He grew up in Mier and married Josefa Gonzalez in the church there. She was born on the north side of the Rio Grande in what is now Texas, and by 1849 they had moved their family to Roma on the north of the Rio Grande. Felipe soon went into the ranching business becoming a *ranchero* and registering his brand on September 25, 1860. The U.S. 1860 census lists Felipe's occupation as stockraiser with $3,000 in real estate and $2,000 in personal estate. Sources say his herdsman was Jesus Ramirez, and his father-in-law was Don Prudencio Gonzalez, a citizen of Roma and also a stockraiser with $4,000 in real estate and $3,000 in personal estate (Salinas, 2018, p. 2).

Felipe left a legacy of being one of the pioneer stockmen who tamed the harsh brush country of Starr County to make it profitable for himself and for future generations to continue in the ranching business. He began buying *ranchos* and *porciónes* and by 1880 he owned Las Escobas, the second largest ranch in Starr County Texas with 25,000 acres and 980 head of cattle, as well as property in other counties. By 1883 according to the Starr County tax rolls, he owned 641 horses, 1404 cattle, 1800 sheep, 500 goats, and five carriages. His net worth in 1884 was estimated at $60,480.

Since his main ranch at Las Escobas was twenty or so miles north of Roma, Felipe and Josefa started a school for their children and the ranch workers. Ezra B. Houston taught in English and lived at the ranch as a boarder. He was also the 1880 enumerator for Starr County. José Angel Salinas taught in Spanish making the Las Escobas children some of the first in Texas to receive a bilingual education (Salinas, 2018, p. 2).

Right: Old stacked mesquite log corral (corral de leños) *at the original home Ranch of Las Escobas, 17 Apr 2019.*

Some of the *ranchos* that Felipe Guerra had an interest in or owned include:

Las Escobas (*Porciónes* 109, 110, 111), Zapata County –inherited by Maria Emilia Guerra. Sources say this was Felipe's original home ranch. He is buried there in a crypt near the original adobe ranch house that dates back to the 1750's.

Las Cuevitas, Jim Hogg County –inherited by Maria Emeteria Guerra. Sources say this ranch is one of the primitive ranches that predates the José Escondon colonization of the mid-1700s. It was a waystop between San Antonio and the early Spanish settlements in the area. The ranch headquarters was built as a fortress against Indian attacks. The homes, many of which are still standing, were built clustered around a plaza using adobe bricks with thick walls and gun ports for windows.

San Roman, Starr County –inherited by José de Jesus Guerra. Sources say some of the original buildings, corrals, and cisterns are still standing (Arteaga & Guerra Jr., 1996, p. 15).

Las Viboras, Starr County –inherited by José Francisco Guerra.

Charco Largo, Jim Hogg County –inherited by Diodoro Vidal Guerra.

San Antonio Viejo, Jim Hogg County –inherited by Maria Josefa Gonzalez.

José Felipe Guerra-Hinojosa and Maria Josefa Gonzalez had the following children:

123. i.   MARIA EMETERIA[9] GUERRA was born in 1846 in Mier, Tamaulipas, Mexico. She married ANTONIO DE LA GARZA FALCÓN.

124. ii. JOSÉ DE JESUS GUERRA was born in 1849 in Roma, Starr, Texas. He died in 1920. He married Manuela Barrera de Guerra about 1869.

125. iii. MARIA EMILIA GUERRA was born on 23 Aug 1857 in Roma, Starr, Texas. She died on 30 Jun 1923 in Rio Grande City, Starr, Texas. She married José Angel Salinas on 12 Feb 1876 in Roma, Starr, Texas.

126. iv. JOSÉ FRANCISCO GUERRA was born on 19 Dec 1863 in Mier, Tamaulipas, Mexico. He died on 11 Jun 1917. He married Mercedes Peña on 20 Sep 1884 in Roma, Starr, Texas.

+127. v. DIODORO VIDAL GUERRA was born on 03 May 1867 in Cuevitas, Jim Hogg, Texas (Rancho Las Cuevitas). He died on 30 Jun 1932 in McAllen, Hidalgo, Texas. He married Maria Matilde Guerra de Guerra, daughter of Jesus Maria Guerra and Maria Andrea Peña, on 26 May 1885 in Rio Grande City, Starr, Texas (Rancho San Antonio Viejo). She was born on 15 Mar 1867 in Mier, Tamaulipas, Mexico. She died on 15 Aug 1939 in McAllen, Hidalgo, Texas.

Generation 9a – *José Manuel Guerra Branch of Guerra Family*

113. **JESUS MARIA[9] GUERRA** (José Lino de Jesus[8], José Manuel[7], José Antonio Albino Hinojosa[6], Joseph Ramon[5], Capitan Cristóbal[4] Guerra-Cañamar, Ignacio[3] Guerra-Cañamar, Antonio[2] Guerra-Cañamal II, Antonio[1] Guerra-Cañamal) was born on 07 May 1827 in Mier, Tamaulipas, Mexico. He died about 1899 in Roma, Starr, Texas (died before grandson Guadalupe born in 1900). He married **Maria Andrea Peña**, daughter of José Francisco De la Peña and Maria Paula Guadalupe Ramirez, on 06 Feb 1851 in Mier, Tamaulipas, Mexico (Immaculate Conception Church). She was born on 23 Jan 1833 in Mier, Tamaulipas, Mexico. She died in 1906 in Laredo, Webb, Texas.

Jesus was the third of José Lino de Jesus Guerra and María del Rosario Peña-Ramírez' five children. His father died when he was three years old, and it is reported that his grandfather José Manuel Guerra was killed by Indians in June 1833. He was raised in Mier by his mother, aunts and uncles and apparently became a merchant there in the 1850s and 1860s.

Freighting with Wagons pulled by mule and oxen teams
–painting by Wayne Cooper, Courtesy Texas A&M University.

His grandson, Guadalupe Guerra, told me about him once, saying:
"My grandfather had a wagon train, oxens and mules, from Corpus Christi. At that time there was nothing but country roads you know, bringing in especially lumber. He had five or six wagons and he used to ride a horse. . . He used to go from Mier straight on

down to Corpus Christi and back with the wagons. . . They tell me that he was such a strong man that he used to pick up sugar and flour in three or four hundred pound barrels." (Guerra G. , 1978).

But growing up in Mier during this period must have been difficult. In 1836 when Jesus was 9 years old, Texas fought for its independence from Mexico. Then in 1842, when he was 15 years old, the Texans conducted the Mier expedition to punish the Mexican Army for raids in the Republic of Texas, culminating in the Battle of Mier on December 25 and 26. Outnumbered ten to one, the Texans were defeated and the 242 that surrendered were held in a stone building belonging to the Guerra family. Then after the end of the US-Mexican War in 1848, when Jesus was 21 years old, heavy Mexican tariffs on consumer goods caused Mexican towns along the Rio Grande border to wither. Unable to compete, many Mexicans moved north across the border (Diaz, 2015, p. 30).

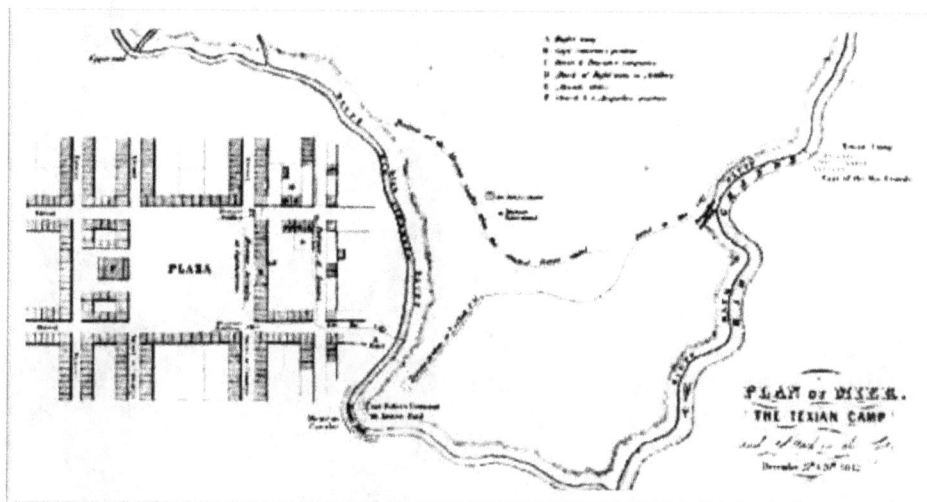

Map of Mier made by the Mier Expedition 1842

In 1851, twenty-four year old Jesus Maria Guerra married eighteen year old Maria Andrea Peña at the Catholic Church in Mier. The Guerra family had claims to land in South Texas that originated in 1767, when José Alejandro Guerra secured two Spanish land grants *(porciónes)* that straddled the Rio Grande. Unlike many Hispanic families with property north of the border, the Guerras did not lose their land to aggressive Anglo ranchers and speculators (Anders, Manuel Guerra, 2010). So after the US Civil War ended in 1865, Jesus Maria Guerra and his wife joined other family members in the vicinity of Rio Grande City in South Texas in the 1870s and became a stockman at Rancho Palangana.

Maria Andrea [8] **Peña (+102.)** (Maria Paula Guadalupe[7] Ramirez, Maria Rita de la[6] Garza Falcón, Maria Candida Francisca[5] Guerra, Antonio[4] Guerra-Cañamar, Ignacio[3] Guerra-Cañamar, Antonio[2] Guerra-Cañamal II, Antonio[1] Guerra-Cañamal) was born on 23 Jan 1833 in Mier, Tamaulipas, Mexico. She died in 1906 in Laredo, Webb, Texas. She married **Jesus Maria Guerra**, son of José Lino de Jesus Guerra and María del Rosario Peña-Ramírez, on 06 Feb 1851 in Mier, Tamaulipas, Mexico (Immaculate Conception Church). He was born on 07 May 1827 in Mier, Tamaulipas, Mexico. He died about 1899 in Roma, Starr, Texas.

Maria Andrea Peña was baptized on 03 Dec 1833 in Mier, Tamaulipas, Mexico. She lived in Mier, Tamaulipas, Mexico in 1850. She lived in Rio Grande City, Starr, Texas in 1870 (Rancho Palangana). (Age 60; cannot write: Y). She arrived in Roma in 1876. She lived in Precinct 3 and 4, Starr, Texas in 1880. (Age 40; Marital Status: Married; Relation to Head of House: Wife). She lived in Justice Precinct 4, Starr, Texas in 1900 (Age 65; Marital Status: Widowed; Relation to Head of House: Mother-in-law).

Right: Undated photo of Maria Andrea Peña, wife of Jesus Maria Guerra –from Fidencio Guerra Collection.

Jesus Maria Guerra and Maria Andrea Peña had the following children:

116. i.   MARIA GABINA DE JESUS[10] GUERRA was born on 22 Feb 1852 in Mier, Tamaulipas, Mexico. She died on 25 Jun 1853 in Mier, Tamaulipas, Mexico.

117. ii.   MARIA DEL REFUGIO PEÑA GUERRA was born on 11 Jul 1854 in Mier, Tamaulipas, Mexico. She married José de los Santos Lopez on 22 Sep 1871 in Rancho San Antonio Viejo, Starr, Texas. He was born in 1852 in Mier, Tamaulipas, Mexico.

118. iii. MARIA ADELAIDA GUERRA was born in 1857 in Mier, Tamaulipas, Mexico. She died in 1916. She married Florentino Bedinghaus in 1889 in Starr, Texas. He was born in 1854.

119. iv.   MARIA CONCEPCION GUERRA was born on 29 Dec 1859 in Mier, Tamaulipas, Mexico. She married Jesus Peña on 03 Sep 1879 in Rio Grande City, Starr, Texas. He was born in Feb 1855 in Mier, Tamaulipas, Mexico. He died on 08 Jan 1939.

+120. v.   JOSÉ ANTONIO GUERRA was born on 07 Nov 1862 in Mier, Tamaulipas, Mexico. He died on 07 Jan 1919 in McAllen, Hidalgo, Texas. He married Tecla Guerra de Guerra, daughter of José Herculano Guerra and Maria Teresa Longoria, on 15 Jun 1892 in Roma, Starr, Texas (Rancho San Antonio Viejo). She was born on 23 Sep 1875 in Roma, Starr, Texas (Rancho Colorado). She died on 27 Oct 1918 in McAllen, Hidalgo, Texas.

+121. vi. MARIA MATILDE GUERRA DE GUERRA was born on 15 Mar 1867 in Mier, Tamaulipas, Mexico. She died on 15 Aug 1939 in McAllen, Hidalgo, Texas (Age 72). She married Diodoro Vidal Guerra, son of José Felipe Guerra-Hinojosa and Maria Josefa Gonzalez, on 26 May 1885 in Rio Grande City, Starr, Texas (Rancho San Antonio Viejo). He was born on 03 May 1867 in Cuevitas, Hidalgo, Texas (Rancho Las Escobas). He died on 30 Jun 1932 in McAllen, Hidalgo,

Texas.

122. vii. JESUS MARIA GUERRA JR. was born on 26 Oct 1872 in Mier, Tamaulipas, Mexico. He died on 23 Oct 1952 in Laredo, Webb, Texas (Jackson Funeral Home). He married Manuela Cruz, daughter of Bartolo Cruz and Juanita Garcia, in 1902 in Zapata County, Texas. She was born on 20 May 1883 in Guerrero, Tamaulipas, Mexico. She died on 27 Jan 1970 in Laredo, Webb, Texas.

Generation 9b - *José de los Angeles Guerra Branch of Guerra Family*

127. DIODORO VIDAL[9] GUERRA (José Felipe[8] Guerra-Hinojosa, José de los Angeles[7] Guerra-Cañamar, José Antonio Albino Hinojosa[6], Joseph Ramon[5], Capitan Cristóbal[4] Guerra-Cañamar, Ignacio[3] Guerra-Cañamar, Antonio[2] Guerra-Cañamal II, Antonio[1] Guerra-Cañamal) was born on 03 May 1867 in Jim Hogg, Texas (Rancho Las Cuevitas). He died on 30 Jun 1932 in McAllen, Hidalgo, Texas. He married **Maria Matilde Guerra de Guerra**, daughter of Jesus Maria Guerra and Maria Andrea Peña, on 26 May 1885 in Rio Grande City, Starr, Texas (Rancho San Antonio Viejo). She was born on 15 Mar 1867 in Mier, Tamaulipas, Mexico. She died on 15 Aug 1939 in McAllen, Hidalgo, Texas.

Diodoro, the youngest of the three sons of pioneer stockman Felipe Guerra, was born and grew up on Rancho Las Cuevitas, north of Roma, Texas. He learned the ranching business from his father and later became a prominent merchant and public official and one of the most influential Hispanics of the Rio Grande River Valley. Diodoro married José Antonio Guerra's sister Matilde in 1885.

In 1906 he was elected Starr County Sheriff as a Democrat and served in Rio Grande City until 1912. However in January 1907, as newly elected sheriff he was involved in a gunfight that killed Republican organizer and customs inspector, Gregorio Duffy. Under pressure from Republican prosecutors, a federal grand jury indicted Diodoro and his cousin Manuel Guerra, two deputies, and a Texas Ranger for conspiring to murder a federal official, but all the defendants eventually won acquittals (Anders, Boss Rule in South Texas: The Progressive Era, 1982).

Meanwhile two of his sons, Enrique and Modesto, left Roma to start "Guerra & Guerra," the first wholesale mercantile company in McAllen. After his term as Sheriff, Diodoro moved his family to McAllen to work with his sons, re-naming their business "D. Guerra & Sons."

Sources say Diodoro (or Deodoro as his name was later spelled) was a gambler and lost a major portion of the property he inherited from his father, but he and his sons were able to re-establish some of the family holdings and by 1936 "D. Guerra & Sons owned several large ranches and ranch headquarters, cotton gins, and 35,000 acres of land and 3,000 cattle (Brownsville Herald, 1936).

Diodoro's first cousin was Manuel Guerra (1856-1915), son of Jesús Guerra-Barrera. He was a banker, rancher, and Democratic leader in Starr County politics. In 1884 he founded one of the first general stores in Roma. The building was used until 1956 and still stands as part of the Roma National Historic Landmark.

Maria Matilde Guerra de[10] Guerra (+121.) (Jesus Maria[9], José Lino de Jesus[8], José Manuel[7], José Antonio Albino Hinojosa[6], Joseph Ramon[5], Capitan Cristóbal[4] Guerra-Cañamar, Ignacio[3] Guerra-Cañamar, Antonio[2] Guerra-Cañamal II, Antonio[1] Guerra-Cañamal) was born on 15 Mar 1867 in Mier, Tamaulipas, Mexico. She died on 15 Aug 1939 in McAllen, Hidalgo, Texas. She married **Diodoro Vidal Guerra**, son of José Felipe Guerra-Hinojosa and Maria Josefa Gonzalez, on 26 May 1885 in Rio Grande City, Starr, Texas (Rancho San Antonio Viejo). He was born on 03 May 1867 in Cuevitas, Hidalgo, Texas (Rancho Las Escobas). He died on 30 Jun 1932 in McAllen, Hidalgo, Texas.

Maria Matilde Guerra de Guerra was baptized in March 1867 in Mier, Tamaulipas, Mexico. She arrived in Roma, Starr, Texas in 1868. She lived at Rancho Las Escobas, Rio Grande, Starr, Texas in 1870 (Age 4; Father Foreign Birth: Y; Mother Foreign Birth: Y). She lived in Precinct 3 and 4, Starr, Texas in 1880 (Marital Status: Single; Relation to Head of House: Daughter). She lived in McAllen, Hidalgo, Texas in 1906. She lived in McAllen, Hidalgo, Texas on 15 Sep 1920 (Street Address: 17th Ave; Age 53; Able To Speak English: No; Can Read: Yes; Can Write: Yes; Enumeration District: 77; Language Spoken: Spanish; Naturalization Status: Naturalized; Relation To Head of House: Wife; Marital Status: Married). She lived in McAllen, Hidalgo, Texas in 1930. She was buried on 16 Aug 1939 in Roma, Starr, Texas [Roma City Cemetery, East Grant (Hwy 83) and North Gladiator St; Find A Grave #199518284]. She was also known as Matilde Guerra y Peña. Her cause of death was Cerebral Embolism (brain bleed or blood clot in the brain).

A frame building housed D. Guerra & Sons, the first wholesale mercantile business in McAllen. It was replaced in 1912 by this masonry one located at the SW corner of Austin and Guerra (now 17th) Street –from (American Studies Class, 1975).

Cousin Manuel Guerra's General Store in Roma, built in 1884 of hand-cast brick and designed by German Architect Heinrich Portscheller, 14 Jan 2019.

Diodoro Vidal Guerra and Maria Matilde Guerra de Guerra had the following children:

146. i. ENRIQUE EPIGMENIO[1] GUERRA was born on 24 Mar 1886 in Rio Grande City, Starr, Texas (Rancho San Antonio Viejo). He died on 23 May 1935 in McAllen, Hidalgo, Texas (heart attack).

147. ii. MODESTO PABLO GUERRA was born on 23 Jan 1888 in Texas. He died on 17 Nov 1927 in San Antonio, Bexar County, Texas.

148. iii. JOSÉ ASUNCION GUERRA was born on 15 Aug 1893 in Rio Grande City, Starr, Texas. He died on 13 Jun 1939 in Edinburg, Hidalgo, Texas. He married Celia Treviño in 1916 in Starr, Texas. She was born on 14 Feb 1897. She died on 05 Mar 1975.

149. iv. RAMON PEDRO GUERRA was born on 29 Apr 1897 in Rio Grande City, Starr, Texas (Rancho San Antonio Viejo). He died on 13 Jun 1981 in McAllen, Hidalgo, Texas. He married Basilia Gonzalez on 09 May 1915 in McAllen, Hidalgo, Texas. She was born in 1898. She died in 1989.

150. v. VIRGINIA GUERRA was born on 16 Nov 1899 in Roma, Starr, Texas. She died on 24 Dec 1954 in San Antonio, Bexar County, Texas (heart attack).

151. vi. GUILLERMO DAVID GUERRA was born on 09 Jan 1902 in Rio Grande City, Starr, Texas (Rancho San Antonio Viejo). He died on 28 Apr 1976 in McAllen, Hidalgo, Texas.

152. vii. DARIO VIDAL GUERRA was born on 28 Apr 1904. He died on 15 Jan 1998 in Edinburg, Hidalgo, Texas.

153. viii. AURORA GUERRA was born on 22 Jul 1907 in McAllen, Hidalgo, Texas. She died on 01 Jan 1992 in San Antonio, Bexar County, Texas.

Maria Matilde Guerra and Diodoro Vidal Guerra –from (Arteaga & Guerra Jr., 1996).

After the Battle of Mier on Christmas Day 1842, this stone building owned by the Guerra family in Mier, Tamaulipas, Mexico, was used to house some of the 242 Texans that were taken prisoner. It is now a museum, 13 Jan 2019.

Chapter 2. José Antonio Guerra and Tecla Guerra

1. JOSÉ ANTONIO[10] **GUERRA** (Jesus Maria[9], José Lino de Jesus[8], José Manuel[7], José Antonio Albino Hinojosa[6], Joseph Ramon[5], Capitan Cristóbal[4] Guerra-Cañamar, Ignacio[3] Guerra-Cañamar, Antonio[2] Guerra-Cañamal II, Antonio[1] Guerra-Cañamal) was born on 07 Nov 1862 in Mier, Tamaulipas, Mexico as the fifth child of Jesus Maria Guerra and Maria Andrea Peña. He had six siblings, namely: Maria Gabina de Jesus, Maria del Refugio Peña, Maria Adelaida, Maria Concepcion, Maria Matilde Guerra, and Jesus Maria Jr. He died on 07 Jan 1919 in McAllen, Hidalgo, Texas (Age 56). When he was 29, he married **Tecla Guerra de Guerra**, daughter of José Herculano Guerra and Maria Teresa Longoria, on 15 Jun 1892 in Roma, Starr, Texas (Rancho San Antonio Viejo).

The only photo known to exist of Tecla Guerra de Guerra and
José Antonio Guerra, taken about 1892 –from Leonardo Guerra Jr. Collection.

José Antonio Guerra was baptized on 15 Nov 1862 in Mier, Tamaulipas, Mexico (Immaculate Conception Church). He lived in Rio Grande City, Starr, Texas in 1870 (Rancho Las Escobas; Age: 4; Father Foreign Birth: Y; Mother Foreign Birth: Y). He lived in Roma, Starr, Texas in 1876. He lived in Precinct 3 and 4, Starr, Texas in 1880 (Age 16; Occupation: No Occupation; Enumeration District: 157; Marital Status: Single; Relation to Head of House: Son). He lived in Justice Precinct 4 El Salineno, Starr, Texas in 1900 (Marital Status: Married; Relation to Head of House: Head). He lived in Justice Precinct 4, Starr, Texas in 1910. He was buried in 1919 in McAllen, Hidalgo, Texas (La Piedad Cemetery Sec B2 Line 16 Space 33 Find A Grave #197162561). He was also known as Antonio Guerra. His cause of death was the 1918 Spanish Flu epidemic. Race: (White) (Mexican).

We do not have many stories about Antonio or Tecla, possibly because they both died during the influenza epidemic when most of their nine children were still quite young. Antonio was born and baptized in Mier, Mexico in the Immaculate Conception Catholic Church where his parents Jesus and Maria were both baptized and later married. In his Mexican War Journal entry for Tuesday Dec 8, 1846 Captain Franklin Smith described this church as well as some of the residents of Mier, "The church is a fine Spanish building elegantly decorated and adorned with many paintings, statues, and gold leaf or gilding of some sort. The prettiest women I ever saw in Mexico I saw in this church piously kneeling on the stone floor" (Chance, 1991, p. 131).

1874 view of the Immaculate Conception Catholic Church in Mier's Main Plaza.

Left: 2019 view of the Immaculate Conception Catholic Church, 25 Apr 2019.

By 1870, however, Antonio's family had moved north across the border to Texas to live and work on their Cousin José Felipe Guerra-Hinojosa's Las Escobas Ranch about twenty-two miles north of Roma. "The famous thing with Mier my dad would tell the story, the wooden wheel fell off the cart, half of the people jumped off the cart and went south and half of them went north" (Guerra F. J., Fidencio Guerra Jr. Family History Video Interview, 2019). Soon they moved further north to Rancho El Colorado where Antonio's future wife Tecla was born in 1875. It is possible that they built their own indigenous housing at that time, known locally as the *Jacal* (Hakal). Many working families lacked the finances and access to materials for wooden houses, so they built houses made of entirely local materials: mesquite wood for the framework, rock and adobe for the walls, and thatched roofs.

Early portrait of a family in a Jacal in the Rio Grande Valley
–photo by Joe Stanley Graham, Courtesy Texas A&M University.

Today the *Rancho* is known as the town of Guerra on Ranch Road 649 forty-five miles south of Hebbronville in southwestern Jim Hogg County. There was no permanent settlement until the late 1800s, when landowner Antonio Guerra established the community. Early Mexican settlers called the town El Colorado, because of the red cattle raised in the area. The Guerra post office, which was still in service in 1990, was founded in 1906, with Don Apolonio Gomez as the first postmaster (Hebbronville, 1963). The post office was reportedly transferred to the community from Rancho San Antonio Viejo. According to Antonio Guerra's son Guadalupe, "My dad got the post office there in 1906. I was six years old when he requested the post office, and it's still there where I was born. . . We left there in 1913." (Guerra G. , 1978).

Right: US Post office, Guerra, Texas. It was established in 1906 and was in service until at least 1990 when the town boasted a population of only fifteen. A nearby welcome sign boasts Guerra as the smallest town in Texas, 16 Jan 2019.

Antonio was a farmer and merchant like his father Jesus according to his son Guadalupe, "Dad had mules. He had a little patch of about thirty-five, forty acres. He always had a man to farm it for him, especially for corn" (Guerra G. , 1978). In 1914 Guerra had 100 residents and sixteen businesses, including Guerra's general store, a blacksmith, a railroad agent, and a number of livestock establishments. The community reported a population of fifty from 1920 to the mid-1960s and seventy-five in 1968. In 1990 Guerra reported a population of fifteen and served as a retail point for nearby cattle ranchers (Elmore, 2010). By 2019 a welcome sign advertised Guerra as the smallest town in Texas.

Antonio and Tecla's four oldest children were born in Guerra at Rancho El Colorado and passed on a few stories told to them about the ranch and the Guerra Mercantile Store. Fidencio's daughter Judy Guerra remembers some of the family folklore including "the *Kukui* is going to get you. . . They call it the *Kukui,* like the boogie man." Also there was "*Laerona,* a lady that crossed the border with her baby, and her baby died. . . So you hear sometimes at night the woman wailing." Mary Guerra remembers, "Daddy (Guadalupe) says about the crying lady . . . that his father (Antonio) went out with the hired hands and what they found were willow branches that in the wind were rubbing together and making the sounds . . . and he proved it wasn't a ghost" (Guerra J. , 2019).

Guadalupe's daughter Mary Guerra also heard that one time, "Daddy was in the store . . . he said he was hiding behind the counter when a Texas Ranger came in, and a bad guy, and they had a shoot-out in the store and he was hiding and looking around the corner at them shooting at each other. And they shot the whole place up; and I asked, 'Did they kill each other?' and Daddy replied, 'Oh no, they were not that good with a pistol.' " Mary Guerra also was told by her father that, "Pancho Villa's men bought all of his supplies through grandpa's store in Guerra, Texas. That's what kept the family solvent; and gave the supplies to the army. Daddy remembers seeing Pancho Villa and the men coming in and getting the supplies. He told my sister and me stories about them all the time" (Guerra J. , 2019).

Left: Pancho Villa mural on building on Calle Allende in the village of Mier, Mexico, 13 Jan 2019.

But in 1913 Antonio and Tecla sold their general store and moved to McAllen. "My Father owned a general store in Guerra, Texas and started one in McAllen," (Guerra, G, 1978). We do not know if he left to help his cousins, nephews, or brother-in-law Diodoro with their mercantile business, or just wanted to take advantage of opportunities in the new and growing community of McAllen, but he spent the remaining five years of his life in McAllen managing his own mercantile store. In 1918 the Spanish flu epidemic swept the country and took Antonio's wife Tecla, then two months later Antonio himself, leaving behind eight orphan children. In the words of Antonio's second son Guadalupe, "When she (Tecla) died he just took it too hard. . . They lived together a good many years and I don't think Dad was ever away more than three or four days from home. . . Nothing could save him. There was three doctors in there trying to save him" (Guerra G. , 1978).

Tecla [9] Guerra de Guerra (+131.) (José Herculano[8] Guerra, Juan José Hermenegildo[7] Guerra,

José Alejandro Hinojosa[6] Guerra, Joseph Ramon[5] Guerra, Capitan Cristóbal[4] Guerra-Cañamar, Ignacio[3] Guerra-Cañamar, Antonio[2] Guerra-Cañamal II, Antonio[1] Guerra-Cañamal) was born on 23 Sep 1875 in Roma, Starr, Texas (Rancho El Colorado) as the fourth child of José Herculano Guerra and Maria Teresa Longoria. She had eight siblings, namely: Paula, Ramona, Cosme, Eugenio, Maria D, Donaciano Ernesto, Agustin, and Dionicio. She died on 27 Oct 1918 in McAllen, Hidalgo, Texas (Age 45). When she was 16, she married José Antonio Guerra, son of Jesus Maria Guerra and Maria Andrea Peña, on 15 Jun 1892 in Roma, Starr, Texas (Rancho San Antonio Viejo).

Tecla Guerra de Guerra lived in Precinct 3 and 4, Starr, Texas in 1880 (Marital status: Single Relation to Head of House: Daughter). She lived in Justice Precinct 4, Starr, Texas in 1900 (Marital Status: Married; Relation to Head of House: Wife). She lived in Roma, Starr, Texas in 1903 (Rancho La Presita). She lived in Jim Hogg, Texas on 07 Aug 1909 (Rancho San Miguel). She lived in Justice Precinct 4, Starr, Texas in 1910 (Marital Status: Married; Relation to Head of House: Wife). She was buried in 1918 in McAllen, Hidalgo, Texas (La Piedad Cemetery Sec B2 Line 16 Space 33 Find A Grave #197162984). She was also known as Teclita. Her cause of death was the 1918 Spanish flu epidemic. Race: (White)

Above: Mary Guerra at the graves of Antonio and Tecla Guerra, buried together at La Piedad Cemetery, McAllen's first cemetery, 11 Jan 2019.

By the year 1875 when Tecla Guerra was born at Rancho El Colorado, Texas had been a state for 26 years and thus unlike Antonio, she was an American citizen at birth. She was the third of nine children of José Herculano Guerra and Maria Teresa Longoria. Tecla's and Antonio's families were both from the town of Mier, Mexico and they shared the same third great grandfather, Joseph Ramon Guerra, who himself married his own third cousin. It is likely that Tecla became the family matriarch after she married. According to her grandson, "My father (Abel) would say that my grandmother (Tecla) was very smart, a go-getter. He said my grandfather was more quiet. The strong personality was hers... Even though she was very short, she was very strong" (Guerra F., 2019). Unfortunately she was the first of the parents to succumb to the Spanish flu epidemic, "My mother died in 1918 . . . double pneumonia . . . Asian flu; and then dad died two months after" (Guerra G., 1978).

José Antonio Guerra and Tecla Guerra de Guerra had the following children:

+2. i.   TERESA[11] GUERRA was born on 15 Oct 1893 in Roma, Starr, Texas (Rancho Colorado). She died on 02 Apr 1990 in Naucalpan de Juárez, Mexico (Age 96). She married Jacobo Garza-Hinojosa on 17 Mar 1921 in McAllen, Hidalgo, Texas (Sacred Heart Church). He was born on 22 Jul 1894 in China, Nuevo León, Mexico. He died on 03 Mar 1957 in McAllen, Hidalgo, Texas (201 W Guerra St).

+3. ii. ABEL EULALIO GUERRA was born on 12 Feb 1896 in Roma, Starr, Texas (Rancho Colorado). He died on 28 Sep 1983 in Conroe, Montgomery, Texas (Age 87), (Ashes scattered near Florencio Guerra home in Conroe). He married Ciria Luz Portilla-Martinez on 28 Jan 1945 in Mexico City, Mexico. She was born on 05 Jun 1918 in Camaguey, Cuba. She died on 01 Jan 1981 in Mexico City, Mexico

4.   iii. VICTORIA GUERRA was born on 24 Mar 1898 in Roma, Starr, Texas (Rancho Colorado). She died on 18 Sep 1978 in Rio Grande City, Starr, Texas (Age 80). She married (1) BERNARDO DE LA GARZA JR., son of Ygnacio De la Garza and Rurara Martinez, on 20 Feb 1925 in McAllen, Hidalgo, Texas. He was born on 03 Jul 1895 in Randado, Texas. He died on 15 Feb 1927 in Laredo, Webb, Texas (Age 31). She married (2) RUBEN GABRIEL VALLE, son of Calixto Cedric Valle and Herminia L. Longoria, on 09 Sep 1939 in Saltillo, Coahuila de Zaragoza, Mexico. He was born on 01 Oct 1900 in Rio Grande City, Texas. He died on 06 Jun 1991 (Age 90).

+5. iv. GUADALUPE FILIBERTO GUERRA was born on 16 Mar 1900 in Roma, Starr, Texas (Rancho Colorado). He died on 27 Dec 1982 in Boise, Ada, Idaho (Age 82). He married Nettie Lavonne Taylor, daughter of Richard Thomas Taylor and Roxie Ann Gibbs, on 18 Apr 1945 in Boise, Ada, Idaho (First Christian Church). She was born on 03 Feb 1915 in Okemah, Okfuskee, Oklahoma. She died on 28 Apr 2002 in Boise, Ada, Idaho (Age 87).

6.   v.   MARGARITA GUERRA was born in 1902 in Cuevitas, Hidalgo, Texas (Rancho La Presita). She died in 1905 in Cuevitas, Hidalgo, Texas (died as an infant at Age 3).

7.   vi. MARIA FLORINDA GUERRA was born on 07 Sep 1903 in Cuevitas, Hidalgo, Texas (Rancho La Presita). She died on 08 Jun 1934 in McAllen, Hidalgo, Texas (Age 30).

8.   vii. HERLINDA GUERRA was born on 12 Mar 1906 in Roma, Starr, Texas (Rancho La Presita). She died on 10 Sep 1989 in Edinburg, Hidalgo, Texas (Age 83); (donated body to University of Texas). She married Elmer Libby Babb on 05 Mar 1943 in McAllen, Hidalgo, Texas (home of Fidencio Guerra). He was born on 30 Jun 1905 in East Lebanon, Maine. He died on 05 Apr 1969 in San Francisco, California (Age 64).

+9. viii. FIDENCIO MIGUEL GUERRA was born on 06 Aug 1909 in Jim Hogg, Texas (Rancho San Miguel). He died on 12 Dec 2004 in McAllen, Hidalgo, Texas (Age 95). He married Estela Guadalupe Margo, daughter of Ruperto Reymundo Margo and Sofia Clarke, on 30 Jan 1941 in Rio Grande City, Starr, Texas. She was born on 15 Aug 1911 in Rio Grande City, Starr, Texas. She died on 29 Jul 1999 in McAllen, Hidalgo, Texas (Age 87).

+10. ix. EVANGELINA GUERRA was born on 30 Mar 1912 in Jim Hogg, Texas (Rancho San Miguel). She died on 13 Jul 1996 in Edinburg, Hidalgo, Texas (Age 84). She married Leonardo Guerra, son of Juan Nepomuceno Guerra and Carlota Vela

Villarreal, on 01 Dec 1943 in San Manuel, Hidalgo, Texas. He was born on 17 Aug 1910 in San Manuel, Hidalgo, Texas (Rancho La Reforma). He died on 02 Apr 2000 in Edinburg, Hidalgo, Texas (smoke inhalation from house fire).

A separate chapter is written for each of José Antonio's children that lived to be adults.

The remains of a plastered adobe house in Guerra, Texas, 17 Apr 2019.

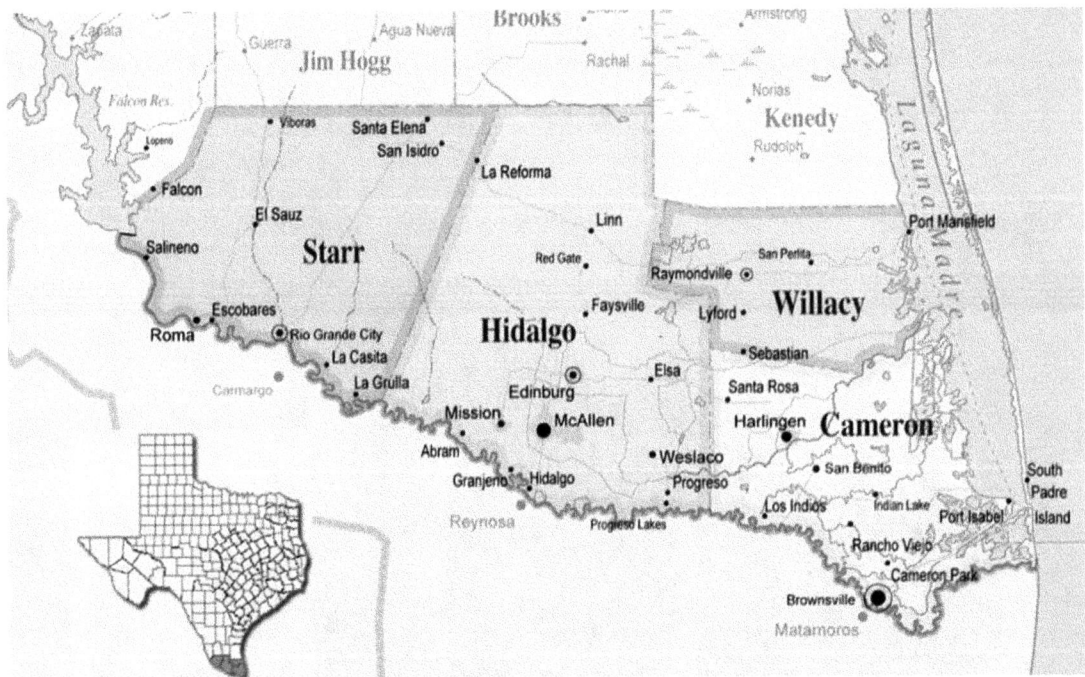

Map of the Rio Grande Valley, Texas. The town of Guerra is shown in the upper left.

Chapter 3. Teresa Guerra and Jacobo Garza

Jacobo y Tere

Generation 1

1. TERESA[I] **GUERRA** (José Antonio[A], Jesus Maria[B], José Lino de Jesus[C], José Manuel[D], José Antonio Albino Hinojosa[E], Joseph Ramon[F], Capitan Cristóbal[G] Guerra-Cañamar, Ignacio[H] Guerra-Cañamar, Antonio[I] Guerra-Cañamal II, Antonio[J] Guerra-Cañamal) was born on 15 Oct 1893 in Roma, Starr, Texas (Rancho El Colorado) as the first child of José Antonio Guerra and Tecla Guerra de Guerra). She had eight siblings, namely: Abel Eulalio, Victoria, Guadalupe Filiberto, Margarita, Maria Florinda, Herlinda, Fidencio Miguel, and Evangelina. She died on 02 Apr 1990 in Naucalpan de Juárez, Mexico, Mexico (Age 96). When she was 27, she married **Jacobo Garza-Hinojosa,** son of Matias Garza-Cantu and Isidra Hinojosa, on 17 Mar 1921 in McAllen, Hidalgo, Texas (Sacred Heart Church).

Teresa Guerra lived in Justice Precinct 4, Starr, Texas in 1900 (Marital Status: Single; Relation to Head of House: Daughter). She lived in Justice Precinct 4, Starr, Texas in 1910 (Marital Status: Single; Relation to Head of House: Daughter). She lived in McAllen, Hidalgo, Texas on 27 Jul 1925. She lived in McAllen, Hidalgo, Texas in 1930 (Street Address: 11th Ave.; Age 36; Able To Speak English: Yes; Attended School: No; Can Read/Write: Yes; Enumeration District: 0023; Homemaker: Yes; Registration District: 23; Marital Status: Married; Relation To Head of House: Wife). She arrived in McAllen, Hidalgo, Texas on 06 Jul 1935. She lived in McAllen, Hidalgo, Texas in 1956. She lived in Saltillo, Coahuila de Zaragoza, Mexico in 1973 (living with daughter Alma who was ill with cancer). She lived in Naucalpan de Juárez, Mexico in 1981 (living with daughter Gloria). She was buried on 03 Apr 1990 in Mexico City, Mexico (Panteon Americano; Fosa-1580, Clase-A, Secc-New, Lote-T). She was also known as *Tia* Tere. Race: (White) Race: (Mexican)

Right: Garza family in 1944, front: Leonel, Gloria, Alma; back: Teresa Guerra and Jacobo Garza –photo from Gloria Garza Collection.

Teresa, or Tere as she was called, was Antonio and Tecla's first child and grew up on Rancho El Colorado. According to Tere's youngest daughter Gloria, "My mother never spoke English. . . because her parents Tecla and Antonio they didn't speak English either." Since she was the oldest child she must have learned to cook, sew, clean, and help her mother to raise her eight siblings on the *ranchos.* Her daughter remembered, "My mother used to be a very good cook.

. . She made good *cabrito* (baby goat)" (Garza G. , 2019). The family moved to McAllen, Texas in 1913 when Tere was twenty years old.

After moving to McAllen, Tere got her first job, possibly working as a shopkeeper, but within five years her parents had both died during the 1918 Spanish flu epidemic. So once again, this time with her younger brother Guadalupe, she helped raise the now orphaned family. Daughter Gloria said Teresa's first boyfriend was a cousin, Juan Guerra, but then she met Jacobo Garza and by 1921 they were married. The family's three children were born in McAllen, Texas. Jacobo was doing well as a businessman and entrepreneur, managing gas stations, theatres and other enterprises. But by the mid-1930s the Great Depression had wiped out Jacobo's enterprises, and Tere began suffering from what Gloria called "hay fever" which was probably emphysema or pulmonary fibrosis. So the family was advised to move to a higher, dryer climate.

Left: Portrait of Gloria Garza and Teresa Guerra in 1935 –photo from Gloria Garza Collection.

By 1936 Jacobo had studied to become an accountant in McAllen, working at one point for Pearl Beer Company. He loved his job and they did not want to move far so he could continue working. But where? Gloria remembered, "When I was two years old my mother came to Saltillo . . . because of health. She was suffering from hay fever. At that time there were no antihistamines and the doctor told my father, 'You need to move to a higher place.' So let's move to Mexico. . . Monterrey is still too low (500 meters). The next town is Saltillo (1500 meters) and they said, 'Okay Saltillo. . . So my mother brought the three children, Leonel, Alma, and myself very little . . . and my father used to come about every fifteen days driving (five hours) from McAllen to Saltillo on the weekends . . . and saw us and saw my mother and went back to McAllen. . . He never did move to Mexico" (Garza G. , 2019).

Jacobo Garza-Hinojosa was born on 21 Jul 1890 in the northern Mexican mining town of China, Nuevo León, as the adopted son and only child of Matias Garza-Cantu and Isidra Hinojosa. He died on 03 Mar 1957 in McAllen, Hidalgo, Texas (Age 62). When he was 30, he married Teresa Guerra, daughter of José Antonio Guerra and Tecla Guerra de Guerra, on 17 Mar 1921 in McAllen, Hidalgo, Texas (Sacred Heart Church).

Right: Portrait of Jacobo Garza in about 1929 when he was 39 years old –photo from Gloria Garza Collection.

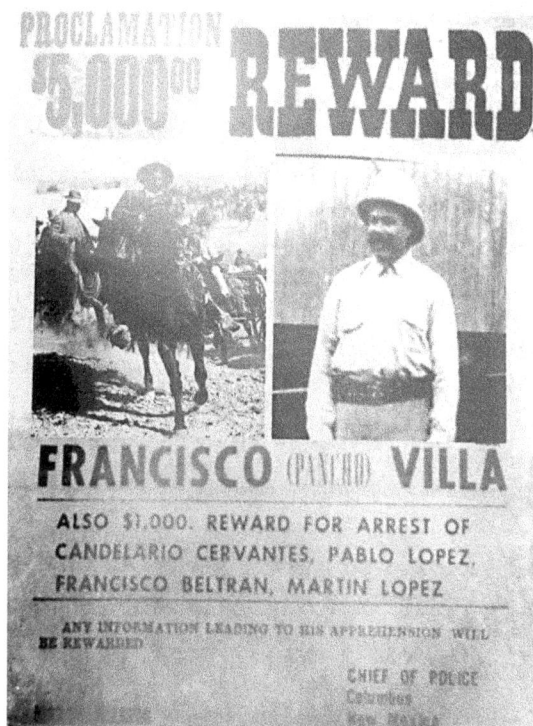

Left: Pancho Villa was wanted in the USA for cross-border raids in New Mexico and Texas.

In 1914 he sailed to Cuba with his family to get to Texas to avoid the Mexican Revolution (Age 24). He lived in McAllen, Hidalgo, Texas in 1920 (Street Address: 17 Street; Age 30; Occupation: Merchant; Able To Speak English: No; Can Read: Yes; Can Write: Yes; Enumeration District: 77; Industry: Retail Store; Is Employed: Own Account; Language Spoken: Spanish; Naturalization Status: Alien; Relation To Head of House: Adopted Son; Marital Status: Single). He arrived in Hidalgo, Texas on 27 May 1920 (Age 26). He lived in McAllen, Hidalgo, Texas in 1930 (Street Address: 11th Ave.; Age 38; Able To Speak English: Yes; Attended School: No; Can Read/Write: Yes; Class of Worker: Wage or salary worker; Enumeration District: 0023; Home Ownership: Owned; Is Employed: Yes; Language Spoken: Spanish; Naturalization Status: Alien; Owned Radio: No; Registration District: 23; Value Of Home: 4000; Marital Status: Married; Relation to Head of House: Head; Occupation: Manager). He arrived in Hidalgo, Texas on 18 Aug 1933 (Age 43). He was buried on 03 Mar 1957 in McAllen, Hidalgo, Texas (La Piedad Cemetery Sec B2 Line 16 Space 35; Find A Grave #197163566). His cause of death was coronary thrombosis due to congestive heart failure. Race: (Mexican).

In 1910 the Mexican Revolution was launched by Francisco Madero just across the border from Laredo, Texas, plunging Mexico into years of civil war that ravaged the country. The dictator Diaz was deposed, then Madero himself was assassinated by the military. During 1913-14 in a second period of civil war, Pancho Villa's troops ravaged northern Mexico and destroyed the regular army. The Garza family in China, Nuevo León was desperate to cross the border to escape the war. Finally twenty-four year old Jacobo and his parents managed to sail to Cuba, then to Florida where they made their way back to Texas, settling in McAllen where he met his future wife Teresa Guerra.

Jacobo managed several businesses in McAllen during the 1920s and did very well. Then came the Great Depression and his enterprises were wiped out. But Jacobo loved numbers and learned the trade of accounting, which served him well for many years. However, family health issues kept him apart from his wife Teresa and their three children for long periods of time. As his nephew Daniel Guerra, MD describes, "That's why they moved to Saltillo, because of the climate. . . It was a little higher, cleaner air, it was easier for them to breathe. That's how that branch of the family ended up in Mexico; because Gloria and Alma were born in McAllen, and so was Leonel" (Guerra D. , 2019). Jacobo became a respected member of the Guerra family and when he died he was buried next to Teresa's parents in La Piedad Cemetery in McAllen. According to Guadalupe Guerra's daughter Mary, "Daddy was really close to her husband

(Jacobo), because when he died I had told Dave this was the first time I ever saw my father cry. . . He really admired that man and they were really close" (Guerra D. , 2019).

Jacobo Garza-Hinojosa and Teresa Guerra had the following children:

+2.   i.   LEONEL[2] GARZA was born on 21 May 1922 in McAllen, Hidalgo, Texas. He died on 09 Jun 2005. He married Carmen Aurora Rubio-Raygadas, daughter of Adan Rubio Raygadas, on 22 Jun 1950 in Azcapotzalco, Distrito Federal, México (Temple of the Immaculate Conception). She was born on 17 Mar 1922 in Pachuca, Hidalgo, Mexico.

+3.   ii.   ALMA NINFA GARZA was born on 27 Jul 1925 in McAllen, Hidalgo, Texas. She died on 30 Nov 1973 in Saltillo, Coahuila, Mexico. She married Joaquin Aguirre, son of Joaquin Aguirre Sr. and Soledad Aguirre de Aguirre, on 22 Oct 1949 in Saltillo, Coahuila de Zaragoza, Mexico. He was born on 27 Feb 1918 in Coahuila de Zaragoza, Mexico. He died on 19 Jul 1957 in Saltillo, Coahuila de Zaragoza, Mexico.

4.   iii.   GLORIA ESTELA GARZA was born on 17 Jan 1934 in McAllen, Hidalgo, Texas. She married Antonio Garza-Montemayor, son of Victoriano Garza and Petra Montemayor, on 17 Dec 1955 in Saltillo, Coahuila de Zaragoza, Mexico (Santiago Cathedral). He was born on 17 Jan 1932 in Saltillo, Coahuila, Mexico. He died on 30 Aug 2011 in San Miguel de Allende, Guanajuato, Mexico.

Generation 2

Left: Alma and older brother Leonel Garza in McAllen, Texas in 1934 –photo from Gloria Garza Collection.

2. LEONEL[2] GARZA (Teresa[1] Guerra, Jacobo-Hinojosa, Matias Garza-Cantu) was born on 21 May 1922 in McAllen, Hidalgo, Texas as the first child of Jacobo Garza-Hinojosa and Teresa Guerra. He had two siblings, namely: Alma Ninfa, and Gloria Estela. He died on 09 Jun 2005 (Age 83). When he was 28, he married **Carmen Aurora Rubio-Raygadas**, daughter of Adan Rubio Raygadas and Carmen Parra de Rubio, on 22 Jun 1950 in Azcapotzalco, Distrito Federal, Mexico (Temple of the Immaculate Conception). She was born on 17 Mar 1922 in Pachuca, Hidalgo, Mexico.

Leonel Garza lived in McAllen, Hidalgo, Texas in 1930 (Street Address: 11th Ave.; Age 7; Attended School: Yes; Enumeration District: 0023; Registration District: 23; Marital Status: Single; Relation To Head of House: Son). He was employed as an MD Internal Medicine-Children in 1950 in Mexico City, Distrito Federal, Mexico. He was buried in 2005 in Saltillo, Coahuila de Zaragoza, Mexico (ashes scattered on hill in Saltillo and a church in Mexico City). He was also known as Leonel Garza de Guerra. He was known by the title of Medical Doctor (MD). Race: (Mexican).

Youngest and oldest of the Leonel Garza family in Sep 1962,
from left: Carmen, little Carmen, Teresa Guerra, Leonel
—photo from Guadalupe Guerra Collection.

Although Leonel was born in McAllen, Texas he graduated from high school in Saltillo where the family had moved. He started body-building and lifting weights when he was a teenager and was a fitness buff all his life. After high school Jacobo sent Leonel to study medicine, first to Monterrey then to Mexico City, where he met his wife Carmen, graduated with an MD Degree (Doctor of Medicine), and became a pediatrician. His original plan was to return to McAllen to practice medicine, and he began his practice in the border town of Reynosa and moved his family there until he could obtain the certificates needed to practice in the U.S.

However, Leonel's plans soon changed. According to his sister Gloria, "His wife was from Mexico City with a very tight family that they didn't like that . . . so Leonel says to my father I have to go back to Mexico City" (Garza G. , 2019). Leonel's cousin Daniel Guerra summarized, "He had actually the opportunity to practice here in McAllen, he was a pediatrician, but his wife didn't want to leave Mexico" (Guerra D. , 2019). So in 1951 they moved back to Mexico City where their four children were born and he worked for many years in the medical profession.

Leonel Garza and Carmen Aurora Rubio-Raygadas had the following children:
   5.   i.   MARIA TERESA[3] GARZA was born on 21 Apr 1951 in Mexico City, Mexico.
+6.   ii.   CARLOS JAVIER GARZA was born on 07 Aug 1952 in Mexico City, Mexico.
   7.   iii.   LEONEL GARZA JR. was born on 07 Dec 1953 in Mexico City, Mexico.

8. iv. CARMEN AURORA GARZA was born on 04 Sep 1958 in Mexico City, Mexico.

3. ALMA NINFA² GARZA (Teresa¹ Guerra, Jacobo-Hinojosa, Matias Garza-Cantu) was born on Jul 1925 in McAllen, Hidalgo, Texas as the second child of Jacobo Garza-Hinojosa and Teresa Guerra. She had two siblings, namely: Leonel, and Gloria Estela. She died on 30 Nov 1973 in Saltillo, Coahuila de Zaragoza, Mexico (Age 48). When she was 24, she married **Joaquin Aguirre**, son of Joaquin Aguirre Sr. and Soledad Aguirre de Aguirre, on 22 Oct 1949 in Saltillo, Coahuila de Zaragoza, Mexico.

Right: 28-year-old Joaquin Aguirre on horseback –photo from Gloria Garza Collection.

Alma Ninfa Garza lived in McAllen, Hidalgo, Texas in 1930 (Street Address: 11th Ave.; Age 4; Attended School: No; Enumeration District: 0023; Registration District: 23; Marital Status: Single; Relation to Head of House: Daughter). Her cause of death was breast cancer. Race: (Mexican). Alma also went to school in Saltillo and studied to become a teacher. But after graduation and only a few years teaching she met her future husband Joaquin Aguirre who was also from Saltillo.

Far Left: Joaquin Aguirre in 1948.
Left: Alma Ninfa Garza in 1940 –photos from Gloria Garza Collection.

Joaquin Aguirre and Alma Ninfa Garza had the following children:

+9. i. BELINDA³ AGUIRRE was born on 14 Aug 1950 in Saltillo, Coahuila de Zaragoza, Mexico. She married Eloy Dewey on 24 Jul 1971 in Saltillo, Coahuila de Zaragoza, Mexico. He was born on 12 Jul 1949. He died on 18 Aug 2013 in Saltillo, Coahuila de Zaragoza, Mexico.

+10. ii. ALMA NORMA AGUIRRE-GARZA was born on 17 Feb 1952 in Saltillo, Coahuila de Zaragoza, Mexico. She married Melchor de los Santos-Ordonez on 13 Oct 1972 in Celaya, Guanajuato, Mexico. He was born on 17 Feb 1950 in Saltillo, Coahuila de Zaragoza, Mexico. He died on 06 Apr 2013 in Mexico City, Mexico.

+11. iii. EDUARDO JOAQUIN AGUIRRE was born on 24 Oct 1954 in Saltillo, Coahuila de Zaragoza, Mexico. He married Consuelo Yolanda Gonzalez-Muzquiz, daughter of Angel Gonzalez and Olga Muzquiz, on 15 Aug 1981 in Querétaro, Queretaro de Arteaga, Mexico (Hacienda San Pedro Martir). She was born on 14 Jul 1961 in Monterrey Nuevo León, Mexico.

4. GLORIA ESTELA² GARZA (Teresa¹ Guerra, Jacobo -Hinojosa, Matias Garza-Cantu) was born on 17 Jan 1934 in McAllen, Hidalgo, Texas as the third child of Jacobo Garza-Hinojosa and Teresa Guerra. She had two siblings, namely: Leonel, and Alma Ninfa. When she was 21, she married **Antonio Garza-Montemayor**, son of Victoriano Garza and Petra Montemayor, on 17 Dec 1955 in Saltillo, Coahuila de Zaragoza, Mexico (Santiago Cathedral).

Gloria Estela Garza lived in McAllen, Texas in 1935 (Street Address: 301 E LaVista Ave). She lived in Saltillo, Coahuila de Zaragoza, Mexico in 1936. She was employed as a University of Georgia Spanish Teacher between 1957 and 1958 in Athens, Clarke, Georgia, USA. She lived in La Piedad Cavadas, Michoacan de Ocampo, Mexico in 1957. She was employed as an Iowa State University Spanish Teacher between 1963 and 1964 in Ames, Story, Iowa, USA. She lived in Celaya, Guanajuato, Mexico in 1965. She lived in San Miguel de Allende, Guanajuato, Mexico in 1970. She lived in Naucalpan de Juárez, Mexico in 1981 (with her mother Teresa Guerra). She lived in San Miguel de Allende, Guanajuato, Mexico in 1996 (Soto Grande #35). She lived at Mesquite #443, Saltillo, Coahuila de Zaragoza, Mexico in 2018.

The Garza Family in front of their home on Maduro Street in Saltillo, Mexico in 1944, front: Gloria; back: Teresa, Jacobo, Alma –photo from Gloria Garza Collection.

Gloria was nine years younger than Teresa's other two children, in some ways being raised as an only child when her older siblings married and moved out of the house. She told me that she was only two years old when the family moved from McAllen to Saltillo. In April 2019, I saw the house she grew up in for ten years. It is still there on Maduro Street, not far from the Santiago Cathedral in central Saltillo. She told me, "I remember a large kitchen with all the shelves . . . and in the back a big yard with lots of trees . . . and I used to go up the trees with *columpios* (swings)." Gloria also told me some of the *dichos* (sayings) her mother Tere used when things weren't going well such as, "*Bucerón el grito en el cielo*" (All shout to the sky), and when she didn't think the children were dressed as she wanted, "*No vas a salir de cotón azul*" (Don't go out in blue jeans; i.e. if you want to impress someone) (Garza G. , 2019).

She went to school in Saltillo and studied to become a teacher like her older sister Alma. Soon Gloria met her future husband Antonio, also from Saltillo. It seems that her older sister Alma wanted her to meet "a very handsome boy" at a school dance that one of her friends knew. They married in 1955 and Gloria followed him as he studied and built a career in agricultural research, spending several years at universities in the U.S. where she was able to practice her English skills. "I went to the university and said I am from Mexico and I want to study American History. . . He said 'Are you from Mexico, and you are an American citizen, and you are a teacher?' . . . I said yes I'm a teacher. He said, 'Can you teach Spanish here?' . . . so I started working, first in Georgia then in Iowa" (Garza G. , 2019).

In the mid-1960s Antonio became a chemist for the Campbell Soup Company and they moved to Celaya, Guanajuato, Mexico. Later they moved to San Miguel de Allende, Guanajuato, Mexico where Antonio worked for the Chevron Oil Company in the agricultural chemicals division. Her mother Teresa lived with them sometime after Jacobo died. Now that Gloria is a widow, she lives in Saltillo again, next door to her nephew Eduardo Aguirre and his family.

Antonio Garza-Montemayor was born on 17 Jan 1932 in Saltillo, Coahuila, Mexico as the first child of Victoriano Garza and Petra Montemayor. He died on 30 Aug 2011 in San Miguel de Allende, Guanajuato, Mexico. When he was 23, he married Gloria Estela Garza, daughter of Jacobo Garza-Hinojosa and Teresa Guerra, on 17 Dec 1955 in Saltillo, Coahuila de Zaragoza, Mexico (Santiago Cathedral).

Left: Antonio and Gloria Garza with their pets in San Miguel de Allende, Guanajuato, Mexico about 1996 –photo from Gloria Garza Collection.

Antonio Garza-Montemayor received a University of Georgia, MS Genetics degree between 1957 and 1960 in Athens, Clarke, Georgia, USA. He received an Iowa State University, PhD Agriculture (Livestock) degree between 1963 and 1964 in Ames, Story, Iowa, USA. He was employed as a Campbell Soup Company agricultural engineer in 1965 in Celaya, Guanajuato, Mexico. He was employed as a Chevron agricultural engineer in 1970 in San

Miguel de Allende, Guanajuato, Mexico. He was cremated in Sep 2011 in Saltillo, Coahuila de Zaragoza, Mexico (ashes in Familia Aguirre-Gonzalez niche at El Ranchito Church). He was also known as Tony.

Antonio Garza-Montemayor and Gloria Estela Garza had no children.

Generation 3

6. CARLOS JAVIER³ GARZA (Leonel², Teresa¹ Guerra, Leonel², Jacobo-Hinojosa, Matias Garza-Cantu) was born on 07 Aug 1952 in Mexico City, Mexico.

Carlos Javier Garza had the following children:
- 12. i. LAUNA⁴ GARZA was born in 1975.
- 13. ii. TACOLEO GARZA was born in 1978.

9. BELINDA³ AGUIRRE (Alma Ninfa² Garza, Teresa¹ Guerra, Joaquin Aguirre, Joaquin Aguirre Sr.) was born on 14 Aug 1950 in Saltillo, Coahuila de Zaragoza, Mexico. She married **Eloy Dewey Sr.** on 24 Jul 1971 in Saltillito, Coahuila de Zaragoza, Mexico. He was born on 12 Jul 1949. He died on 18 Aug 2013 in Saltillo, Coahuila de Zaragoza, Mexico.

Right: Mary Guerra (on left) goes shopping with her cousins Belinda Aguirre and Gloria Garza (on right) in Saltillo, Mexico, 24 Apr 2019.

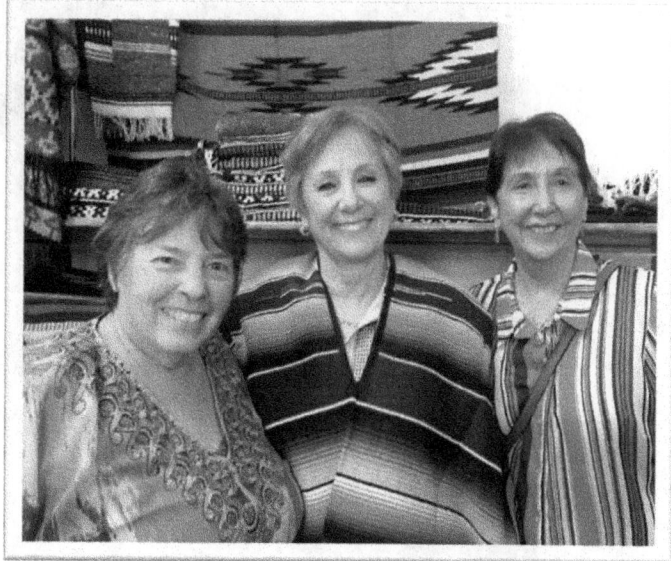

Eloy Dewey Sr. and Belinda Aguirre had the following children:
- +14. i. BELINDA⁴ DEWEY was born on 25 Jun 1973 in Saltillo, Coahuila de Zaragoza, Mexico.
- +15. ii. LINSAY DEWEY was born on 05 Apr 1977 in Saltillo, Coahuila de Zaragoza, Mexico. She married David Mendel on 03 Nov 2000. He was born on 24 Aug 1977.
- +16. iii. ELOY DEWEY was born on 14 Mar 1979 in Saltillo, Coahuila de Zaragoza, Mexico. He married Linda Cavazos on 16 Dec 2006. She was born on 09 Nov 1988.
- +17. iv. GALWIN DEWEY was born on 07 Feb 1981 in Saltillo, Coahuila de Zaragoza, Mexico. He married Alejandra Flores Garza on 03 May 2014. She was born on 22 Nov 1987.

10. ALMA NORMA³ AGUIRRE-GARZA (Alma Ninfa² Garza, Teresa¹ Guerra, Joaquin Aguirre Sr.)

was born on 17 Feb 1952 in Saltillo, Coahuila de Zaragoza, Mexico. She married **Melchor de los Santos-Ordonez** on 13 Oct 1972 in Celaya, Guanajuato, Mexico. He was born on 17 Feb 1950 in Saltillo, Coahuila de Zaragoza, Mexico. He died on 06 Apr 2013 in Mexico City, Mexico.

Melchor de los Santos-Ordonez and Alma Norma Aguirre-Garza had the following children:

18. i.   MELISSA DE LOS[4] SANTOS-ORDONEZ was born on 21 Aug 1976 in Saltillo, Coahuila de Zaragoza, Mexico.

+19. ii. MELCHOR DE LOS SANTOS-AGUIRRE was born on 19 Oct 1979 in Mexico City, Mexico. He married Mardana Fernandez-Godoy on 29 Apr 1999 in Mexico City, Mexico. She was born on 20 Apr 1979 in Mexico City, Mexico.

20. iii. ADRIAN MATIAS DE LOS SANTOS-AGUIRRE was born on 30 Oct 1990 in Mexico City, Mexico.

11. EDUARDO JOAQUIN[3] AGUIRRE (Alma Ninfa[2] Garza, Teresa[1] Guerra, Joaquin Aguirre Sr) was born on 24 Oct 1954 in Saltillo, Coahuila de Zaragoza, Mexico. He married **Consuelo Yolanda Gonzalez-Muzquiz**, daughter of Angel Gonzalez and Olga Muzquiz, on 15 Aug 1981 in Querétaro, Queretaro de Arteaga, Mexico (Hacienda San Pedro Martir). She was born on 14 Jul 1961 in Monterrey, Nuevo León, Mexico. He was employed as an architect in 2019 in Saltillo, Mexico.

Eduardo Aguirre family about 2009, from left in front: Yolanda, Eduardo; from left in back: Ricardo, Kiara, Rodrigo –photo from Gloria Garza Collection.

Eduardo Joaquin Aguirre and Consuelo Yolanda Gonzalez-Muzquiz had the following children:

21. i.   RODRIGO ALEJANDRO[4] AGUIRRE-GONZALEZ was born on 25 Jun 1984 in Conroe,

Montgomery, Texas. . He was employed as a Graphic Designer in 2019 in Saltillo, Coahuila de Zaragoza, Mexico.

22. ii.   KIARA AGUIRRE-GONZALEZ was born on 16 Apr 1988 in Saltillo, Coahuila de Zaragoza, Mexico.

23. iii.   RICARDO AGUIRRE-GONZALEZ was born on 12 Jul 1990 in Saltillo, Coahuila de Zaragoza, Mexico. He was employed as an architect in 2019 in Saltillo, Mexico.

Generation 4

14. BELINDA⁴ DEWEY (Belinda³ Aguirre, Alma Ninfa² Garza, Teresa¹ Guerra, Eloy Sr.) was born on 25 Jun 1973 in Saltillo, Coahuila de Zaragoza, Mexico.

Belinda Dewey had the following children:
24. i.   BELINDA SOFIA MEDRANO⁵ DEWEY was born on 22 Jul 1996.
25. ii.   MARIEL MEDRANO DEWEY was born on 26 Jul 1999.
26. iii. REGINA MARIA MEDRANO DEWEY was born on 09 Dec 2002.
27. iv.   JUAN PABLO MEDRANO DEWEY was born on 20 Feb 2007.

15. LINSAY⁴ DEWEY (Belinda³ Aguirre, Alma Ninfa² Garza, Teresa¹ Guerra, Eloy Sr.) was born on 05 Apr 1977 in Saltillo, Coahuila de Zaragoza, Mexico. She married David Mendel on 03 Nov 2000. He was born on 24 Aug 1977.

David Mendel and Linsay Dewey had the following children:
28. i.   ANDREA⁵ MENDEL was born on 16 Mar 2001.
29. ii.   DAVID MENDEL JR. was born on 03 Jul 2002 (Twin of Leo).
30. iii. LEO MENDEL was born on 03 Jul 2002 (Twin of David).
31. iv.   DANIEL MENDEL was born on 25 Nov 2004.
32. v.   LINLY MENDEL was born on 01 Nov 2009.

16. ELOY⁴ DEWEY (Belinda³ Aguirre, Alma Ninfa² Garza, Teresa¹ Guerra, Eloy Sr.) was born on 14 Mar 1979 in Saltillo, Coahuila de Zaragoza, Mexico. He married Linda Cavazos on 16 Dec 2006. She was born on 09 Nov 1988.

Eloy Dewey and Linda Cavazos had the following children:
33. i.   ELOY⁵ DEWEY JR. was born on 28 Jun 2007.
34. ii.   LYNETTE DEWEY was born on 16 Feb 2009.
35. iii. MATTEO DEWEY was born on 10 Jul 2011.

17. GALWIN⁴ DEWEY (Belinda³ Aguirre, Alma Ninfa² Garza, Teresa¹ Guerra, Eloy Sr.) was born on 07 Feb 1981 in Saltillo, Coahuila de Zaragoza, Mexico. He married Alejandra Flores Garza on 03 May 2014. She was born on 22 Nov 1987.

Galwin Dewey and Alejandra Flores Garza had the following children:
36. i.   BERNARDO⁵ DEWEY was born on 19 May 2017.
37. ii.   ALLE DEWEY was born on 13 Apr in 2015.

19. MELCHOR DE LOS⁴ SANTOS-AGUIRRE (Alma Norma³ Aguirre-Garza, Alma Ninfa² Garza, Teresa¹ Guerra, Melchor de los Santos-Ordonez) was born on 19 Oct 1979 in Mexico City, Mexico. He married Mardana Fernandez-Godoy on 29 Apr 1999 in Mexico City, Mexico. She was born on 20 Apr 1979 in Mexico City, Mexico.

Melchor de los Santos-Aguirre and Mardana Fernandez-Godoy had the following children:

38. i. MARIA JOSÉ DE LOS⁵ SANTOS-FERNANDEZ was born on 12 Dec 2011 in Mexico City, Mexico.
39. ii. MANUEL DE LOS SANTOS-FERNANDEZ was born on 15 Sep 2014 in Mexico City, Mexico.

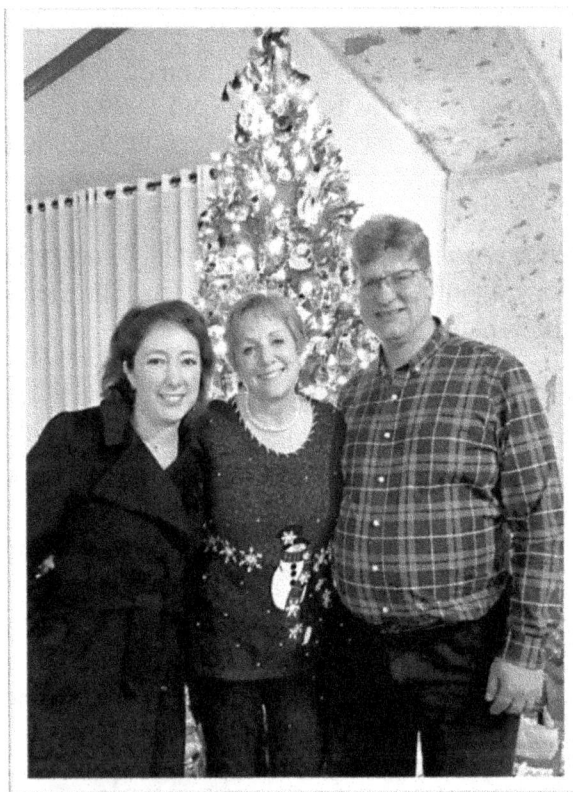

Alma Norma Aguirre (left) with her mother Belinda Aguirre and spouse Melchor de los Santos-Ordonez celebrate Christmas together --photo from Gloria Garza Collection.

Chapter 4. Abel Eulalio Guerra and Ciria Luz Portilla

Generation 1

1. ABEL EULALIO[J] GUERRA (José Antonio[A], Jesus Maria[B], José Lino de Jesus[C], José Manuel[D], José Antonio Albino Hinojosa[E], Joseph Ramon[F], Capitan Cristóbal[G] Guerra-Cañamar, Ignacio[H] Guerra-Cañamar, Antonio[I] Guerra-Cañamal II, Antonio[J] Guerra-Cañamal) was born on 12 Feb 1896 in Roma, Starr, Texas (Rancho El Colorado) as the second child of José Antonio Guerra and Tecla Guerra de Guerra. He had eight siblings, namely: Teresa, Victoria, Guadalupe Filiberto, Margarita, Maria Florinda, Herlinda, Fidencio Miguel, and Evangelina. He died on 28 Sep 1983 in Conroe, Montgomery, Texas (Age 87) (ashes scattered near Florencio Guerra home in Conroe, Texas). When he was 41, he married **Ciria Luz Portilla-Martinez**, daughter of Manuel Portilla-Bolado and Elvira Martinez-Morales, in Havana, Cuba; and again on 28 Jan 1945 in Mexico City, Mexico.

Abel Eulalio Guerra lived in Justice Precinct 4, Starr, Texas in 1900 (Marital Status: Single, Relation to Head of House: Son). He lived in Justice Precinct 4, Starr, Texas in 1910 (Age 14; Marital Status: Single; Relation To Head of House: Son). He lived in McAllen, Hidalgo, Texas on 05 Jun 1917. He was described as Spanish American, Tall, Slender, Brown Hair, Brown Eyes on 05 Jun 1917 in McAllen, Hidalgo, Texas. He lived in Mexico in 1918. He lived in Cuba from 1924 to 1939. He lived in Mexico City, Distrito Federal, Mexico on 28 Oct 1942. He lived in Mexico City, Distrito Federal, Mexico on 22 Apr 1954 (La Joya, Tlalpan). He lived in Houston, Texas on 08 Feb 1983 (2501 Westerland Dr). He was also known as Abel Guerra y Guerra. His cause of death was heart failure during cataract surgery. Race: (White).

Abel Guerra (on right) was 20 years old when this photo was taken with his younger brother Guadalupe (left) and friend Manuel Tijerina (sitting) in 1916 in McAllen, Texas –photo from Guadalupe Guerra Collection.

Abel was born and grew up on Rancho El Colorado at what is now Guerra, Texas. According to his son Florencio, by the time he was seventeen Abel really wanted to study English and learn how to run a business. So, in 1913 when he was seventeen years old the family talked his Uncle Diodoro Guerra, who was opening the Guerra & Sons grocery store in McAllen, into hiring him so he would be able to go to school in McAllen. He started as a delivery boy and his uncle allowed him to sleep in the back of the store and work during the day (Guerra F. , 2019).

Abel probably would have remained in the lower Rio Grande River Valley with its large Hispanic population if it had not been for world events. The first was the beginning of the Mexican Revolution in the fall of 1910 followed by the outbreak of World War I in 1914. As required, Abel registered for the draft when he was 21 years old in June 1917. But some sources say that his Uncle paid off the draft board to have Abel switched with one of his own sons and be drafted first.

Left: Abel Guerra World War I draft registration card showing his requested exemption on line 12 due to working as Deputy Constable, 5 Jun 1917.

"There's that rumor when the war broke out, World War I. So Diodoro wouldn't have to have his kids drafted he volunteered *Tio* (uncle) Abel to go in their place. . . That's how he ended up in Mexico. To avoid the war here, he went to Mexico and ended up being in the war there. And then was on the wrong side of the war and he had to flee to Cuba" (Guerra F. J., Fidencio Guerra Jr. Family History Video Interview, 2019).

So Abel decided that rather than being forced into conscription, he would go to Mexico, and ended up fighting in the Mexican Revolution instead. According to his son, "He had some friends on the Mexican side and he crossed the border. They went to the Revolution, these guys, and he went with them to get out of this area" (Guerra F. , 2019). In Mexico a radical new constitution was passed in 1917, and in 1918 Alvaro Obregón resigned as General of the Federal Army. Then on Apr 22, 1920, the three Sonoran generals: De la Huerta (then-governor of Sonora), Obregón and Calles formulated the Revolution of Agua Prieta where the military, backed by labor unions and Zapatistas, ousted and killed President Carranza.

During the 1920 Revolution, Abel became a Colonel under General Tiburcio Garza Zamora. At one point some sources say that Abel was engaged in providing weapons and ammunition. Mary Guerra remembers her father telling her the story, "Abel was running guns across the border and he wanted Daddy (Guadalupe) to help him and he goes 'Nooo. I'm taking care of the children and if I get caught who's going to take care of the children? (Guerra J. , 2019).

Apparently after the revolution was victorious, Abel Guerra decided to go to southern Mexico. His son Florencio says that Abel published his memoirs of this period in a book. So far I have not located any copies of the book, but according to his son the memoirs indicate that he got a job (possibly at Pavo Obispo) near the border of British Honduras (now Belize) with the Customs Bureau. The Bureau was under the Secretary of Finance and Public Credit, who at this time was Adolfo de la Huerta, the past President of Mexico before Alvaro Obregón.

In November 1923, Abel's boss, De la Huerta, launched a rebellion and Abel joined him, in part protesting President Obregón's Bucareli Treaty, an agreement that attempted to resolve important issues in Mexico–United States relations. Obregón returned to the battlefield and crushed the rebellion by Jan 24, 1924. In his victory, he was aided by the United States with arms and 17 U.S. planes that bombed De la Huerta's supporters. Obregón ordered that all rebel officers captured above the rank of Major be executed. So by 1924 Colonel Abel Guerra, forced to flee Mexico, was now in Cuba.

President Obregón's Mexican Artillery shells De la Huerta's rebel army in 1924.

His son tells the story:
> "When his boss began fighting with the federal government, he joined his boss. There were 300 of them, not well armed, with very little ammunition, fighting against 2,000 soldiers. The battle lasted only three hours and those that knew how to swim crossed the Rio Hondo into British Honduras. They were thrown in jail there, but because Abel was white, tall, and spoke very good English, he was treated a little better. After a few weeks they allowed him to get on a ship to get out of there without going back to Mexico by going to Cuba where he lived for ten years. His English language skills helped him find a job and he also helped other Mexican veterans. They decided to write a magazine with memoirs about the Mexican Revolution, so he went back to Mexico (about 1930) to start the business, which was a failure, so he came back to Cuba (about 1937) and got a job in pharmaceuticals and married his sweetheart Lulu Portilla who had been waiting for him for seven years."

"My father's English is what got him a good job in Cuba when he was there. . . He got a job with a U.S. corporation in pharmaceuticals. Then just before the Second World War (about 1939) Mexico's borders were closed to German pharmaceuticals, and the U.S. companies in Cuba offered him a job selling their products in Mexico. That's why he moved from Cuba back to Mexico (in 1942), because he speaks English and he was Mexican" (Guerra F. , 2019).

Right: Abel Guerra acknowledgement of Mexican Revolution service, 1954 –from Guadalupe Guerra Collection.

When Abel returned to Mexico he established a very successful pharmaceutical business with Paul Lewis and PABTS Laboratories. He also started a pet food business in Mexico called Nutre-Can. Then he got into real estate, bought a home in Cuautla, and later as his son remembers, "We moved to Tlalpan outside of Mexico City and bought a house with three acres and my dad loved all the fruit trees we had" (Guerra F. , 2019).

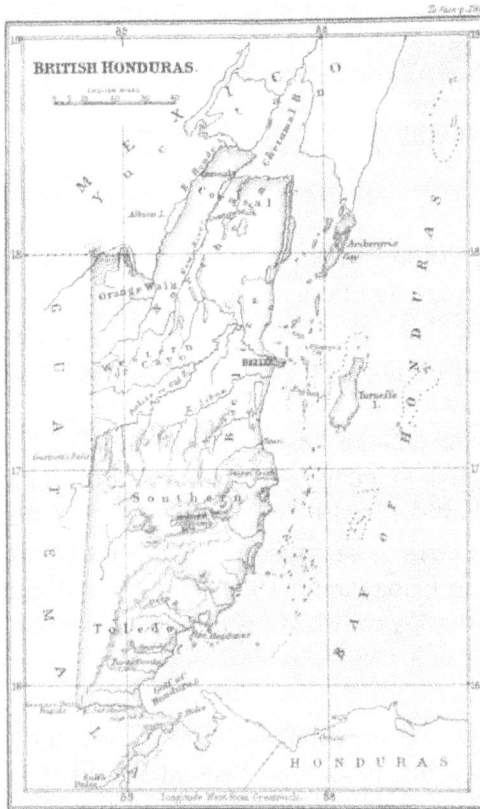

After he retired, Abel lived between Mexico City and Texas where his sons live today. Many of Abel's and Lulu's descendants still live in Mexico.

Left: 1888 map of British Honduras showing the Rio Hondo border on the, upper left –from British Library.

Right: Grass house on the Rio Hondo –from Thomas William Francis Gann, Bureau of American Ethnology.

Ciria Luz Portilla-Martinez was born on 05 Jun 1918 in Camaguey, Cuba as the eighth of nine children of Manuel Portilla-Bolado and Elvira Martinez-Morales. She died on 01 Jan 1981 in Mexico City, Distrito Federal, Mexico. When she was 19, she married Abel Eulalio Guerra, son of José Antonio Guerra and Tecla Guerra de Guerra, in 1937 in Havana, Cuba, then again on 28 Jan 1945 in Mexico City, Mexico. She died of leukemia and was cremated in Jan 1981 in Mexico City, Distrito Federal, Mexico (ashes reported to be interred in Mexico City Cathedral). She was also known as Lulu Portilla.

We do not know much about Lulu, as she was known, other than what her two sons remember about her. We know that she was from a "well-to-do" Cuban landowner family. We know she was a talented musician, played the piano, and was a big influence on her niece, Cuban singer-songwriter Angela Alvarez. According to her cousin Florencio Guerra, Angela was born in Cuba in 1927 and now lives in Baton Rouge, LA. She published her first album of Cuban songs *"Un Nuevo Amanecer"* (A New Dawn) in 2017 when she was 90 years old (Alvarez, 2017).

Lulu married Abel Guerra in Havana, Cuba in 1937 and had two sons that were stillborn, one in Havana, Cuba in 1940, and one in Mexico City in 1942. To validate their civil marriage in Cuba, they married again in Mexico City in 1945, Lulu giving birth to Abel Jr. the same year and Florencio two years later. Youngest son Florencio remembers his mother:

> "My mother Lulu was one of six sisters and three brothers and her mother became a widow when the oldest was nineteen. My mother moved from Cuba to Mexico when she married Abel. Her sisters all moved to Mexico by the 1960s. Lulu played very good piano and was very friendly with everyone. She worked at home helping Abel with his business, with accounting, and even with breaking down barrels of tablets into small containers for retail sale. Abel and Lulu always worked very well together" (Guerra F. , 2019).

Apparently she was also a good cook as her son recalls with fondness, "We ate a lot of Cuban food made by my mother. I love those things . . . *arroz con pollo* (rice with chicken) . . . *congri* (rice, beans and pork) . . . *Moros y Cristianos* (black beans and white rice) . . . all kinds of Cuban food" (Guerra F. , 2019).

Abel Eulalio Guerra and Ciria Luz Portilla-Martinez had the following children:

+2.   i.   ABEL LUIS^2 GUERRA was born on 05 Jan 1945 in Mexico City, Mexico (Hospital Frances). He married Susana Blanca Gasque e Sol on 15 Jul 1967 in Mexico City, Mexico. She was born on 27 Apr 1949 in Mexico City, Mexico.

+3.   ii.   FLORENCIO IGNACIO GUERRA was born on 05 May 1947 in Mexico City, Mexico (Hospital Frances). He married Evelyn Audrey Muller-Gandolfo on 05 Jun 1977 in Mexico City, Mexico (Senora de Los Angeles Church). She was born on 27 Dec 1957 in Manhattan, New York, New York, USA (Doctors Hospital).

Abel Guerra family in 1952 (from left to right: Florencio, Lulu Portilla, Abel Luis, Abel Eulalio) –photo from Guadalupe Guerra Collection.

Generation 2

2. ABEL LUIS^2 GUERRA (Abel Eulalio^1, José Antonio^A, Jesus Maria^B, José Lino de Jesus^C, José Manuel^D, José Antonio Albino Hinojosa^E, Joseph Ramon^F, Capitan Cristóbal^G Guerra-Cañamar, Ignacio^H Guerra-Cañamar, Antonio^I Guerra-Cañamal II, Antonio^J Guerra-Cañamal) was born on 05 Jan 1945 in Mexico City, Mexico (Hospital Frances). He married **Susana Blanca Gasque e Sol** on 15 Jul 1967 in Mexico City, Mexico. She was born on 27 Apr 1949 in Mexico City, Mexico.

Left: Abel Luis Guerra and Florencio Guerra, Jul 1948 –photo from Guerra Family History Collection.

Abel Jr. was a very friendly child, like his mother Lulu. Both he and his younger brother Florencio were home-schooled by a tutor until fourth grade. By then his mother Lulu had convinced her husband Abel that the boys needed to socialize with others their age so they were sent to parochial schools through high school. But Abel Jr. did not take to school like his brother did. According to his cousin Fidencio Guerra Jr. (Guerra F. J., Abel Guerra Jr. Phone call Video Interview, 2019), Abel Jr. would walk to school with his brother Florencio but sometimes "played hooky." But he was a smart entrepreneur, even as a youngster. A story also told by his cousin Fidencio Jr. involved cousins Carlos Guerra and Leonardo Guerra Jr. driving from Texas to Mexico City on a high school graduation trip, visiting Abel's family. So Abel Jr. became their local guide, and when they went out to eat in a local restaurant and left a five dollar tip, Abel Jr. went back in and replaced it with one dollar.

After Abel Jr. finished high school he told his father he preferred work rather than college, so his father made sure he worked. Abel Jr. got different jobs; selling signs, then clothing, then cars. He liked selling cars and soon started his own car sales business. Then he decided to open a swimming academy close to where he lived in Tlalpan and ran that for a few years before going into the real estate business with his father Abel. He was always a very friendly guy and made many friends.

Abel Luis Guerra and Susana Blanca Gasque e Sol had the following children:

4.   i.   SUSANA MARIA^3 GUERRA.
5.   ii. LETICIA MARIA GUERRA.
6.   iii. PATRICIA MARIA GUERRA.
7.   iv. MONICA MARIA GUERRA.

3. FLORENCIO IGNACIO^2 GUERRA (Abel Eulalio^1, José Antonio^A, Jesus Maria^B, José Lino de Jesus^C, José Manuel^D, José Antonio Albino Hinojosa^E, Joseph Ramon^F, Capitan Cristóbal^G Guerra-Cañamar, Ignacio^H Guerra-Cañamar, Antonio^I Guerra-Cañamal II, Antonio^J Guerra-Cañamal) was born on 05 May 1947 in Mexico City, Mexico (Hospital Frances). He married **Evelyn Audrey Muller-Gandolfo** on 05 Jun 1977 in Mexico City, Mexico (Senora de Log Angeles Church). She was born on 27 Dec 1957 in Manhattan, New York, NY, USA (Doctors Hospital).

Florencio was also a very friendly child. Both he and his brother Abel Jr. were home-schooled. After his mother Lulu convinced her husband Abel that the boys needed to socialize with others their age, they were both sent to parochial schools. Later, when Florencio was ten or twelve years old his father bought a beautiful place in Tlalpan southwest of Mexico City where they moved.

Right: Nuevo León Governor Pedro Zorrilla (2nd from right) explains Florencio's (left) project to Mexican President Luis Echeverria (right) –1976 photo from Florencio Guerra Collection.

In the 1960s Florencio went to a Catholic High School and then studied law in college in Mexico City, graduating in 1968. He practiced law for four years while helping his father in the real estate business as well. In 1972 his former college professor became the Mexico City District Attorney and invited Florencio to work with him which he did. Later his boss, the former college professor, campaigned for the Governor of Nuevo León in Monterrey, and with Florencio's help he won the election in August 1973. Florencio worked for the new governor on special projects and later public relations. Also in 1976, he coordinated Lopez Portillo's presidential campaign (Guerra F. , 2019).

After that, he went back to his real estate business. He also got into the construction business as well when he and his future wife Evelyn were in Houston to get a wedding dress in 1977. While waiting for the fitting, they stayed at a new subdivision in nearby Conroe, Texas. He liked the area, bought land, and started Conco Grande Construction Company to build houses. Now he has businesses both in Texas and Nuevo León, Mexico which he is involved in with his sons and daughters and their families.

Florencio learned French in college, but learned English on his own over the past thirty years as he jokingly says, "Just like a good wetback, I practice it. My kids all of them are bilingual. They studied in Monterrey but in the American School and they got everything in English" (Guerra F. , 2019).

On the move

wife Holly live in Rivershire.

Florencio I. Guerra is the owner of Conco Grande, a residential and commercial construction group near Lake Conroe on Highway 105 West. Guerra received his law degree in 1968 and practiced law from 1968 through 1972. He has been involved in real estate, a travel agency and a printing company. Florencio, has wife Evelyn and their two children live at Walden on Lake Conroe.

MCCLAIN

John A. Tatum Jr., president and CEO of InterFirst Bank, Conroe, has announced the election of STEPHEN W. MCCLAIN to the bank's board of directors. McClain, a lifetime resident of Conroe, is a partner in the law firm of McClain, Harrel & McClain.

McClain serves as vice chairman of the administrative board at First United Methodist Church in Conroe.

GUERRA

Jim Lawrence, President Dailey Petroleum Services Co and Gene Hoffman, Vice Presid of Marketing, have announced p sonnel appointments in light of company's recent reorganizat and the addition of several n downhole drilling products to its c rent line.

Clif Cook has been appointed tional accounts sales manag Reporting to Cook in national counts sales are Gene Dillman, M Reid, and Tom Preseau. Rudy O and Bill Brand have responsibili as product line managers.

Ken Mills has been appoi Domestic Marketing Manager. Jeff Wells is eastern reg marketing manager. Steve Gree western region marketing manag

Left: Page B1 of The Courier, Conroe, Texas, highlights Florencio Guerra after he was designated as advisory director of Interfirst Bank, 19 Oct 1983 –from Florencio Guerra Collection.

His wife Evelyn's side of the family is from Argentina, but her father is German and her mother is Italian. So once their children were of high school age, Florencio and Evelyn sent them to Germany each summer to learn German plus one semester in Germany as exchange students.

He met his wife Evelyn in a restaurant in Monterrey. He says he was with a group of friends in the lounge and saw her passing through with her boyfriend. He liked her and asked his friend who she was. His friend said he knew who she was. Florencio then asked about her boyfriend. His friend said, "He is a foreigner, he just came to study here, he just finished and is going back home." So Florencio said, "Well, he just lost her." They married a year later and have been married for more than forty-two years (Guerra F. , 2019).

Florencio Ignacio Guerra and Evelyn Audrey Muller-Gandolfo had the following children:

+8. i. MARIEL ALEXANA[3] GUERRA-MULLER was born on 01 Feb 1980 in Monterrey, Nuevo León, Mexico (Hospital Maternidad Conchita). She married Manuel Regules-Rojas on 10 Nov 2007 in Monterrey, Nuevo León, Mexico. He was born on 29 Jan 1976.

+9. ii. FLORENCIO ANTONIO GUERRA was born on 30 Jul 1983 in Conroe, Montgomery, Texas. He married Rebeca Alessandra Vannesa on 04 Feb 2012. She was born on 14 May 1985.

10. iii. GUNTHER GUILLERMO GUERRA was born on 06 Apr 1990 in Conroe, Montgomery, Texas. He married Sofia Hernandez on 01 Sep 2017 in Monterrey, Nuevo León, Mexico. She was born on 09 Oct 1990.

11. iv. ALEXIA ROMINA GUERRA was born on 27 May 1993 in Conroe, Montgomery, Texas.

Generation 3

8. MARIEL ALEXANA[3] GUERRA-MULLER (Florencio Ignacio[2] Guerra, Abel Eulalio[1] Guerra, José Antonio[A] Guerra, Jesus Maria[B] Guerra, José Lino de Jesus[C] Guerra, José Manuel[D] Guerra, José Antonio Albino Hinojosa[E] Guerra, Joseph Ramon[F] Guerra, Capitan Cristóbal[G] Guerra-Cañamar, Ignacio[H] Guerra-Cañamar, Antonio[I] Guerra-Cañamal II, Antonio[J] Guerra-Cañamal) was born on 01 Feb 1980 in Monterrey, Nuevo León, Mexico (Hospital Maternidad Conchita).

She married **Manuel Regules-Rojas** on 10 Nov 2007 in Monterrey, Nuevo León, Mexico. He was born on 29 Jan 1976.

Left: Mariel Guerra and Manuel Regules pose for a Christmas portrait with their children, Dec 2019, from left: Mariel Arianne, Manuel, Manuel Andreu, Mariel, Christian Alexander –from Florencio Guerra Collection.

Manuel Regules-Rojas and Mariel Alexana Guerra-Muller had the following children:

12. i. MARIEL ARIANNE[4] REGULES-GUERRA was born on 04 Feb 2014 in Conroe, Montgomery, Texas.
13. ii. MANUEL ANDREU REGULES-GUERRA was born on 03 Jun 2015 in Conroe, Montgomery, Texas.
14. iii. CHRISTIAN ALEXANDER REGULES-GUERRA was born in Sep 2017 in Conroe, Montgomery, Texas.

9. FLORENCIO ANTONIO[3] GUERRA (Florencio Ignacio[2], Abel Eulalio[1], José Antonio[A], Jesus Maria[B], José Lino de Jesus[C], José Manuel[D], José Antonio Albino Hinojosa[E], Joseph Ramon[F], Capitan Cristóbal[G] Guerra-Cañamar, Ignacio[H] Guerra-Cañamar, Antonio[I] Guerra-Cañamal II, Antonio[J] Guerra-Cañamal) was born on 30 Jul 1983 in Conroe, Montgomery, Texas. He married **Rebeca Alessandra Vanessa** on 04 Feb 2012. She was born on 14 May 1985.

Florencio Antonio Guerra and Rebeca Alessandra Vanessa had the following children:

15. i. REBECA ALESSANDRA[4] GUERRA was born on 26 Aug 2016 in Edinburg, Hidalgo, Texas.
16. ii. SARA VANESSA GUERRA was born on 24 Mar 2019 in Edinburg, Hidalgo, Texas.

Abel Luis Guerra and Susana Blanca Gasque e Sol (fourth and fifth from left in back row), with children and grandchildren --2019 photo from Abel Guerra Jr. Collection.

Florencio Guerra (fourth from left) and Evelyn Audrey Muller-Gandolfo (fifth from right), with children and grandchildren --2019 photo from Florencio Guerra Collection.

Chapter 5. Victoria Guerra and Ruben Gabriel Valle

Generation 1

1. VICTORIA^I **GUERRA** (José Antonio^A, Jesus Maria^B, José Lino de Jesus^C, José Manuel^D, José Antonio Albino Hinojosa^E, Joseph Ramon^F, Capitan Cristóbal^G Guerra-Cañamar, Ignacio^H Guerra-Cañamar, Antonio^I Guerra-Cañamal II, Antonio^J Guerra-Cañamal) was born on 24 Mar 1898 in Roma, Starr, Texas (Rancho El Colorado) as the third child of José Antonio Guerra and Tecla Guerra de Guerra. She had eight siblings, namely: Teresa, Abel Eulalio, Guadalupe Filiberto, Margarita, Maria Florinda, Herlinda, Fidencio Miguel, and Evangelina. She died on 18 Sep 1978 in Rio Grande City, Starr, Texas (Age 80). When she was 26, she married (1) **BERNARDO DE LA GARZA JR.**, son of Ygnacio De la Garza and Aurora Martinez, on 20 Feb 1925 in McAllen, Hidalgo, Texas. He was born on 03 Jul 1895 in Randado, Jim Hogg County, Texas (Rancho De la Garza). He died on 15 Feb 1927 in Laredo, Webb, Texas (Age 31). When she was 41, she married (2) **RUBEN GABRIEL VALLE**, son of Calixto Cedric Valle and Herminia L. Longoria, on 09 Sep 1939 in Saltillo, Coahuila de Zaragoza, Mexico. He was born on 01 Oct 1900 in Rio Grande City, Texas. He died on 06 Jun 1991 (Age 90).

Left: Undated portrait of Victoria Guerra, possibly around the time of her first marriage in the 1920s –photo from Guadalupe Guerra Collection.

Victoria Guerra lived in Justice Precinct 4, Starr, Texas in 1900 (Marital Status: Single; Relation to Head of House: Daughter). She lived in Justice Precinct 4, Starr, Texas in 1910 (Marital Status: Single; Relation to Head of House: Daughter). She lived in Rio Grande City, Starr, Texas in 1941 (103 N Corpus St). She had a medical condition of Parkinson's disease, then a botched brain operation made her an invalid about 1954. She lived in Rio Grande City, Starr, Texas in 1978. She was buried on 20 Sep 1978 in Rio Grande City, Starr, Texas (Rio Grande City Cemetery, N Fairgrounds Rd and W 3rd St, Find A Grave #197169262). She was also known as *Tia* Vira. Her primary cause of death was Pneumonia.

Victoria spent the first thirteen years of her life with her brothers and sisters on Rancho El Colorado at Guerra, Texas before the family moved into McAllen in about 1913. By 1919 her parents had died during the Spanish flu epidemic, her older brother Abel had moved to Mexico, and her younger brother Guadalupe had become the head of household, working as a merchant in a retail store. The five Guerra sisters were very pretty and by 1921 Victoria's older sister Teresa was married. Four years later 26 year old Victoria married 29 year old Bernardo De la Garza Jr. of the De la Garza Ranching family of Randado and she moved to Laredo, Texas.

Right: News clipping of Bernardo De la Garza's suicide, Feb 16, 1927 —from Laredo Daily Times.

Victoria's life was just beginning and a bright future seemed assured. But storm clouds were on the horizon. For as yet unknown reasons, after they had been married for only two years, her husband Bernardo committed suicide. According to the Feb 16, 1927 edition of the Laredo Daily Times, "Bernardo De la Garza returned from the Mexican side of the Rio Grande, telephoned goodbye to a sister, told his wife (Victoria) goodbye; procured his 45-caliber revolver, proceeded to the bathroom of this home at 2019 Chacon street in Montrose, and sent a bullet crashing through his brain producing instant death" (Laredo Daily Times, 1927, p. 1).

Victoria was devastated and soon moved back to Rio Grande City to be closer to her sisters and brothers. There, twelve years after her first husband died, she met and married Ruben Valle in 1939, hoping for a new life with him. He was 38, two years younger than Victoria, and some said he married her for her money, as she did receive the remaining property of Bernardo De la Garza Jr., but we do not know what it was or what value it had. Her niece Mary Guerra remembers, "I heard that *Tio* (Uncle) Ruben bought her a new car and parked it in front of their house to show her, even though he knew she did not know how to drive."

Even with a new husband and a new car, Victoria's life got more complicated. By the time she was fifty-six years of age she was said to have developed serious tremors attributed to Parkinson's disease. To make matters worse, her niece Mary Guerra says that a botched deep brain stimulation operation to stop the tremors made her an invalid and by 1954 she could no longer walk. Victoria's nephew George Guerra's family visited her often and George recalls, "From what my mother tells me, she had Parkinson's, and back then there were not the kind of medicines you have today to treat Parkinson's, and so they tried an experimental surgery that supposedly the neurologist back then felt would help and it ended up paralyzing her" (Guerra G. , 2019). Ruben cared for her, but her main caregiver became her younger sister

Herlinda, who moved in with them at one point. Victoria died in 1978 at age 80 from pneumonia complications from Parkinson's disease.

Bernardo De la Garza Jr. was born on 03 Jul 1895 in Randado, Jim Hogg County, Texas (Rancho De la Garza) as the first child of Ygnacio De la Garza and Aurora Martinez). He died on 15 Feb 1927 in Laredo, Webb, Texas (Age 31). When he was 29, he married Victoria Guerra, daughter of José Antonio Guerra and Tecla Guerra de Guerra, on 20 Feb 1925 in McAllen, Hidalgo, Texas.

Bernardo De la Garza Jr. was employed as a Stockman at Rancho De la Garza in 1917 in Randado, Jim Hogg County, Texas. He lived in Laredo, Webb, Texas on 05 Jun 1917 (Street Address: 1708 Victoria St; Marital Status: Single). He lived in Laredo, Webb, Texas in 1927 (2019 Chacon St). He was buried on 17 Feb 1927 in Laredo, Webb, Texas (Calvary Catholic Cemetery, 3600 McPherson St; Block 16, Find A Grave #177488081). His cause of death was suicide (gunshot wound to head). Race: Spanish American).

Portrait of five Guerra brothers and sisters in about 1941, from left, front: Fidencio, Abel; back: Evangelina, Teresa, Victoria –photo from Guadalupe Guerra Collection.

Ruben Gabriel Valle was born on 01 Oct 1900 in Rio Grande City, Texas as the first child of Calixto Cedric Valle and Herminia L. Longoria. He died on 06 Jun 1991 (Age 90). When he was 38, he married Victoria Guerra, daughter of José Antonio Guerra and Tecla Guerra de Guerra, on 09 Sep 1939 in Saltillo, Coahuila de Zaragoza, Mexico.

Ruben Gabriel Valle lived in Justice Precinct 1, Starr, Texas in 1910 (Age 9; Marital Status: Single; Relation to Head of House: Son). He lived in Justice Precinct 1, Starr, Texas in 1920

(Street Address: East Street; Age 19; Able to Speak English: Yes; Attended School: Yes; Can Read: Yes; Can Write: Yes; Enumeration District: 154; Language Spoken: Spanish; Relation to Head of House: Son; Marital Status: Single). He was employed by the Grulla Common School District No 1 in 1942 in Rio Grande City, Starr, Texas. He lived in Rio Grande City, Starr, Texas in 1942 (Age 42; Relation to Head of House: Self). He was described as Complexion: Light; Eye Color: Brown; Hair Color: Black; Height: 5'5"; Weight: 142 on 16 Feb 1942 in Rio Grande City, Starr, Texas. He lived in Rio Grande City, Texas in 1991; Street Address: 108 N Pope St). He was buried in Jun 1991 in Rio Grande City, Starr, Texas (Rio Grande City Cemetery, N Fairgrounds Road and West 3rd St; Find A Grave #197169455). Race: (White)

Above: Victoria (front) and Ruben Valle, Jan 1962
–photo from Guadalupe Guerra Collection.

Bernardo De la Garza Jr. and Victoria Guerra had no children.
Ruben Gabriel Valle and Victoria Guerra had no children.

Victoria & Ruben Valle house
103 N Corpus Street, Rio Grande City,
13 Jan 2019.

Victoria & Ruben Valle graves
Rio Grande City Cemetery,
13 Jan 2019.

Chapter 6. Guadalupe Filiberto Guerra and Nettie LaVonne Taylor

Generation 1

1. GUADALUPE FILIBERTO[1] GUERRA (José Antonio[A], Jesus Maria[B], José Lino de Jesus[C], José Manuel[D], José Antonio Albino Hinojosa[E], Joseph Ramon[F], Capitan Cristóbal[G] Guerra-Cañamar, Ignacio[H] Guerra-Cañamar, Antonio[I] Guerra-Cañamal II, Antonio[J] Guerra-Cañamal) was born on 16 Mar 1900 in Roma, Starr, Texas (Rancho El Colorado) as the fourth child of José Antonio Guerra and Tecla Guerra de Guerra. He had eight siblings, namely: Teresa, Abel Eulalio, Victoria, Margarita, Maria Florinda, Herlinda, Fidencio Miguel, and Evangelina. He died on 27 Dec 1982 in Boise, Ada, Idaho (Age 82). When he was 45 he married **Nettie LaVonne Taylor**, daughter of Richard Thomas Taylor and Roxie Ann Gibbs, on 18 Apr 1945 in Boise, Ada, Idaho (First Christian Church). He was also known as Lupe.

Guadalupe and the younger Guerra children in 1915 in McAllen, Texas, three years before their parents died. Front: Evangelina, Guadalupe, Fidencio; back: Maria Florinda and Herlinda –photo from Guadalupe Guerra Collection.

Guadalupe Filiberto Guerra lived in Justice Precinct 4, El Salineno, Starr, Texas on 15 Jun 1900 (Marital Status: Single; Relation to Head of House: Son). He lived in Justice Precinct 4, Starr, Texas in 1910 (Relation to Head of House: Son). Draft Registration: Bet. 1917–1918 in Hidalgo County, Texas. He lived in McAllen, Hidalgo, Texas in 1920 (Marital Status: Single; Relationship: Head). He lived in McAllen, Hidalgo, Texas in 1930 (Marital Status: Single; Relation to Head of House: Head). He lived at 1716 Beaumont Ave, McAllen, Hidalgo, Texas in 1935 (Agent, Magnolia Coffee Company). He lived in McAllen, Hidalgo, Texas on 01 Apr 1940 (Age 40); Marital Status: Single; Relation to Head of House: Head. He was employed as a Salesman for Lee Auto Company at age 41 on 15 Feb 1942 in McAllen, Hidalgo, Texas. He was described on 15 Feb 1942 in McAllen, Hidalgo, Texas as: Complexion: Light; Eye Color: Brown; Hair Color: Brown; Height: 71in; Weight: 192 lbs; mole on right temple. He served in the military between 30 Jun 1942 to 11 Sep 1945 at Fort Sam Houston, TX; and Gowen Army Airfield, Idaho (Sgt 141st Bomb Wing). He was employed as a VA Hospital Statistician Clerk in 1950 in Boise, Ada, Idaho, USA. He lived in Boise, Ada, Idaho, USA in 1960 (308 Clithero Dr). He lived in Boise, Ada, Idaho, USA in 1982 (308 Clithero Dr). He was buried on 30 Dec 1982 in Boise, Ada, Idaho, USA (Cloverdale Memorial Park, Find A Grave #193540388). He was also known as Lupe. His cause of death was a heart aneurism after several heart attacks. Race: (White)

Guadalupe was the fourth of nine children and was born and grew up on Rancho El Colorado at what is now Guerra, Texas as did his brother Abel who was four years older. Like many ranch kids, "Lupe" as he was known, rode horses, helped with the livestock and loved to hunt. Although he hunted white-tailed deer, he also liked Javalina, saying, "The wild hogs, I used to get lots of them. . . Get a young one, barbeque them especially, they are good meat. . . They say they never have heard of anybody getting sick eating Armadillo or Javelina meat at any time, because they are raised on roots." Lupe also helped chop down more than a few native mesquite trees to build the stacked *corrales de leños* (log corrals) commonly used in Texas (see photo in Chapter 1, page 39) saying, "All the fences was built like that at that time. I saw some that were almost a hundred years old. . . and by God not even a cat could go through there" (Guerra G. , 1978).

Left: Portrait of Guadalupe Guerra in Tampico, Mexico on 24 Sep 1921 –photo from Guadalupe Guerra Collection.

But ranch life ended for Lupe at age thirteen. He explained, "In 1912 after I finished Spanish school on the ranch I went to Laredo to the English school. . . Heck there wasn't any English-speaking kids in my class. . . I passed first, second, and third grade all in one year. That's when I learned to say good morning in English" (Guerra G. , 1978). When his family moved to McAllen the next year, Lupe went to school there, but only through seventh grade. José Antonio Guerra and his wife Tecla died during the 1918 influenza epidemic, leaving eight orphan children. Since oldest son Abel was fighting in the revolution in Mexico, it was left up to the next oldest son, 18 year old Guadalupe, to get a job if he wanted to keep his orphaned family together and raise his three sisters and younger brother, which he did for the next fifteen years.

As Lupe recounted, "I had a rich aunt, dad's sister, (Matilde Guerra) that wanted to take two of the girls. Tere was the oldest one and I told her I don't know if you consider myself capable, but I think I will (raise the family) . . . and we all lived together in the same house." When his last parent died, Lupe said his older sister Tere told him, "You have just lost your father. The responsibility of your little brothers and sisters is too big. But God always tries his favored children and see if they have faith in God. You are one of the favored children evidently. Have faith in God. He will help you" (Guerra G. , 1978).

Right: Guadalupe Guerra in his Picador clothes, McAllen, Sep 1924 –photo from Guadalupe Guerra Collection.

Since it was traditionally the Spanish custom, the oldest male child, Lupe Guerra, became the head of household for his four younger siblings: Florinda, Herlinda, Fidencio, and Evangelina. His oldest sister Teresa helped out until she married in 1921. They all loved him for keeping them together. To do this he worked as a storekeeper, agent for the Magnolia Coffee Company, salesman for the Lee Auto Company, and even a Picador at the Reynosa, Mexico bull ring in 1926. He said he worked as a Picador in Reynosa "just to kill time" and they used three and four-year-old bulls. "We never killed the bulls. The ranchmen would donate the bulls. . . They used to charge a dollar, dollar and a half you know. We used to have some pretty good crowds" (Guerra G. , 1978). By 1933 Guadalupe's youngest sister Evangelina was 21 years old, and all the orphans were now old enough to support themselves. Lupe, with his limited education, worked as a salesman during the Great Depression after his responsibilities to his family had been completed.

Left: 1941 Texas Poll Tax Receipt –Guadalupe Guerra Collection.

When World War II broke out in 1941, Guadalupe was already a corporal in the Texas National Guard. He told me, "Three of us were in the automobile business but couldn't get any cars to sell because of the war. I was 43 years old and couldn't be drafted." But, he went to the draft board anyway and said, "I don't have a damn thing to do and I want to go see the world. . . Why don't you send me and see if San Antonio will take me." They did, and after enlisting in the U.S. Army Air Corps, Corporal Guerra completed seven weeks of military training or "hard labor" as he called it, at Sheppard Field in Wichita Falls, Texas. After basic and advanced training there, he was sent to Salt Lake City to wait for assignment. He along with eight others in his group were assigned to Gowen Field, Idaho. From there he was tasked to the 15th Bomb Wing training squadron in Sioux City, Iowa. Soon he returned with the Bomb Wing which was de-activated, and Guadalupe was reassigned to the 141st Bomb Wing at Gowen Field. For three and a half years Guadalupe kept the same job as a file clerk and was promoted to sergeant (Guerra G. , 1978).

Left: Guadalupe Guerra and Nettie Taylor on their wedding day 18 Apr 1945 –photo from Guadalupe Guerra Collection.

In April 1945 Germany was overrun by the Allies, U.S. President Franklin D. Roosevelt died, and Sergeant Guadalupe Guerra married a young pediatrics nurse, Nettie Taylor, in Boise with his good friend and Army buddy Cruz Bettencourt as best man. In September of that same year Japan surrendered and Lupe was honorably discharged from the Army Air Corps. Lupe told me that he and his new wife Nettie bought a 1937 Dodge automobile to drive to Texas and find a job and place to live. But Nettie's father Richard Taylor was selling his farm near Eagle, Idaho and asked if they would stay and help them for a couple of months. Guadalupe agreed and went to the unemployment office to look for a temporary job. He found that the Veterans Administration was looking for file clerks and was willing to hire him for a couple of months. So he took the job and ended up staying with the VA for seventeen and a half years. Along the way, he went to Business College part-time for 5 years to learn accounting and was promoted to Statistician Clerk. Lupe and Nettie lived in Boise for the rest of their lives.

Far Left: Painting of Guadalupe Guerra done by Nettie Taylor in Jan 1983 shortly after he died.

Left: Nettie (Taylor) Guerra sketch, 8 Oct 1945 –from Guadalupe Guerra Collection.

Nettie LaVonne Taylor was born on 03 Feb 1915 in Okemah, Okfuskee, Oklahoma, USA as the sixth child of Richard Thomas Taylor and Roxie Ann Gibbs. She had six siblings, namely: Elsie Blanche, Nommie Lee, Bessie Amanda, Richard Lamuel II, Artice Raymond, and Marjorie Ellen. She died on 28 Apr 2002 in Boise, Ada, Idaho (Age 87). When she was 30, she married Guadalupe Filiberto Guerra, son of José Antonio Guerra and Tecla Guerra de Guerra, on 18 Apr 1945 in Boise, Ada, Idaho, USA (First Christian Church).

For more information on Nettie LaVonne Taylor see *"The Descendants of Richard Thomas Taylor-Chapter 8"* (Conklin D. G., 2020).

Guadalupe Filiberto Guerra and Nettie Lavonne Taylor had the following children:

+2.   i.   TECLA ANN[2] GUERRA was born on 14 Oct 1946 in Boise, Ada, Idaho, USA (St Alphonis Hospital). She married Daniel Oakley Blood, son of Harold Clifton Blood and Marjorie Alene Jones, on 14 Jul 1973 in Boise, Ada, Idaho, USA (St Stephens Church). He was born on 27 Apr 1937 in Moscow, Latah, Idaho, USA. He died on 04 May 1977 in Potlatch, Latah, Idaho, USA.

+3.   ii. MARY LAVONNE GUERRA was born on 15 Jun 1949 in Boise, Ada, Idaho, USA. She married David Gene Conklin on 22 Nov 1969 in Moscow, Latah, Idaho, USA (Trinity Baptist Church).He was born on 03 Nov 1948 in Lynwood, Los Angeles, California, USA.

4.   iii. ANTONIO RICHARD GUERRA was born on 20 Mar 1954 in Boise, Ada, Idaho, USA. He died on 17 Apr 1954 in Boise, Ada, Idaho, USA (Age 28 days). He was described as red hair, bluish green eyes in Apr 1954 in Boise, Ada, Idaho, USA. He was buried in Apr 1954 in Boise, Ada, Idaho, USA (Cloverdale Memorial Park, 11825 W Fairview Ave; Find A Grave #132078861). His cause of death was congenital heart disease with harelip and cleft palate.

Guerra family prepares for a feast in Boise, Idaho in about 1956.
From left: Tecla, Guadalupe, Nettie, and Mary –photo from Guadalupe Guerra Collection.

Generation 2

2. TECLA ANN[2] **GUERRA** (Guadalupe Filiberto[1], José Antonio[A], Jesus Maria[B], José Lino de Jesus[C], José Manuel[D], José Antonio Albino Hinojosa[E], Joseph Ramon[F], Capitan Cristóbal[G] Guerra-Cañamar, Ignacio[H] Guerra-Cañamar, Antonio[I] Guerra-Cañamal II, Antonio[J] Guerra-Cañamal) was born on 14 Oct 1946 in Boise, Ada, Idaho, USA (St Alphonis Hospital as the first child of Guadalupe Filiberto Guerra and Nettie LaVonne Taylor). She had two siblings, namely: Mary LaVonne and Antonio Richard. When she was 26, she married **Daniel Oakley Blood**, son of Harold Clifton Blood and Marjorie Alene Jones, on 14 Jul 1973 in Boise, Ada, Idaho, USA (St Stephens Church).

Tecla Ann Guerra lived in Boise, Idaho, USA in 1962 (Age 16). She graduated in Jun 1964 in Boise, Ada, Idaho, USA (Boise High School). She was employed as a McCall Elementary School music teacher between 1968 and 1971 in McCall, Valley, Idaho, USA. She received a University of Idaho, BS (Music Education) degree in May 1969 in Moscow, Latah, Idaho, USA. She was employed as an Elementary music and orchestra teacher between 1971 and 1973 in Boise, Ada, Idaho, USA. She lived in Potlatch, Latah, Idaho, USA in 1973 (Duffield Flat Rd). She lived in Potlatch, Latah, Idaho, USA in 1993 (Duffield Flat Rd). She was described in 2014 in Moscow, Latah, Idaho as having a ruddy complexion, brown hair, brown eyes, height 5'6" weight 225lbs (Idaho driver license).

Tecla remembers her childhood fondly as the older of two sisters:

"One of the fun things we used to do with Granddad Taylor: We would go to Lake Lowell and rent a rowboat and granddad would take a whole stack of gunny sacks and we would fish until those gunny sacks were full of catfish, hundreds of them. Then we would take them back to granddad's place and dump them into galvanized tubs. The catfish would stay alive until we would have a little butchering party which took about a week. We liked catfish!" (Guerra T. , 2018).

Left: Tecla Guerra with her Grandpa Richard Taylor's catalog-ordered violin, 17 Aug 2018.

Why Tecla became a music teacher is no mystery. She says, "I'm musical. I like to sing, to play the piano. I used to play the violin and the guitar. I started playing violin in the 4th grade. Grandpa Taylor bought a violin from the Sears & Roebuck catalog in 1906, and I still have it" (Guerra T. , 2018). Tecla learned the piano in high school from a friend during lunchtime and school breaks.

Not only does Tecla like to sing, some say she is a very good singer. In 1969 she sent a tape recording of her songs to her Aunt Evangelina Guerra, a school teacher, who wrote back, "I took it to school and when my principal heard the songs from his office, he came and asked, 'Mrs. Guerra, I am so happy to hear you can sing so well. It sounds beautiful. May I listen to the rest?' I said, 'Yes of course Mr. West,' and never told him it was my niece until the songs had finished" (Guerra E. , 1969). Tecla studied Music Education in college and after graduation taught music in McCall and Boise, Idaho, then moving to Palouse, WA and Potlatch, ID where she married Dan Blood in 1973. They had two children before his untimely death from heart failure in 1977.

Tecla was left with two babies at Dan's death. Casey was three years old and Ellery was seven months old. Her parents wanted her and the boys to move back to Boise with them, but Tecla did not want to leave her widowed mother-in-law Marjorie Blood alone on the farm. Also Tecla's home was debt free. So she and "Marge" created an informal partnership. Marge took care of her own land and all the milk cows while Tecla leased her own land to a neighbor and took care of all the cattle, sheep, horses, chickens, and later goats while Marge helped her with the boys. They had a very good working relationship and did many things together over the years until Marge passed away in 2006. When her youngest son Ellery started first grade Tecla began working for the Palouse school district where she worked for 20 years.

Tecla Guerra with her parents on her wedding day 14 Jul 1973. From left: Nettie, Tecla, Guadalupe Guerra –photo from Guadalupe Guerra Collection.

Tecla has remained very active in the nearby communities of Palouse and Potlatch. She sang for 10 years with their large Community Chorus. In 1994 Tecla and her mother Nettie Guerra went with the chorus to sing in Austria and Hungary. They rehearsed in the same palace Hayden, Beethoven, Mozart, and other famous musicians worked, studied and performed. Her mother was thrilled to make such a trip with Tecla and they brought back many happy memories. A year later, in 1995, Tecla was badly injured in a traffic accident near her home and as a result had to sell her livestock and curtail many of her farm activities. Then in 2017 she was injured in a second traffic accident and since then has had to really slow down. But she still lives on the family farm with her oldest son Casey and his family who remodeled and moved into Grandma Marge's house next door.

Daniel Oakley Blood was born on 27 Apr 1937 in Moscow, Latah, Idaho, USA as the first child of Harold Clifton Blood and Marjorie Alene Jones. He died on 04 May 1977 in Potlatch, Latah, Idaho, USA. When he was 36, he married Tecla Ann Guerra, daughter of Guadalupe Filiberto Guerra and Nettie LaVonne Taylor, on 14 Jul 1973 in Boise, Ada, Idaho, USA (St Stephens Church).

Right: Daniel Blood on his and Tecla's wedding day on 14 Jul 1973 –photo from Guadalupe Guerra Collection.

Daniel Oakley Blood lived in Palouse, Latah, Idaho, USA in 1940 (Marital Status: Single; Relation to Head of House: Son). He graduated in Jun 1955 in Potlatch, Latah, Idaho, USA (Potlatch High School). He was employed as a grain and legume Farmer (peas and lentils) and Electrician in 1973 in Potlatch, Latah, Idaho, USA. He lived on Rt. 1, Potlatch in 1977. He was buried on 07 May 1977 in Potlatch, Latah, Idaho (Freeze Cemetery; Find A Grave #24849229). His cause of death was a streptococcus infection leading to heart failure from a previously unknown defective heart valve.

Daniel Oakley Blood and Tecla Ann Guerra had the following children:

+5. i.   CASEY GUERRA[3] BLOOD was born on 29 Apr 1974 in Moscow, Latah, Idaho, USA (Gritman Memorial Hospital). He married Cathy Hui-Ju Woo, daughter of George Tai Mei Woo and Nancy Fong Ju Chen, on 01 Jun 1996 in Palouse, Whitman, Washington, USA (Palouse Federated Church). She was born on 14 May 1976 in T'ai-pei, Taiwan.

+6. ii. ELLERY ABNER BLOOD was born on 26 Sep 1976 in Moscow, Latah, Idaho, (Gritman Memorial Hospital). He married Alexa Braughton, daughter of William Braughton and Zena Marie Dickenson, on 25 Sep 2005 in Shawnee-on-Delaware, Monroe, PA. She was born on 19 Jul 1984 in Moscow, Latah, Idaho.

3. MARY LAVONNE[2] GUERRA (Guadalupe Filiberto[1], José Antonio[A], Jesus Maria[B], José Lino de Jesus[C], José Manuel[D], José Antonio Albino Hinojosa[E], Joseph Ramon[F], Capitan Cristóbal[G] Guerra-Cañamar, Ignacio[H] Guerra-Cañamar, Antonio[I] Guerra-Cañamal II, Antonio[J] Guerra-Cañamal) was born on 15 Jun 1949 in Boise, Ada, Idaho, USA as the second child of Guadalupe Filiberto Guerra and Nettie LaVonne Taylor. She had two siblings, namely: Tecla Ann and Antonio Richard. When she was 20, she married **David Gene Conklin** on 22 Nov 1969 in Moscow, Latah, Idaho, USA (Trinity Baptist Church).

Left: Tecla and Mary Guerra (on right) pose in their new dresses in about 1953, --photo from Guadalupe Guerra Collection.

Mary LaVonne Guerra graduated in June 1967 in Boise, Ada, Idaho, USA (Capital High School). She was employed at the Helena Public Library in 1974 in Helena, Lewis and Clark County, Montana. She was employed as a Veterinarian Assistant in 1977 in Helena, Lewis and Clark, Montana. She was employed as a Montana Legislative Council Librarian in 1983 in Helena, Lewis and Clark, Montana. She received an AS Degree (Business Management) in May 1997 from Flathead Valley Community College. She was employed as a Flathead Valley Community College Instructor in 2001 in Kalispell, Flathead, Montana. She was described as: fair complexion, brown hair, blue eyes, height 5'3" weight 190 lbs (MT driver license) on 13 Jun 2014 in Kalispell, Flathead, Montana. She tested her DNA on 07 Jan 2017 in Ancestry Kit #A022185. DNA Match: 22 Nov 2018 (1st cousins: Leonard Guerra Jr., Daniel Guerra, Gloria Garza, Arlene Taylor, Dennis Taylor) She has a medical condition of osteo-arthritis.

Born and raised in Boise, the Idaho summers were some of Mary's fondest memories:
"I remember just summer times running through the neighborhood. We would do our chores first thing in the morning and then we were outside. . . We kids rode our bikes, we played in the dirt, and we went to the (Boise) River . . . and we would eat baloney sandwiches on white bread and drink Kool-Aid . . . and we had no helmets or seat belts or any kind of security, and we all lived through it somehow" (Guerra M. , 2015).

Upon graduation from Capital High School in 1967 she attended the University of Idaho where her sister Tecla was a senior at the time. Mary sang in the University's Vandaleer Chorale and played string bass in the orchestra.

She met and married her lifelong partner Dave Conklin in 1969 while in college. Their daughter Dacia was born the next year and in 1972 they moved to Helena, Montana where Dave worked for State Parks while Mary worked for the Lewis & Clark County Library and later the Montana Legislative Council Library. In 1980 they moved to Miles City where their son Christopher was born in 1982. They returned to Helena in 1983 and in 1990 moved to Kalispell where Mary received her Associates Degree in 1997 from Flathead Valley Community College and later joined the faculty.

Mary explained, "I had numerous professions because Dave kept moving. I started out as an artist, then librarian, which I enjoyed the most because I loved books and research, especially trivia questions. I worked at a veterinary clinic. I taught computer classes both overseas and in Montana" (Guerra M. , 2015).

Mary Guerra and David Conklin on their
Wedding day, 22 Nov 1969.

Mary and Dave's 50th Wedding Anniversary,
22 Nov 2019.

Mary also took on the burden of managing the home, children, pets, and finances during the many times Dave was training or deployed overseas as an Army Reserve officer. In 1998 she and son Chris were able to join him for a year where she taught computer classes at the Anglo-American School in Sofia, Bulgaria. During that time they were able to travel throughout Europe together. After Dave returned from two years in Iraq in 2006, she retired from teaching and moved with him to Hawaii for 7 years where he worked as an IT technician and where Mary made many friends, became a Sea Turtle Guardian, and rescued and trained her service and therapy dog Mai Tai. During that time she also loved to travel throughout the Islands and to Australia with friends and family. Always ready for a new adventure, Mary again moved with Dave when his job was relocated to Camp Pendleton, California in 2012. When Dave retired, they bought a winter home and moved to Sun City, AZ where she has been active in crafts and other clubs.

Although she was raised in the city of Boise, Mary was always around horses, dogs, and cats and became an avid horsewoman, gardener, and dog trainer. The family home in Boise always included pet dogs, cats, and a garden full of flowers and vegetables. She was also an excellent cook, seamstress, and nurse which she learned from her mother and spent many loving hours passing her talents and skills on to her children Dacia and Chris, as well as grandchildren Justin and Isabelle. As for hobbies Mary says, "I like to read, I like to sew, crochet and knit, and cook, and go for walks" (Guerra M. , 2015).

David Gene Conklin was born on 03 Nov 1948 in Lynwood, California (St Francis Hospital) as the first child of Charles Franklin Conklin and Betty Marinkovic. He had three siblings, namely: Rita Marie, Joan Louise, and Lorie Ann. When he was 21, he married Mary LaVonne Guerra on 22 Nov 1969 in Moscow, Latah, Idaho (Trinity Baptist Church).

Right: Mary (Guerra) and Staff Sergeant Dave Conklin, U.S. Army Reserve, attend the Marine Corps Birthday Ball in Honolulu, Hawaii, 11 Nov 2006.

David Gene Conklin graduated in May 1966 in South Gate, Los Angeles, California (South Gate High School). He served in the military between Jun 1969 and Oct 2008 in the US Army Reserve/National Guard (Combat Engineer/Broadcast Journalist). He received a BS Degree (Forestry) in Jun 1970 at the Univ of Idaho. He received a MS Degree (Natural Resources) in Dec 1972 at Univ of Montana. Public Service: Bet. 1973 and 1999 as a Montana State Park Ranger. He received a MBA degree in Jun 1998 at the Univ of Montana. He was described as: Gray hair, blue eyes, left-handed, 5'8" 145 lbs. in 2006 in Honolulu, Hawaii (Hawaii driver license). He had the medical condition of Parkinson's disease; O+ blood type on 03 Nov 2014 in Kalispell, Flathead, Montana. He tested his DNA on 07 Jan 2017 in Ancestry Kit #A858700 (Haplogroup Y= R1a (most common group in Tatars). DNA Match: 07 Jan 2017 (1st/2nd cousins: Diane Berg, Charlene Elfers, Savo Marinkovic, Ginger Walston, Alice Kirkman, James Mauzey). He had a heart attack while hiking on 08 Jun 2017 in Kalispell, Flathead, Montana. He tested his DNA on 08 Jun 2018 in Family Tree Y-DNA37 Kit #MK36621 (Haplogroup Y= R-M269). He tested his DNA on 23 Nov 2018 in 23andMe Kit #72-9118-1743-3929 (Haplogroup Y= R-L1066), X= H1c). He is also known as Dave and by the title of Lieutenant Colonel. He was affiliated with the Serbian Orthodox religion. For more information about David Gene Conklin see *"Conklin-Marinkovic Family History"* (Conklin D. G., 2018, p. 64).

David Gene Conklin and Mary LaVonne Guerra had the following children:

+7. i. DACIA MARIE³ CONKLIN was born on 06 Feb 1970 in Moscow, Latah, Idaho, USA (Gritman Memorial Hospital). She had a child with (1) MYRON TROY KUNZ, son of Myron Logan Kunz and Sandra Lucille Nelson, on 21 Jul 1994 in Mesa, Maricopa, Arizona, USA (Partner split-up in 1998). He was born on 12 May 1968 in Sandy, Utah, USA. She married (2) RANDAL WILLIAM ENGLISH on 16 Mar 2000 in Bullhead City, Mohave, Arizona, USA. He was born on 26 Jan 1970 in Montana.

+8. ii. CHRISTOPHER ANDREW CONKLIN was born on 29 Apr 1982 in Miles City, Custer, Montana (Holy Rosary Hospital). He had a child with (1) BRITTANY SMITH on 29 Apr 2004 in Kalispell, Flathead, Montana (Partner split-up in 2006). She was born in Kalispell, Flathead, Montana (adopted daughter). He met his current partner (2) JESSICA SWANSON about 2007 in Kalispell, Flathead, Montana. She was born on 13 Apr 1984 in St Paul, Hennepin, Minnesota.

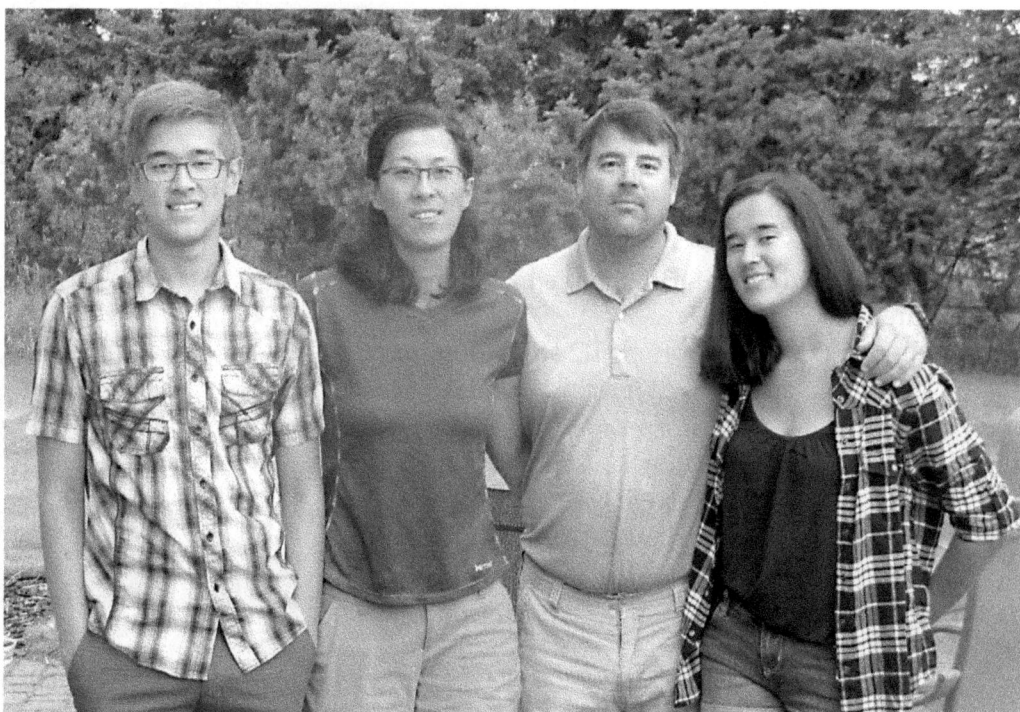

Casey Blood family, from left: Derrick, Cathy Woo, Casey, and Lyssa, 13 Aug 2017

5. CASEY GUERRA³ BLOOD (Tecla Ann² Guerra, Guadalupe Filiberto¹ Guerra, Daniel Oakley, Harold Clifton) was born on 29 Apr 1974 in Moscow, Latah, Idaho, USA (Gritman Memorial Hospital). He married **Cathy Hui-Ju Woo**, daughter of George Tai Mei Woo and Nancy Fong Ju Chen, on 01 Jun 1996 in Palouse, Whitman, Washington, USA (Palouse Federated Church). She was born on 14 May 1976 in T'ai-pei, Taiwan. Casey has worked for fifteen years for the Wilbur Ellis Agribusiness Company providing seed and fertilizer for local pea, lentil, and wheat farmers and enjoys being a Boy Scout Troop and Venture Crew leader. Cathy works at nearby Washington State University in Pullman and also volunteers with Habitat for Humanity and Boy Scouts.

Casey Guerra Blood and Cathy Hui-Ju Woo had the following children:
9. i. DARRICK⁴ BLOOD was born on 07 Sep 1996 in Spokane, Spokane, Washington, USA (Sacred Heart Hospital).
10. ii. LYSSA WOO BLOOD was born on 13 Sep 1998 in Moscow, Latah, Idaho, USA (Gritman Memorial Hospital).

6. ELLERY ABNER³ BLOOD (Tecla Ann² Guerra, Guadalupe Filiberto¹ Guerra, Daniel Oakley, Harold Clifton) was born on 26 Sep 1976 in Moscow, Latah, Idaho, USA (Gritman Memorial Hospital). He married **Alexa Braughton**, daughter of William Braughton and Zena Marie Dickenson, on 25 Sep 2005 in Shawnee-on-Delaware, Monroe, Pennsylvania, USA. She was born on 19 Jul 1984 in Moscow, Latah, Idaho, USA.

Ellery Abner Blood and Alexa Braughton had the following children:

11. i. OLIVER⁴ BLOOD was born on 02 Nov 2009 in Annapolis, Anne Arundel, Maryland.
12. ii. IAN BLOOD was born on 12 Sep 2012 in Moscow, Latah, Idaho, USA.
13. iii. ANNEMARIE PEARL BRAUGHTON BLOOD was born on 07 Dec 2014 in Moscow, Latah, Idaho, USA.

Alexa Braughton and Navy Commander Ellery Blood, 2019.

7. DACIA MARIE³ CONKLIN (Mary LaVonne² Guerra, Guadalupe Filiberto¹ Guerra, David Gene) was born on 06 Feb 1970 in Moscow, Latah, Idaho (Gritman Memorial Hospital) as the first child of David Gene Conklin and Mary LaVonne Guerra. She had one sibling, namely: Christopher Andrew. When she was 24, she had a child with Myron Troy Kunz, son of Myron Logan Kunz and Sandra Lucille Nelson, on 21 Jul 1994 in Mesa, Maricopa, Arizona, USA (Partner split-up in 1998). When she was 30, she married **Randal William English** on 16 Mar 2000 in Bullhead City, Mohave, Arizona, USA.

Left: At age 3 Dacia Conklin was a flower girl for her Aunt Tecla's wedding on 14 Jul 1973.

Dacia Marie Conklin was baptized in 1970 in Spokane, Spokane, Washington, USA (Serbian Orthodox). She lived in Helena, Montana in 1985. She graduated in Jun 1988 in Helena, Lewis and Clark, Montana (Helena High School). She lived in Mesa, Maricopa, Arizona, USA in Aug 1988 (Street Address: 930 S Dobson Road Rd). She lived in Helena, MT in 1990 (Postal Code: 59601-9656; Street Address: 1919 Grizzly Gulch Dr; Postal Code: 85202-1055; Street Address: 2107 W Broadway Rd Apt 159; Postal Code: 85202-2910 (1996); Street Address: 930 S Dobson Rd; Postal Code: 85201 (1993); Street Address: 2060

North Cn 412; Age 20). She lived in Kalispell, Flathead, Montana in 1998. She received AAS, AAA Degrees (Business) in May 2002 at Flathead Valley Community College. She lived in Bozeman, Gallatin, Montana in Aug 2002. She received a BS Degree (Business) in Dec 2003 at Montana State University. Dacia was employed as an EMC2 Environmental Engineering Project Assistant in 2004 in Bozeman, Gallatin, Montana. She was employed as a Blue Cross-Blue Shield Health Insurance Claims Adjuster in 2008 in Helena, Lewis and Clark, Montana. She lived in Helena, Lewis and Clark, Montana in 2008. She was employed as a Montana Dept of Revenue Liquor Control Division compliance supervisor in Aug 2014 in Helena, Lewis and Clark, Montana. She was described in 2016 in Helena, Lewis and Clark, Montana as: Blonde hair, blue eyes, right-handed, 5'2" 167 lbs. (Montana driver license).

Some of the Blood, Conklin and English families at the Conklin home in Kalispell, MT. From front row on left: Mary Guerra, Tecla Guerra, Dacia Conklin, Dave Conklin with family dog Mai Tai. Back row on left: Casey Blood, Randy English, Cathy Woo Blood, Derrick Blood, Lyssa Blood, 13 Aug 2017.

Randal William English was born on 26 Jan 1970 in Helena, Montana. When he was 30, he married Dacia Marie Conklin, daughter of David Gene Conklin and Mary LaVonne Guerra, on 16 Mar 2000 in Bullhead City, Mohave, Arizona, USA.

Randy as he was known, graduated in 1988 in Helena, Lewis and Clark, Montana (Helena High School). He was employed as a Tower Meats meat cutter in 1988 in Helena, Lewis and Clark, Montana. He was employed as an American Chemet maintenance man in 1992 in East Helena, Lewis and Clark, Montana. He received an AA Degree (Surveying) in May 2002 at

Flathead Valley Community College. He lived in Bozeman, Gallatin, Montana in Aug 2002. He received a BS Degree (Civil Engineering) in Dec 2006 at Montana State University. He was employed as a Tetra Tech Environ Engineering (Civil Engineer) in Apr 2007 in Helena, Lewis and Clark, Montana. He lived in Helena, Lewis and Clark, Montana in 2008. He is also known as Randy.

Randal William English and Dacia Marie Conklin have no children.
Myron Troy Kunz and Dacia Marie Conklin had the following children:
14. i.   JUSTIN TROY^4 KUNZ was born on 21 Jul 1994 in Mesa, Maricopa, Arizona, USA (Mesa Lutheran Hospital).

8. CHRISTOPHER ANDREW^3 CONKLIN (Mary LaVonne^2 Guerra, Guadalupe Filiberto^1 Guerra, David Gene) was born on 29 Apr 1982 in Miles City, Custer, Montana (Holy Rosary Hospital). He had a child with (1) **BRITTANY SMITH** on 29 Apr 2004 in Kalispell, Flathead, Montana (Partner split-up in 2006). She was born in Kalispell, Flathead, Montana (adopted daughter). He met his current partner (2) **JESSICA SWANSON** about 2007 in Kalispell, Flathead, Montana. She was born on 13 Apr 1984 in St Paul, Hennepin, Minnesota, USA.

Christopher Andrew Conklin and Jessica Swanson have no children.
Christopher Andrew Conklin and Brittany Smith had the following children:
15. i.   ISABELLE IONA^4 CONKLIN was born on 29 Apr 2004 in Kalispell, Flathead, Montana.

Annual Independence Day gathering at Randy English family ranch in the Sweetgrass Hills of Montana, from left: Justin Kunz, Dave Conklin, Dacia Conklin, Randy English, Jessica Swanson, Chris Conklin, Isabelle Conklin, Mary Guerra, 5 Jul 2016.

Chapter 7. Maria Florinda Guerra

Generation 1

1. MARIA FLORINDA[I] GUERRA (José Antonio[A], Jesus Maria[B], José Lino de Jesus[C], José Manuel[D], José Antonio Albino Hinojosa[E], Joseph Ramon[F], Capitan Cristóbal[G] Guerra-Cañamar, Ignacio[H] Guerra-Cañamar, Antonio[I] Guerra-Cañamal II, Antonio[J] Guerra-Cañamal) was born on 07 Sep 1903 in Cuevitas, Hidalgo, Texas (Rancho La Presita) as the sixth child of José Antonio Guerra and Tecla Guerra de Guerra. She had eight siblings, namely: Teresa, Abel Eulalio, Victoria, Guadalupe Filiberto, Margarita, Herlinda, Fidencio Miguel, and Evangelina. She died on 08 Jun 1934 in McAllen, Hidalgo, Texas (Age 30).

Maria Florina Guerra in 1915
–photo from Guadalupe Guerra Collection.

Maria Florinda Guerra in about 1925
–photo from Leonard Guerra Jr. Collection.

Maria Florinda Guerra lived in Justice Precinct 4, Starr, Texas in 1910 (Age 8; Relation To Head of House: Daughter). She lived in McAllen, Hidalgo, Texas in 1920 (Street Address: 16th Ave; Age 14; Attended School: No; Can Read: Yes; Can Write: Yes; Enumeration District: 77; Marital Status: Single; Relation To Head of House: Sister). She lived in McAllen, McAllen, Hidalgo, Texas in 1930 (Street Address: 16th Ave; Age 21; Able To Speak English: Yes; Attended School: No; Can Read Write: Yes; Enumeration District: 0023; Registration District: 23; Marital Status: Single; Relation To Head of House: Sister). She lived in McAllen, Hidalgo, Texas in 1934 (Street Address: 2304 E Augusta St). She was buried in Jun 1934 in McAllen, Hidalgo, Texas (La Piedad Cemetery Sec B2 Line 16 Space 34; Find A Grave #197164087). She was also known as Florencia. Her primary cause of death was Tuberculosis. Race: (White) Race: (Mexican).

She was known as Florinda although her 1903 birth certificate says Maria Guerra without her middle name of Florinda. She was the second of three Guerra children that were born at Rancho La Presita in Cuevitas, Texas. Florinda spent the first ten years of her life with her brothers and sisters at La Presita before the family moved to McAllen in 1913. By 1919 her parents had died during the Spanish flu epidemic, her older brother Abel had moved to Mexico, and her younger brother Guadalupe had become the head of household, working as a merchant in a retail store.

According to Fidencio Guerra Jr., "My dad said she was a very sickly girl. She was always very sick" (Guerra F. J., Fidencio Guerra Jr. Family History Video Interview, 2019). Although she lived to age 30, I have found very little information or any stories about Maria Florinda other than her death certificate, witnessed by her older brother Guadalupe, which lists her cause of death as Tuberculosis of the lungs. But also listed as a contributing factor in her death was the clinical diagnosis of infantilism. Infantilism in a general sense is childlike behavior in adults, particularly lack of judgement and poor ability to make conclusions based on logical reasoning as well as actions driven more by immediate impressions and impulses rather than by rationale. Depending on degree of expression can range from mental disorder, to behavioral disorder or simply psychological makeup and personality trait of otherwise healthy person (Wikipedia, 2020).

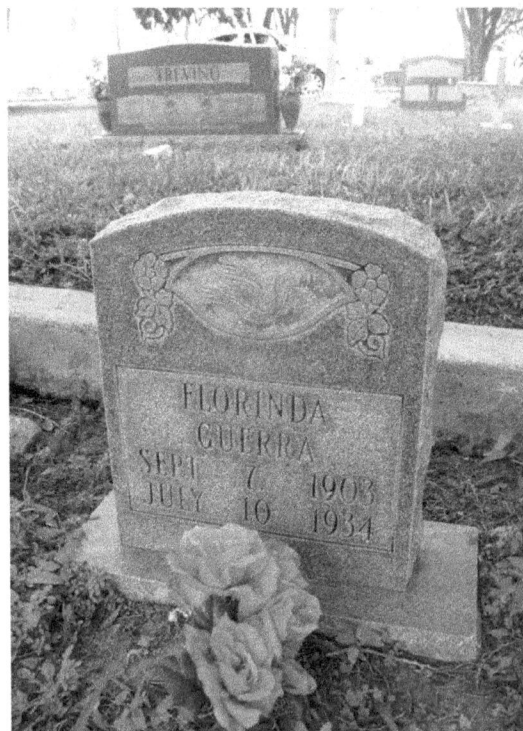

Maria Florinda Guerra is buried near her parents in La Piedad Cemetery,
McAllen, Texas, 10 Jan 2019 photo.

So we do not know the circumstances of her life or how she contracted tuberculosis and died from the disease. Maria Florinda was buried next to her parents In McAllen's La Piedad Cemetery.

Maria Florinda Guerra had no children.

Chapter 8. Herlinda Guerra and Elmer Libby Babb

Generation 1

1. HERLINDA[1] GUERRA (José Antonio[A], Jesus Maria[B], José Lino de Jesus[C], José Manuel[D], José Antonio Albino Hinojosa[E], Joseph Ramon[F], Capitan Cristóbal[G] Guerra-Cañamar, Ignacio[H] Guerra-Cañamar, Antonio[I] Guerra-Cañamal II, Antonio[J] Guerra-Cañamal) was born on 12 Mar 1906 in Roma, Starr, Texas (Rancho La Presita) as the seventh child of José Antonio Guerra and Tecla Guerra de Guerra). She had eight siblings, namely: Teresa, Abel Eulalio, Victoria, Guadalupe Filiberto, Margarita, Maria Florinda, Fidencio Miguel, and Evangelina. She died on 10 Sep 1989 in Edinburg, Hidalgo, Texas (Age 83). She donated her body to the Univ. of Texas. When she was 36, she married **Elmer Libby Babb** on 05 Mar 1943 in McAllen, Hidalgo, Texas (in the home of her brother Fidencio Guerra).

Right: Sisters Teresa and Herlinda Guerra (right) pose by a lemon tree in McAllen, Texas in the 1930's –photo from Guadalupe Guerra Collection.

Herlinda Guerra lived in Justice Precinct 4, Starr, Texas in 1910 (Relation to Head of House: Daughter). She lived in McAllen, Hidalgo, Texas in 1920 (Street Address: 16th Ave; Age 13; Able To Speak English: Yes; Attended School: Yes; Can Read: Yes; Can Write: Yes; Enumeration District: 77; Relation To Head of House: Sister; Marital Status: Single). She arrived in Hidalgo, Texas on 04 Aug 1923 (Age 16). She lived in McAllen, Hidalgo, Texas in 1930.

Left: Visiting Teresa Guerra and grandson Eduardo in Saltillo, Mexico in April, 1973. From left: Eduardo Aguirre, Teresa Guerra, Herlinda Guerra, Mary Guerra and daughter Dacia Conklin –photo from Guadalupe Guerra Collection.

(Street Address: 16th St; Age 22; Able To Speak English: Yes; Attended School: No; Can

Read Write: Yes; Enumeration District: 0023; Registration District: 23; Marital Status: Single; Relation To Head of House: Sister). She lived at 1716 Beaumont Ave, McAllen, Hidalgo, Texas in 1935 (Marinello Beauty Shop Hairdresser). She lived in McAllen, Hidalgo, Texas in 1940; Age 32; Occupation: Saleswoman; Attended School: No; Class of Worker: Wage or salary worker in private work; Employment Code: 1; Employment Details: No; Employment History: No; Enumeration District: 108-19; Grade Completed: High School, 4th year; Hours Worked: 40; Income: $700; Income Other Sources: No; Is Employed: Yes; Language Spoken: Spanish; Public Emergency Work: No; Seeking Work: No; Usual Class Of Worker: Wage or salary worker in private work; Usual Industry: Ladies Clothes; Usual Occupation: Saleswoman; Usual Occupation Code: 298 65 1; Veteran: No; Weeks Worked: 52; Marital Status: Single; Relation To Head of House: Sister). She lived in McAllen, Hidalgo, Texas in 1973. She had a medical condition of a broken hip, then she stopped eating and died in 1989 in McAllen, Hidalgo, Texas. She was buried in Sep 1989 in McAllen, Hidalgo, Texas (La Piedad Cemetery Sec B2 Line 16 Space 32 Find A Grave #197164330). She was also known as Linda. Race: (White) Race: (Mexican).

Linda as she was called, or *Tia* Linda (Aunt Linda) as her nieces and nephews knew her, was the last of Antonio Guerra's children to be born on Rancho La Presita. She was very close to two of her older sisters, Victoria and Florinda, and later after Florinda died and Victoria contracted Parkinson's decease, she became Victoria's live-in caregiver until Victoria died. In McAllen she worked as a hairdresser at the Marinello Beauty Shop until 1939 when she left to manage a ladies ready-to-wear shop on Main Street and Austin Avenue for her friend Maria Resendez (Monitor, 1939, p. 2). In 1943 Linda became the bride of Elmer Babb, a recent PhD graduate of Georgetown University and resident of Washington D.C. who was stationed in Mexico City working for the U.S. Public Health Service helping to move Mexican farm workers to the U.S. during World War II. The wedding was held in Linda's brother Fidencio's home in McAllen (Monitor, 1943, p. 8). So off she went to live in Mexico City while Elmer was working there.

Elmer Babb and Herlinda Guerra Babb in Mexico City, 1943
–photo from Guadalupe Guerra Collection.

A few months later, Elmer was to report back to Washington for re-assignment. So Linda took a train from Mexico City to visit her family in McAllen before joining Elmer. Her trip turned out to be newsworthy when her train was delayed by a cattle train that wrecked ahead of her train and another train full of VIPs. So the two trains spent two days in the remote backcountry of Delores, Mexico without fresh food or water waiting for crews to clear stock cars and dead cattle from the tracks (Monitor, 1943, p. 4).

By January 1944 Linda and Elmer were on their way to his next Public Health Service assignment in Trinidad in the British West Indies (Monitor, 1944, p. 4). But for some reason, five months later she was back in Saltillo, Mexico taking courses at the business college "while her husband is in Trinidad on government business" (Monitor, 1944, p. 2). We do not know when their relationship began to fray, but one story circulated was that Elmer beat his wife Linda, and her brother Guadalupe Guerra, helped her get away from him until she was able to get a divorce. She never remarried.

Left: Herlinda Guerra Babb is buried to the left of her parents at La Piedad Cemetery in McAllen, Texas, 11 Jan 2019 photo.

Much later, in the summer of 1973, I remember when Linda came with my wife Mary's parents to visit us at our home in Helena, Montana and we put her on a horse for her first time. Mary always said, "Although other cousins complained about her being so strict when she was babysitting, she was always so sweet to me. Our favorite phrase was 'I love you a bushel and a peck and a hug around the neck.'

Elmer Libby Babb was born on 30 Jun 1905 in East Lebanon, Maine, USA. He died on 05 Apr 1969 in San Francisco, California (Age 64). When he was 37, he married Linda Guerra, daughter of José Antonio Guerra and Tecla Guerra de Guerra, on 05 Mar 1943 in McAllen, Hidalgo, Texas.

Elmer Libby Babb lived in Belmont, Middlesex, Massachusetts, USA in 1910. He lived in Boston, Suffolk, Massachusetts, USA in 1920. He arrived in Fort Shafter, Honolulu, Hawaii, USA in 1932 (Tripler Army Hospital). He arrived in the C.G. Hawaiian Department, from Ft. McDowell, California on 07 Oct 1932. He departed from Fort Slocum, New York on 07 Oct 1932. He lived in Honolulu, Hawaii Territory in 1935. He departed from San Francisco, California, USA on 05 Sep 1936 (Fort McDowell on Angel Island). He lived in High Point, North Carolina, USA in 1940 (Occupation: Salesman). He lived in Washington, District of Columbia, USA in 1940 (Age 35). He arrived in Laredo, Texas on 22 Oct 1943 (Age 36). He arrived in Miami, Florida, USA on 13 Sep 1944. He arrived in New York, New York on 17 May 1946. He arrived in New York, New York on 10 Jan 1953. He lived in San Francisco, California, USA in 1958. Race: (White).

Elmer was born the youngest of three children and spent much of his life in government service traveling the world. He was born in Maine, lived in Boston, and by 1925 was married to Nora Wilkinson and had a child in Washington, D.C. Then from 1920 to about 1936 was in the U.S. Army Medical Corps and spent time at Tripler Army Hospital in Hawaii. By 1940 he was in the U.S. Public Health Service working on assignments in Mexico, Trinidad and elsewhere.

We do not know when he and his first wife Nora split up, but in 1943 he married Herlinda Guerra in Texas. After he and Herlinda split up he worked for the U.S. Public Health Service in Europe and managed to get captured and held by the Russians in East Germany during the cold war (Santa Maria Times, 1952, p. 5). Apparently he remarried again and moved to San Francisco where he died in 1969.

Elmer Babb in 1912   Elmer Babb about 1950
–photos from Daniel Babb Collection, Dallas, Texas.

Soviets Free Three Allies

BERLIN, (U.P.) — The Russians today released an American official and two British Army officers who were swept up in a sudden wave of arrests in East Berlin and East Germany.

Three British soldiers who disappeared on the highway between Berlin and Western Germany apparently still were held by the Russians.

The American official is Elmer L. Babb, of Lebanon, Me., attached to the United States Public Health Service. It was disclosed he was held more than 48 hours after a truck he was driving skidded off the Western Germany-Berlin highway into a ditch. Babb was bringing X-ray equipment to the American consulate here.

Left: News article about Elmer Babb release by the Russians in East Germany –from (Santa Maria Times, 1952, p. 5).

Elmer Libby Babb and Nora Elizabeth Wilkinson had the following children:
1. Raymond Babb was born in 1925 in Washington, District of Columbia, USA. He died in 2015.

Elmer Libby Babb and Herlinda Guerra had no children.

Chapter 9. Fidencio Miguel Guerra and Estela Guadalupe Margo

Generation 1

1. FIDENCIO MIGUEL[1] GUERRA (José Antonio[A], Jesus Maria[B], José Lino de Jesus[C], José Manuel[D], José Antonio Albino Hinojosa[E], Joseph Ramon[F], Capitan Cristóbal[G] Guerra-Cañamar, Ignacio[H] Guerra-Cañamar, Antonio[I] Guerra-Cañamal II, Antonio[J] Guerra-Cañamal) was born on 07 Aug 1909 in Jim Hogg, Texas (Rancho San Miguel) as the eighth child of José Antonio Guerra and Tecla Guerra de Guerra. He had eight siblings, namely: Teresa, Abel Eulalio, Victoria, Guadalupe Filiberto, Margarita, Maria Florinda, Herlinda, and Evangelina. He died on 12 Dec 2004 in McAllen, Hidalgo, Texas (Age 95). When he was 31, he married **Estela Guadalupe Margo**, daughter of Ruperto Reymundo Margo and Sofia Clarke, on 30 Jan 1941 in Rio Grande City, Starr, Texas.

Fidencio Guerra's bilingual abilities and law degree allowed him to serve the U.S. State Department in Embassies in Columbia and then Spain during World War II.
Above left: Fidencio Guerra in Bogotá, Columbia, 1943.
Above right: Guerra family in Bogotá, Jan 1944; from left: Roberto, Estela, Fidencio, Diana –photos from Fidencio Guerra Collection.

Fidencio Miguel Guerra lived in Justice Precinct 4, Starr, Texas in 1910 (Relation to Head of House: Son). He graduated about 1928 in McAllen, Hidalgo, Texas (McAllen High School). He lived in Austin, Texas in 1932 (Univ. of Texas). He lived at 1716 Beaumont Ave, McAllen, Hidalgo, Texas in 1935 (School Teacher). He was employed as a City Commissioner between 1937 and 1942 in McAllen, Hidalgo, Texas. He received a JD (Juris Doctor) degree in 1940 at the University of Texas, Austin. He lived in McAllen, Hidalgo, Texas in 1940 (Address: Beaumont Ave; Age 30; Occupation: Salesman; Class of Worker: Wage or salary worker in private work; Enumeration District: 108-19; Grade Completed: College, 4th year; Hours Worked: 50; Income: $750; Income Other Sources: Yes; Is Employed: Yes; Weeks Worked: 52; Marital Status: Single; Relation To Head of House: Brother). In 1940 he was described as Complexion: Light; Eye Color: Brown; Hair Color: Brown; Height: 5'10"; Weight: 145 lbs.

He served the U.S. State Department as an attorney in Washington D.C., Bogotá, and Madrid. He lived in Bogotá, Colombia in 1943 (U.S. Embassy). He lived in Madrid, Spain in 1945 and 1946 (U.S. Embassy). He was employed as a Justice of the Peace between 1946 and 1949 in Edinburg, Hidalgo County, Texas. He was employed as a Texas Asst. Attorney General from 1949 to1952 in Austin, Travis, Texas. He was employed as an attorney at law in private practice between 1952 and 1954 in McAllen, Hidalgo, Texas. He was employed as the 139th District Court Judge between 1954 and 1980 in Edinburg, Hidalgo County, Texas. He lived in McAllen, Hidalgo, Texas in 1963 (Postal Code: 78501; Street Address: 704 W Maple Ave; Age 54). He lived in McAllen, Hidalgo, Texas in 2000 (704 W Maple Ave). He was buried on 15 Dec 2004 in Mission, Hidalgo, Texas (Valley Memorial Gardens Sec B Lot 226 Space 2; Find A Grave #12636155). He was known by the title of Judge. He was affiliated with the Catholic religion. Race: (White).

In 1954 Fidencio Guerra was appointed as judge of the newly formed 139th District Court, becoming the first Hispanic District Judge in the Rio Grande Valley, Texas –undated photo from Fidencio Guerra Collection.

Fidencio was the second youngest child in his family. His closest brother Guadalupe was nine years older and raised him from the age of ten after their parents died in the 1918 Spanish flu epidemic. After graduation from McAllen High School, he attended the University of Texas in Austin where he was a handball champion, graduating with a law degree. He returned to McAllen and began a career in public service starting with his election to the City Commission in 1937. He met his future wife Estela Margo in Rio Grande City due to the efforts of their mutual cousin Arturo Guerra, grandson of Diodoro and Matilde Guerra. According to Fidencio Guerra Jr., "Arturo was an orphan like my father and would spend a week or two in Rio Grande City with my mother's family, and would spend time in McAllen. . . They grew up together so he (Fidencio) would go along with him (Arturo) to Rio Grande and that's how he met my mom" (Guerra F. J., Fidencio Guerra Jr. Family History Video Interview, 2019). They were married in 1941 with Arturo serving as best man.

During World War II Fidencio and his older brother Guadalupe both signed up for the draft, but when the officials noted that Fidencio had a law degree and was bilingual, he was given a job at the U.S. State Department in 1942. By 1943 Fidencio was in Bogotá assisting Columbian officials in the handling of German, Italian and Japanese assets in that country. His wife and daughter Diana were with him and his first son, Roberto, was born there. In 1945 he was reassigned with his family to the U.S. Embassy in Madrid, Spain where he processed cases against Germans and Italians for war crimes there. His second son, Carlos, was born there. In 1946 Fidencio returned to McAllen and was appointed as Justice of the Peace. In 1949 he accepted a position for two years as a Texas Assistant Attorney General and began commuting to Austin while Estela kept the home together.

His oldest son Roberto remembers that he would come home on weekends, and on Saturday night "We would all get into our little car and for a dollar or something we'd all go to the movies at the drive-in" (Guerra R. , 2019). The family always had Sunday dinner together, and Fidencio always ate at noon. Daughter Judy recalled, "Mother would make roast beef, peas, mashed potatoes, and we would all have dinner together every Sunday" (Guerra J. , 2019).

According to his younger son Carlos, another tradition every summer for the family was to go to the beach at Corpus Christi or Brownsville for ten days or so (Guerra C. , 2018). Daughter Judy added, "All of us would get together in the old station wagon, we would be like the 'Clampets.' We'd go to Corpus Christi for a few days and rent a cabana there. Poor mother she worked like a lunatic and all of us would get our inner tubes; Daddy would blow them up; and then we'd all go like little ducks holding hands on the beach" (Guerra J. , 2019).

News clipping of Fidencio Guerra appointment as 139th District Court Judge. –from (The Daily Review, 1954, p. 1).

Fidencio was back in McAllen by 1954, appointed as judge of the newly formed 139th District Court, becoming the first Hispanic District Judge in the Rio Grande Valley. Two years later he was elected at large, and re-elected until he retired in May, 1980. Fidencio continued to serve as a substitute judge for several years. His seven children say that all his life he was a voracious reader of both Spanish and English books, magazines, poetry and newspapers. He loved to write as well. Daughter Brenda recalled, "He was either reading or writing, or on the typewriter, and walking back and forth" (Guerra B. , 2019). My wife Mary Guerra and I often used to get typed or hand-written letters from Fidencio, both in Spanish and English, many of which we still have.

Review

Independent Daily Newspaper
...rnoon, September 14, 1954   — Price 5 Cents —   NO. 172

Fidencio Guerra Picked As 139th Court Judge

Named As Compromise Candidate

Fidencio Guerra of McAllen today was named judge of the new 139th District Court by Gov. Allan Shivers as a compromise candidate.

Hidalgo County's delegation to the state Democratic convention at Mineral Wells accepted Guerra as a compromise candidate after the delegation voted 22-6 for Joe B. Alamia, district attorney, over Jackson Littlehm, Edinburg lawyer.

Alamia supporters pressed to get a unanimous vote but the eight would not change. Then Charley Thompson, former county Democratic chairman, Bill Whalen and other McAllenites pushed for Guerra when the delegation began to look for a compromise candidate.

Hidalgo County is joining hands with the Harris County liberal delegation and voted 16 to 8 to join the Yarborough liberals.

Guerra is a native of Jim Hogg County and has lived at McAllen since 1914. He was graduated from high school there and attended the University of Texas. He was admitted to the bar in 1940.

The new judge served on the McAllen city commission from 1939 to 1943 and was with the U. S. Department of State in Bogota, Colombia and Madrid, Spain from 1945 to 1947, during World War II.

He was a Justice of the peace in McAllen in 1948 and 1949.

Then he became an assistant attorney general of Texas, serving from 1949 to 1953.

In the last primary election he ran against Mrs. Helen Singleton for county treasurer but was the unsuccessful candidate.

Guerra is a member of the McAllen Public Library Board and the board of directors of the county March of Dimes. He is married and has six children.

FIDENCIO GUERRA

Estela Guadalupe Margo was born on 15 Aug 1911 in Rio Grande City, Starr, Texas as the first child of Ruperto Reymundo Margo and Sofia Clarke. She died on 29 Jul 1999 in McAllen, Hidalgo, Texas (Age 87). When she was 29, she married Fidencio Miguel Guerra, son of José

Antonio Guerra and Tecla Guerra de Guerra, on 30 Jan 1941 in Rio Grande City, Starr, Texas.

Estela Margo portrait as an infant in 1911 –photo from Fidencio Guerra Collection.

Estela Guadalupe Margo lived in Justice Precinct 1, Starr, Texas in 1920. She lived in Rio Grande, Starr, Texas in 1930. She lived in Austin, Texas in 1932. She graduated about 1932 in Austin, Travis, Texas (St Mary's Academy Catholic High School). She lived in Justice Precinct 1, Starr, Texas in 1935. She received a BS (Language, Music) degree about 1937 in University of Texas, Austin. She was employed as an elementary school teacher between 1938 and 1941 in Rio Grande City, Starr County, Texas. She lived in Justice Precinct No 1, Starr, Texas in 1940 (Street Address: Second Street; Age 28; Occupation: Teacher; Attended School: No; Class of Worker: Wage or salary worker in Government work; Employment Code: 1; Enumeration District: 214-1; Grade Completed: College, 1st to 4th year; Income: $990; Income Other Sources: No; Occupation Code: V34 91 2; Weeks Worked: 36; Marital Status: Single; Relation To Head of House: Daughter). She lived in Bogotá, Bolivar, Colombia in 1943 (U.S. Embassy). She lived in Madrid, Spain between 1945 and 1946 (U.S. Embassy). She was employed as an Edinburg, McAllen High School Spanish teacher between 1957 and 1977 in Hidalgo County, Texas. She lived in McAllen, Hidalgo, Texas in 1963 (Postal Code: 78501-2422; Street Address: 704 W Maple Ave; Age 52). She lived in McAllen, Hidalgo, Texas in 1992 (Postal Code: 78501-4460 (1992); Street Address: 1400 N 16th St Apt 204). She was buried on 31 Jul 1999 in Mission, Hidalgo, Texas (Valley Memorial Gardens Sec B Lot 226 Space 3; Find A Grave #111728886). She had a medical condition of asthma as does her daughter Judy. She was affiliated with the Catholic religion. Race: (White).

Right: Estela Margo's now vacant home on Washington & Main Street, Rio Grande City, 13 Jan 2019.

Estela Margo grew up in Rio Grande City, Texas. Her great grandfather Robert Margo came to Mexico from France; and her mother Sofia Clarke was Irish. Estela's daughter Brenda remembers her grandmother (Sofia) as, "having very long hair and when I used to go to Rio Grande City and spend the night, I can remember my grandmother brushing her hair, and I used to just watch her because she had beautiful hair. . . Her (Estela's) uncle had a ranch in the Margo family where she used to go horseback riding and they used to have gatherings with her grandmother. . . Those were really fond memories for her" (Guerra B. , 2019). Brenda's sister Judy added, "My grandmother (Sofia) was a very hard-working woman. . . She was real fair (complexion) like my mom, and sort of grayish eyes, and she only spoke Spanish" (Guerra J. , 2019).

Left: Sofia Clarke wedding portrait, 18 Apr 1910 –photo from Fidencio Guerra Collection.

Estela attended the Catholic elementary school in Rio Grande City and then attended high school at St. Mary's Academy in Austin. After graduation in about 1932, she enrolled at Our Lady of the Lake College in San Antonio, Texas. After two years, she transferred to the University of Texas at Austin where she graduated in about 1937 with a degree in language and music. She returned to Rio Grande City and taught Spanish and Piano there for three years until she married Fidencio Guerra in 1941.

In the early years of World War II, Estela accompanied Fidencio, who had been appointed on special assignment with the U.S. embassies in Bogotá, Colombia, and Madrid, Spain. While abroad, Estela occupied her time rearing her first two children, Diana and Roberto, and taking classes in language, history and the arts at the universities of these capital cities. Upon their return to Texas in 1946, she spent the next twelve years raising her seven children.

Her children remember her as an average cook, but an outstanding baker who made delicious cakes and pies for special occasions. Her son Roberto says, "She had a wonderful upside down cake, potato cake, and would make *turkos* for Christmas. She had a lemon cake, orange cake, wonderful coffee cake, and *arroz con pollo*" (rice with chicken) (Guerra R. , 2019). Also Roberto recalled, "My mother was a very strict Catholic, confessions every weekend, prayers at night." Estela was a strict disciplinarian also. "We were taught to mind our P's and Q's, and keep family business a secret. . . No one told us a thing. We didn't know why *Tia* Linda's last name was Babb. I was thirty-five not knowing she had been divorced" (Guerra R. , 2019).

In 1957, Estela resumed her teaching career in Edinburg where she taught Spanish for ten years at Edinburg High School, then transferred to McAllen High School and taught Spanish for ten more years until her retirement in 1977. In 1971, Estela was the recipient of the prestigious American Association of Spanish and Portuguese Cervantes Award. This recognition is presented to an outstanding teacher of the Alamo-Valley Chapter, which includes San Antonio.

Upon her retirement, Estela remained active in her community with memberships in organizations including Our Lady of Sorrows Altar Society, the Pan American College Round Table, McAllen Music Club and the Retired Teachers Association, to name a few.

*Margo family picnic at the Margo Ranch near Rio Grande City
—undated photo from Fidencio Guerra Collection.*

*Surviving children of Fidencio Guerra and Estela Margo meet in McAllen, 5 Aug 2018.
From left: Brenda, Fidencio Jr., Judy, Roberto (Bobby), Carlos, Daniel
—from Guadalupe Guerra Collection.*

Estela enjoyed spending time with her family, traveling, reading, baking and tending to her rose garden.

Fidencio Miguel Guerra and Estela Guadalupe Margo had the following children:

+2. i. DIANA MARIA² GUERRA was born on 20 Oct 1941 in McAllen, Hidalgo, Texas. She died on 14 Aug 1994 in Austin, Travis, Texas (Age 52). She married Roger J. Levesque in Jun 1966 in McAllen, Hidalgo, Texas (Our Lady of Sorrows Catholic Church). He was born on 04 Dec 1939 in Bristol, Hartford, Connecticut, USA.

3. ii. ROBERTO MIGUEL GUERRA was born on 20 Nov 1943 in Bogotá, Bolivar, Colombia.

+4. iii. CARLOS ANTONIO GUERRA was born on 28 Jul 1946 in Madrid, Spain. He married Elizabeth Susan Good on 04 Jul 1987 in Scottsdale, Maricopa, Arizona, USA. She was born on 27 Jan 1961 in Hollywood, Los Angeles, California, USA.

5. iv. FIDENCIO MIGUEL GUERRA JR. was born on 19 Dec 1947 in McAllen, Hidalgo, Texas (fraternal twin of Brenda).

6. v. BRENDA ESTELA GUERRA was born on 19 Dec 1947 in McAllen, Hidalgo, Texas (fraternal twin of Fidencio Jr.). She married Bennett Franklin Brooke on 16 Jun 1984 in Austin, Travis, Texas. He was born on 29 Sep 1945 in Sherman, Grayson, Texas.

+7. vi. JUDITH ANN GUERRA was born on 06 Dec 1949 in McAllen, Hidalgo, Texas. She married Mark Edward Arnold on 23 Jun 1973 in McAllen, Hidalgo, Texas. He was born on 13 Nov 1952 in New York, USA.

+8. vii. DANIEL JOSÉ GUERRA was born on 13 May 1955 in McAllen, Hidalgo, Texas. He married Sabrina S. Garza on 25 May 1985 in Hidalgo, Texas. She was born on 02 Feb 1961.

Generation 2

2. DIANA MARIA² GUERRA (Fidencio Miguel¹, José Antonio^A, Jesus Maria^B, José Lino de Jesus^C, José Manuel^D, José Antonio Albino Hinojosa^E, Joseph Ramon^F, Capitan Cristóbal^G Guerra-Cañamar, Ignacio^H Guerra-Cañamar, Antonio^I Guerra-Cañamal II, Antonio^J Guerra-Cañamal) was born on 20 Oct 1941 in McAllen, Hidalgo, Texas as the first child of Fidencio Miguel Guerra and Estela Guadalupe Margo. She had six siblings, namely: Roberto Miguel, Carlos Antonio, Fidencio Jr., Brenda Estela, Judith Ann, and Daniel José. She died on 14 Aug 1994 in Austin, Travis, Texas (Age 52). When she was 24, she married **Roger J. Levesque** in Jun 1966 in McAllen, Hidalgo, Texas.

Diana Maria Guerra lived in McAllen, Texas in 1957. She received a BA degree on 22 Feb 1963 from Our Lady of the Lake College, San Antonio. She received a Master of Arts degree in 1965 from Our Lady of the Lake College, San Antonio. She lived in Dallas, Texas in 1968.

She was employed as a Middle School teacher and counselor about 1970 in Austin, Texas. She was employed as a High School Teacher and counselor about 1980 in Austin, Travis, Texas. She lived in Austin, Travis, Texas in 1990. She was buried on 19 Aug 1994 in Mission, Hidalgo, Texas (Valley Memorial Gardens Sec B Lot 226 Space 1; Find A Grave #111728451). She was also known as Princess. Her cause of death was metastatic breast cancer.

Left: The Levesque family in Kailua, Hawaii in 1974, from left: Diana, Jon, Michelle, and Roger Levesque –photo from Guadalupe Guerra Collection.

Diana Maria Guerra was the first of Fidencio and Estela's children. She was born in McAllen after her father became a lawyer and before the U.S. became involved in World War II. Her middle name honors both of her father Fidencio's grandmothers who were named Maria. She was the first of their children to attend Our Lady of Sorrows Catholic School in McAllen. Her family nickname was said to be given to her by her father, but her sister Judy says, "In our first house at 1225 N. 16th street in McAllen five of us slept in one bedroom, except for Diana, who as the oldest, had her own bedroom. That's why we called her princess. . . Diana was called princess, I was called *fadonga* (hippy), and Brenda was called *tusa* which is squirrel" (Guerra J. , 2019).

Right: Diana Guerra & Roger Levesque family, Jul 1987; from left: Shari, Diana, Roger, Michelle, Jon –photo from Guadalupe Guerra Collection.

After graduating from McAllen High School Diana studied to be a teacher like her mother Estela. She received a Bachelor's degree and a Master's degree from Our Lady of the Lake College in San Antonio. Diana met Roger Levesque, a U.S. Air Force veteran from Hartford, Connecticut who also became a teacher. They were married in her home church of Our Lady of Sorrows in McAllen, Texas. Diana became a middle school teacher and counselor in Austin, Texas. They also lived and taught in Kailua Kona, Hawaii, and Okinawa, Japan before moving back to Austin where she was a high school teacher and counselor until she lost her five-year battle with metastatic breast cancer. Diana died at the age of fifty-two, leaving behind a husband and three children.

In the words of her sisters, "Diana was always princess to Daddy, that's why it was such a blow when she passed. . . We all loved her so much. We all couldn't wait for her to come and visit. . . Diana was a butterfly. She was always on the phone with her friends, always in the streets. . . She loved to socialize. She wasn't so much of a housekeeper at all, that wasn't her priority" (Guerra J. , 2019).

Roger J. Levesque and Diana Maria Guerra had the following children:
+9.   i.   Jon Michael[3] Levesque. He married Tracy Ann Vincik on 08 Jun 1991 in   Austin, Travis, Texas (St Theresa Catholic Church).
10.   ii.   Michelle Judette Levesque.   She married Bryan Combes in 1994.
11.   iii.   Shari Malia Levesque.

Left: Roberto (Bobby) Miguel Guerra, Mar 1950 –photo from Guadalupe Guerra Collection.

Far Left: Diana Maria Guerra, Mar 1950 –photo from Guadalupe Guerra Collection.

3. Roberto Miguel[2] Guerra (Fidencio Miguel[1], José Antonio[A], Jesus Maria[B], José Lino de Jesus[C], José Manuel[D], José Antonio Albino Hinojosa[E], Joseph Ramon[F], Capitan Cristóbal[G] Guerra-Cañamar, Ignacio[H] Guerra-Cañamar, Antonio[I] Guerra-Cañamal II, Antonio[J] Guerra-Cañamal) was born on 20 Nov 1943 in Bogotá, Bolivar, Colombia (U.S. Embassy) as the second child of Fidencio Miguel Guerra and Estela Guadalupe Margo. He had six siblings, namely: Diana Maria, Carlos Antonio, Fidencio Jr., Brenda Estela, Judith Ann, and Daniel José.

Roberto Miguel Guerra had a medical condition of Infantile Paralysis (polio) in 1950. He received a BS Degree (History) in 1964 from Pan American College in Edinburg. He was employed as a Brown High School History Teacher between 1964 and 1994 in McAllen, Hidalgo, Texas. He lived in McAllen, Hidalgo, Texas in 2018 (704 W Maple Ave). He is also known as Bobby.

His sister Brenda remembers how they used to listen to classical music together and exchange novels. She also remembers how he did so well on an exam when they had a class together at the University. After that she wanted to be sure and sit next to him the rest of the semester (Guerra B. , 2019). Even though confined to crutches due to the effects of Polio, Roberto earned two college degrees (BS and MS in History), and was a history teacher for thirty years before retiring in 1994. He says, "We were mostly in education. Diana was a teacher, I was a teacher,

Brenda was a teacher, and Judy was a teacher, and the others went into law" (Guerra R. , 2019).

Right: Portrait of Roberto Miguel Guerra –undated photo from Fidencio Guerra Collection.

Roberto Guerra, or Bobby as he is commonly known, is the first of Fidencio's four sons, born two years after his older sister Diana. He was born in Bogotá in 1943 while his father was working on war assets at the U.S. Embassy. His middle name Miguel honors his father Fidencio Miguel Guerra. As a child Roberto went to Our Lady of Sorrows Catholic School in McAllen. During the 1950 polio epidemic both he and his three-month-old sister Judy came down with the disease, which put Roberto in a coma for two weeks. His parents not only had two sick children, but five more to raise at the time. Yet Roberto says, "My mother and father pushed me into realizing that this wasn't the end, that I could do whatever I wanted, and I did" (Guerra R. , 2019).

4. Carlos Antonio[2] Guerra (Fidencio Miguel[1], José Antonio[A], Jesus Maria[B], José Lino de Jesus[C], José Manuel[D], José Antonio Albino Hinojosa[E], Joseph Ramon[F], Capitan Cristóbal[G] Guerra-Cañamar, Ignacio[H] Guerra-Cañamar, Antonio[I] Guerra-Cañamal II, Antonio[J] Guerra-Cañamal) was born on 28 Jul 1946 in Madrid, Spain as the third child of Fidencio Miguel Guerra and Estela Guadalupe Margo. He had six siblings, namely: Diana Maria, Roberto Miguel, Fidencio Jr., Brenda Estela, Judith Ann, and Daniel José. When he was 40, he married **Elizabeth Susan Good** on 04 Jul 1987 in Scottsdale, Maricopa, Arizona, USA (St Maria Goretti Church).

Undated portrait of Susan Good and Carlos Guerra.
–photo from Fidencio Guerra Collection.

Susan and Carlos Guerra children, Dec 1997, From left: Anthony, Richard, and Elizabeth --photo from Guadalupe Guerra Collection.

Carlos Antonio Guerra graduated about 1964 in McAllen, Hidalgo County, Texas (McAllen High School). He received a BS Degree (electrical engineering) about 1968 from the

University of Texas, Austin. He received a JD Degree (Juris Doctor) in 1976 from the University of Houston. He lived in Scottsdale, AZ in 1993; Street Address: 7721 E North Ln; Postal Code: 85267-2999 (1995); Street Address: PO Box 12999; Street Address: 11604 Village Place Dr; (Age 47). He lived in Scottsdale, Arizona, USA in 2000. He lived in Scottsdale, Maricopa, Arizona, USA in 2018. He tested his DNA on 19 Jan 2019 in Scottsdale, Maricopa, Arizona (Family Tree Y-DNA37 Kit #MK36622; Haplogroup Y= R-M269). He is also known as Carlin. He was employed as an Oil & Gas attorney for Giant Industries in Phoenix, Maricopa, Arizona.

Carlos was Fidencio's third child and second son, three years younger than Roberto. He was born in Madrid in 1946 while his father was still working on war crimes cases at the U.S. Embassy. His middle name Antonio honors his grandfather José Antonio Guerra. Carlos remembers growing up with his brothers and sisters in McAllen. His youngest brother Daniel remembered, "Carlos was the bully of the family, but when it came to me he was protective because Junior would pick on me a lot and beat me up and so Carlos would beat him up" (Guerra D. , 2019).

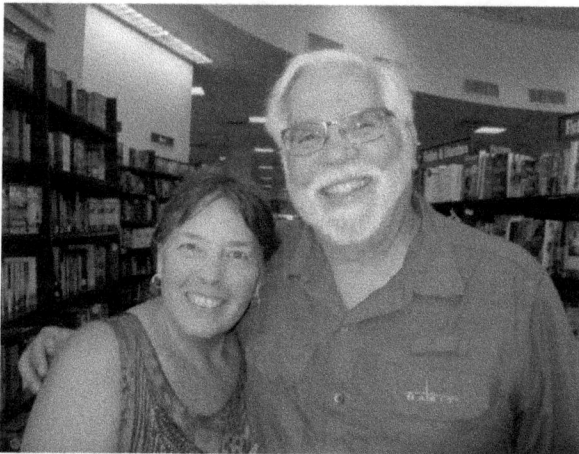

Mary (Guerra) Conklin with Cousin Carlos Guerra in Scottsdale, Arizona, 21 Apr 2018.

Carlos agrees, saying, "My brothers and sisters thought I was a bully . . . but I only bullied them when they antagonized me. When my three sisters needed to be put in line I was more than happy to do it" (Guerra C. , 2018). His sister Brenda also says that he excelled in Math and often had friends over to work on math homework. She also said that Carlos was the organizer of many informal football and soccer matches in the field near their house on Maple Avenue (Guerra B. , 2019).

But sometimes Carlos and his "accomplices" got into trouble for their efforts. His sister Judy said when she was age seven, "My brothers, when we were little we played a lot of cowboys and Indians, and they tied me to a tree – and gagged me!" It was getting dark and Judy did not come in for dinner as she was tied to a tree – exhausted, sweating, crying, gagged, with rope burns. She said her brothers Carlos and Juno got in big trouble that time (Guerra J. , 2019).

Carlos probably knew his maternal grandmother more than any of his brothers and sisters, because as he said, "I spent a lot of time in the summer with my maternal grandmother (Sofia Clarke) because my brother and sister were twins born 18 months after me and it was a big burden for my mother" (Guerra C. , 2018).

Carlos went to college at the University of Texas, Austin where he received a Bachelor's degree in electrical engineering. In 1976 he received a law degree from the University of Houston and by 1987 he was in Scottsdale, Arizona where he married his wife Susan. He spent many years as an oil and gas attorney for Giant Industries before retiring in Scottsdale.

Carlos Antonio Guerra and Elizabeth Susan Good had the following children:

12. i. ELIZABETH ANNE[3] GUERRA was born on 29 Apr 1989 in Phoenix, Maricopa, Arizona, USA.

13. ii. ANTHONY MICHAEL GUERRA was born on 29 Oct 1990 in Phoenix, Maricopa, Arizona, USA.

14. iii. RICHARD ROBERT GUERRA was born on 26 Jun 1996 in Scottsdale, Maricopa, Arizona, USA.

5. FIDENCIO MIGUEL [2] GUERRA JR. (Fidencio Miguel[1], José Antonio[A], Jesus Maria[B], José Lino de Jesus[C], José Manuel[D], José Antonio Albino Hinojosa[E], Joseph Ramon[F], Capitan Cristóbal[G] Guerra-Cañamar, Ignacio[H] Guerra-Cañamar, Antonio[I] Guerra-Cañamal II, Antonio[J] Guerra-Cañamal) was born on 19 Dec 1947 in McAllen, Hidalgo, Texas (fraternal twin of Brenda) as the fourth child of Fidencio Miguel Guerra and Estela Guadalupe Margo. He had six siblings, namely: Diana Maria, Roberto Miguel, Carlos Antonio, Brenda Estela, Judith Ann, and Daniel José.

Right: Undated portrait of Fidencio Guerra Jr.
–from Fidencio Guerra Collection.

Fidencio Miguel Guerra Jr. graduated in May 1966 in McAllen, Hidalgo County, Texas (McAllen High School). He received a BA Degree (Government) in May 1971 from Pan American College, Edinburg. He received a JD Degree (Juris Doctor) on 10 May 1974 from St Mary's University, San Antonio. He was employed as an Asst. County District Attorney in Nov 1974 in Edinburg, Hidalgo County, Texas. He was employed as an attorney at law in private practice between 1978 and 2015 in McAllen, Hidalgo County, Texas. He was elected 370th District Court Judge between 1991 and 1994 in Edinburg, Hidalgo, Texas. He lived in McAllen, TX in 1993; Street Address: 705 W Maple Ave; Street Address: PO Box 4227; Age 46. He lived in McAllen, Hidalgo, Texas in 2018. He is also known as Juno (junior).

Although he was the third of Fidencio's sons, he was named after his father Fidencio so everyone called him *Juno* (Junior). According to him, "I was the 'gray sheep' of the family and they didn't know how to control me" (Guerra F. J., Fidencio Guerra Jr. Family History Video Interview, 2019). He was also an altar boy at church, but his older brother Bobby remembers, "Fidencio was always in trouble. He was like Dennis the Menace, primarily with the nuns (at school). . . But my mother made it plain that if the nuns punish you, you're going to be punished twice" (Guerra R. , 2019).

Judge Fidencio M. Guerra Administers Lawyer's Oath To Son

Judge Fidencio M. Guerra administers the lawyer's oath to his son, Fidencio Guerra, Jr. Judge Guerra is in his 18th year of presiding over the 139th Judicial District Court in Edinburg. Fidencio Jr. is a graduate of McAllen High School and Pan American College. He graduated last May from St. Mary's Law School in San Antonio. He plans to practice in McAllen. (Photo by Slymen Showery)

Left: News clipping of Judge Fidencio Guerra (on right) administering the lawyer's oath to his son Fidencio Jr. after his graduation from law school –from (Monitor, 1974, p. 8).

Like his older brother Carlos, Fidencio Jr. became a lawyer. He received a Bachelor's degree in Government from Pan American College in 1971, and in May 1974 a law degree from St. Mary's University School of Law in San Antonio, Texas. For the next four years he was an Assistant County District Attorney for Hidalgo County in Edinburg before going into private practice in McAllen. In 1991 Fidencio Jr. was elected as the 370th District Court Judge for four years before returning to private practice until retiring in 2015.

Fidencio Guerra Jr. lives in McAllen across the street from his parents' house and did not marry. He also arguably has the best memory among all his siblings. Thus he often became the family representative when others had commitments. In the 1980s Fidencio and his twin sister Brenda together escorted their retired parents on a tour of Europe. Fidencio also went on ski trips together with Brenda and her husband Bennett. I (the author) remember one snowy December in Boise, Idaho in 1982 when Juno got off an airplane with not even a winter coat to be at his Uncle Guadalupe's funeral. He managed to return to southern Texas without frostbite and still serves when called upon to represent the Guerra family.

6. **Brenda Estela**[2] **Guerra** (Fidencio Miguel[1], José Antonio[A], Jesus Maria[B], José Lino de Jesus[C], José Manuel[D], José Antonio Albino Hinojosa[E], Joseph Ramon[F], Capitan Cristóbal[G] Guerra-Cañamar, Ignacio[H] Guerra-Cañamar, Antonio[I] Guerra-Cañamal II, Antonio[J] Guerra-Cañamal) was born on 19 Dec 1947 in McAllen, Hidalgo, Texas (fraternal twin of Fidencio Jr.) as the fifth child of Fidencio Miguel Guerra and Estela Guadalupe Margo. She had six siblings, namely: Diana Maria, Roberto Miguel, Carlos Antonio, Fidencio Jr., Judith Ann, and Daniel José. When she was 36, she married **Bennett Franklin Brooke** on 16 Jun 1984 in Austin, Travis, Texas (Green Pastures Church).

Brenda Estela Guerra lived in McAllen, Texas in 1965 (Street Address: 704 W Maple Ave). She graduated in 1966 in McAllen, Hidalgo County, Texas (McAllen High School). She received a BA degree in 1971 from Pan American College, Edinburgh. She received a Master of Education Degree (Counseling) in May 1975 from Pan American College, Edinburg. She received an MA Degree (Public Admin) about 1980 from Texas State University. She was employed as a Teacher and counselor in 1993 in Austin, Travis, Texas. She lived in Austin, TX in 1993; Street Address: 3908 Greystone Dr; (Age 46). She lived in Austin, Travis, Texas in 2018. She is also known as *tusita* (little squirrel).

Brenda was the second of Fidencio and Estela's three daughters, and a fraternal twin to Fidencio Jr. Her father nicknamed her *"tusita"* (little squirrel). She has fond memories of her childhood and the family's first house in McAllen, Texas. She says, "We grew up on 16th street. We played a lot outside because we didn't have air conditioning." The family also took annual vacations together. "I remember going to the beach in the summertime, Corpus Christi. My parents rented a cabana there and we would go for a week, I think, and we looked forward to it. My dad would take us out into the ocean. . . Each of us had inner tubes and dad was at the forefront." As a young woman Brenda remembers, "I would go to New York with my girlfriend and (my brother) Bobby many summers, and we would catch Broadway plays and go out to eat. It was so much fun. . . Growing up we were close and still are very close" (Guerra B. , 2019).

Right: Undated portrait of Brenda Guerra –from Fidencio Guerra Collection.

Far Right: Undated portrait of Judy Guerra – from Fidencio Guerra Collection.

Like several of the Guerra children, Brenda became a teacher like her mother Estela. She received Bachelor and Master of Education degrees from Pan American College in Edinburg and later a Master of Public Administration from Texas State University in San Marcos. She met her future husband Bennett Brooke in Austin who was the brother of one of her teacher friends. Brenda's father, Judge Fidencio Guerra, performed the civil ceremony for them. Brenda spent her career teaching and counseling until she retired in Austin where she lives with her husband Bennett.

Bennett Franklin Brooke and Brenda Estela Guerra have no children.

7. JUDITH ANN[2] GUERRA (Fidencio Miguel[1], José Antonio[A], Jesus Maria[B], José Lino de Jesus[C], José Manuel[D], José Antonio Albino Hinojosa[E], Joseph Ramon[F], Capitan Cristóbal[G] Guerra-Cañamar, Ignacio[H] Guerra-Cañamar, Antonio[I] Guerra-Cañamal II, Antonio[J] Guerra-Cañamal) was born on 06 Dec 1949 in McAllen, Hidalgo, Texas as the sixth child of Fidencio Miguel Guerra and Estela Guadalupe Margo. She had six siblings, namely: Diana Maria, Roberto Miguel, Carlos Antonio, Fidencio Jr., Brenda Estela, and Daniel José. When she was 23, she married **Mark Edward Arnold** on 23 Jun 1973 in McAllen, Hidalgo, Texas (Our Lady of Sorrows Catholic Church).

Judith Ann Guerra had a medical condition of Infantile Paralysis (polio) and asthma about 1950. She was employed as a Special Education Teacher between 1989 and 2018 in McAllen, Hidalgo, Texas. She lived in McAllen, Hidalgo, Texas in 2018 (701 W Maple Ave). She is also known as Judy and *fadonga* (hippy).

Judith Ann or Judy as she was called, is the youngest girl in her family. She believes she was named after an aunt. In her words, Judy says she was always a friendly, smiling, laughing, outgoing child. But in 1950 both Judy and her older brother Roberto contracted Polio during the Polio epidemic of that year. She was only three months old and had a full cast; later only a brace for her right leg. As a child with a brace she could not climb the trees or keep up with her brothers and sisters. As Judy told me, "I was in a full-length cast until they finally put braces on me. . . I was always breaking it because I loved to jump-rope. The nuns (at school) had to call my daddy during the day, 'Judy broke her brace again' so I would have to go with him in the car to the welders" . . . (Guerra J. , 2019).

HELPING MARCH OF DIMES—Little Roberto Miguel Guerra and his sister, Judith Ann, children of Mr. and Mrs. Fidencio Guerra, 1225 North 16th Street, McAllen, want everyone to know what March of Dimes funds have done for them. Recovering from infantile paralysis and able to walk now with the aid of crutch and leg brace, the children are shown with an iron lung replica being placed in cafes to collect "coffee money" and publicize the county-wide drive for polio funds. (Monitor Photo)

Left: News clipping of March of Dimes campaign for polio funds features Bobby Guerra (left) and Judy Guerra –from The (Monitor, 1950), *McAllen, Texas.*

But in many other ways she was a normal child. One time Judy got into trouble at Our Lady of Sorrows Catholic School when she wasn't chosen for the softball team because she had a brace on her right leg and couldn't run fast. She remembers, "Two girls and I, we weren't chosen, so we stuffed the toilets with baseball bats, gloves, mittens, everything. . . I was hurt and I said, 'I'll show them' " (Guerra J. , 2019). She also has many good memories of her childhood. "I loved my bicycle. Daddy got me a bicycle one Christmas . . . and it was good exercise for my leg. . . So you would see me on my bicycle every day . . . up and down . . . up and down . . . up and down. . . I wasn't one to play with dolls because we were outside" (Guerra J. , 2019).

Judy says her brothers and especially sisters didn't have time for hobbies because mother always kept them busy with things like pasting "green stamps" into books and wrapping clothes hangers. But she did have time for quite a few activities it seems. Judy remembered, "I was also a girl scout and a brownie and my daddy he went with me to all these places anytime we had a banquet. I had one girlfriend whose daddy passed away . . . so daddy was like her dad. When daddy could, he would always be involved" (Guerra J. , 2019).

Judy did indeed grow up, meet and marry her husband Mark Arnold, and raise a daughter, Natalie Colleen Arnold. In the meantime Judy also had a career as a special education teacher, retiring in 2018 to spend more time with her granddaughter Colleen Nicole Gross.

Mark Edward Arnold and Judith Ann Guerra had the following child:
+15. i. NATALIE COLLEEN[3] ARNOLD was born on 03 Apr 1974 in San Antonio, Bexar, Texas. She married Kurt David Gross on 25 Oct 2003 in McAllen, Hidalgo, Texas. He was born on 11 Jun 1966 in Kenmore, Erie, New York, USA.

8. DANIEL JOSÉ[2] GUERRA (Fidencio Miguel[1], José Antonio[A], Jesus Maria[B], José Lino de Jesus[C], José Manuel[D], José Antonio Albino Hinojosa[E], Joseph Ramon[F], Capitan Cristóbal[G] Guerra-Cañamar, Ignacio[H] Guerra-Cañamar, Antonio[I] Guerra-Cañamal II, Antonio[J] Guerra-Cañamal) was born on 13 May 1955 in McAllen, Hidalgo, Texas. He married **Sabrina S. Garza** on 25 May 1985 in Hidalgo, Texas. She was born on 02 Feb 1961.

Daniel José Guerra lived in Corpus Christi, Nueces, Texas in 1968 (Seminary School). He lived in San Antonio, Bexar, Texas in 1973 (College of St Marys). He received a Bachelors Degree in 1976 from Rice University. He received an MD Degree (Doctor of Medicine) on 31 May 1980 at the University of Texas, Austin. He lived in Fort Worth, Johnson, Texas in 1982 (MD Resident, John Peterson Hospital). He was employed as a Medical Doctor (General Practice) between 1983 and 2019 in McAllen, Hidalgo, Texas. He lived in McAllen, TX in 1993 (Postal Code: 78504-2215 (1993); Street Address: 100 Canary Ave; Postal Code: 78502-4091; Street Address: PO Box 4091 #43; (Age 38). He tested his DNA on 22 Apr 2017 in McAllen, Hidalgo, Texas (Ancestry DNA Kit). He lived in McAllen, Hidalgo, Texas in 2019. He is also known as Danny.

Left: Daniel Guerra, M.D. works at the Family Physicians Clinic in McAllen as a general practitioner and family doctor.
–photo from www.familyphysiciansclinic.com

Daniel Guerra is the youngest of Fidencio's seven children, born almost six years after his older sister Judy. His middle name José honors his grandfather José Antonio Guerra. As for his first name he says, "I am named after Daniel Boone I think. At the time I was born in 1955 Daniel Boone and Davy Crockett were really popular on TV. So my father unfortunately left it up to my siblings to choose which name, and they chose Daniel" (Guerra D. , 2019).

Daniel remembers his childhood fondly and his Grandmother Sofia who came to babysit him when his parents were out, "I remember walking with her to the kitchen for a snack one evening. She would make me a little corn tortilla and she would scrape a little bar of *Piloncillo* which is like brown sugar and she would roll it into a tortilla and it was like a little candy snack." He also remembers their house on Maple Avenue still not having enough bedrooms for all the kids, "I was like the gypsy sleeper. I didn't have my own bedroom. For many years I slept with the housekeeper . . . and I spent many nights on the sofa when company would come. . . Then once Carlos left (to attend college) I was extremely excited because I went and took over his bed in the corner of the bedroom" (Guerra D. , 2019).

After attending Catholic elementary school in McAllen, at age 13 he went to Seminary school in Corpus Christi for four years to become a priest. Danny says, "I wanted to help people. I could see the hundreds of people I would be able to guide and convert as a priest." But instead of becoming a priest, he decided help people by becoming a doctor (Guerra D. , 2019).

Daniel graduated from Rice University in 1973. He received his doctorate from the University of Texas Medical School in San Antonio where he graduated with honors in 1980. He did his Residency training at John Peter Smith Hospital in Fort Worth. Daniel returned to McAllen and in 1983 he joined the Family Physicians Clinic as a Family Practice Specialist and later married Sabrina Garza and had two children. He now has spent more than 39 years in the medical field, especially in family practice. Daniel is a Fellow of the American Academy of Family Physicians, a member of the Texas Medical Association and the Hidalgo-Starr Counties Medical Society. In his spare time, he enjoys spending time with his family and friends.

Guerra Family Primos (Cousins) Reunion in McAllen, Texas 13 Apr 2019.
Front, from left: Mary, George, Tecla.
Back, from left: Florencio, Judy, Fidencio Jr., Leonard Jr., Brenda.
Not shown: Abel Jr., Roberto, Carlos, Daniel, Rose Marie, Gloria Garza.

Daniel José Guerra and Sabrina S. Garza had the following children:

 16. i. STEPHEN[3] GUERRA was born on 21 Feb 1991 in McAllen, Hidalgo, Texas.

 17. ii. ANDREA GUERRA was born on 17 Feb 1994 in McAllen, Hidalgo, Texas.

Generation 3

9. JON MICHAEL[3] LEVESQUE (Diana Maria[2] Guerra, Fidencio Miguel[1] Guerra, Mark Edward) He married **Tracy Ann Vincik** on 08 Jun 1991 in Austin, Travis, Texas (St Theresa Catholic Church). She was born on 18 Apr 1966 at Fort Sill, Comanche, Oklahoma, USA.

Jon Michael Levesque and Tracy Ann Vincik had the following child:

 18. i. BRONTE[4] LEVESQUE was born in 1993.

15. NATALIE COLLEEN[3] ARNOLD (Judith Ann[2] Guerra, Fidencio Miguel[1] Guerra, Mark Edward) was born on 03 Apr 1974 in San Antonio, Bexar, Texas. She married **Kurt David Gross** on 25 Oct 2003 in McAllen, Hidalgo, Texas. He was born on 11 Jun 1966 in Kenmore, Erie, New York, USA.

Kurt David Gross and Natalie Colleen Arnold had the following child:

 19. i. COLLEEN NICOLE[4] GROSS was born on 16 Feb 2005 in McAllen, McAllen, Hidalgo, Texas.

Left: Undated photo of Judy Guerra's daughter Natalie Arnold (on right) and granddaughter Colleen Gross –photo from Judy Guerra.

Chapter 10. Evangelina Guerra and Leonardo Guerra

Tia Eva é tio Lalo

Generation 1

1. EVANGELINA[I] **GUERRA** (José Antonio[A], Jesus Maria[B], José Lino de Jesus[C], José Manuel[D], José Antonio Albino Hinojosa[E], Joseph Ramon[F], Capitan Cristóbal[G] Guerra-Cañamar, Ignacio[H] Guerra-Cañamar, Antonio[I] Guerra-Cañamal II, Antonio[J] Guerra-Cañamal) was born on 30 Mar 1912 in Jim Hogg, Texas (Rancho San Miguel) as the ninth child of José Antonio Guerra and Tecla Guerra de Guerra. She had eight siblings, namely: Teresa, Abel Eulalio, Victoria, Guadalupe Filiberto, Margarita, Maria Florinda, Herlinda, and Fidencio Miguel. She died on 13 Jul 1996 in Edinburg, Hidalgo, Texas (Age 84). When she was 31, she married **Leonardo Guerra**, son of Juan Nepomuceno Guerra and Carlota Vela Villarreal, on 01 Dec 1943 in San Manuel, Hidalgo, Texas.

Right: Portrait of Evangelina Guerra and husband Leonardo Guerra, 1976 –from Leonard Guerra Jr. Collection.

Evangelina Guerra lived in McAllen, Hidalgo, Texas in 1920 (Street Address: 17 Ave; Age 7; Enumeration District: 77; Relation To Head of House: Sister; Marital Status: Single). She lived in McAllen, Hidalgo, Texas in 1930 (Street Address: 16th St; Age 17; Able To Speak English: Yes; Attended School: Yes; Can Read Write: Yes; Enumeration District: 0023; Registration District: 23; Marital Status: Single; Relation To Head of House: Sister). She lived at 1716 Beaumont Ave, McAllen, Hidalgo, Texas in 1935 (Occupation: Saleslady). She lived in McAllen, Hidalgo, Texas in 1940 (Street Address: Beaumont Avenue; Age 26; Attended School: No; Employment Code: 5; Employment Details: Home Housework; Employment History: No; Enumeration District: 108-19; Grade Completed: College, 2nd year; Income: 0; Income Other Sources: Yes; Is Employed: No; P). She received a BS (Education) degree about 1950 in Pan American College, Edinburg. She was employed as a Brewster Elementary School Teacher between 1956 and 1979 in Linn, Hidalgo, Texas. She lived in Edinburg, Texas in 1957. She lived in McAllen, TX in 1996 (Postal Code: 78503 (1996); Street Address: 731 Francisca Alamo). She was buried on 15 Jul 1996 in Mission, Hidalgo, Texas (Valley Memorial Gardens Sec O Lot 383 Space 3; Find A Grave #197168847). She was also known as *Tia* Eva and Chita. Her cause of death was metastatic breast cancer. Race: (White) Race: (Mexican).

Evangelina, or Eva as she was called, was the youngest of the nine children of Antonio and Tecla Guerra, born on Rancho San Miguel a year before the Guerra family moved to McAllen. She did not remember much about ranch life and both of her parents died during the Spanish flu epidemic when she was six years old. She was raised by her older sisters and brother Guadalupe and worked with her sisters as a saleslady after she graduated from high school.

Left: Dave Conklin and spouse Mary Guerra visit Evangelina Guerra's family at the Guerra Grocery in San Manuel, Texas, Apr 1973. From left to right: Dave Conklin, Leonard Guerra Jr., Evangelina, Herlinda (Eva's sister), Mary Guerra, Rose Marie Guerra –photo from Guerra Family History Collection.

Eva met and married her husband Leonardo Guerra during the War in 1943. He was a Guerra from another branch of the family. She lived with her mother-in-law Carlota Villarreal until they could get their own house. Eva worked as a housewife at first, raising three children. But she began teaching elementary school as a substitute teacher when the regular teacher had a nervous breakdown. So she went back to school and received her bachelor's degree in education at Pan American College. Eva taught school in the Edinburg School district for over 30 years, including 23 years

Right: Handwritten page from Eva Guerra's personal diary dated 10 Oct 1995, nine months before she died of breast cancer –from Leonard Guerra Jr. Collection.

at Brewster Elementary School in Linn, Texas, retiring in 1979. Eva's son George remembered, "She taught fifth grade and when I got to fifth grade she was my teacher and I didn't like it because she was so tough on me. . . . But she was a good teacher . . . and the strange thing now is that Rose Marie teaches at Brewster, back where my mother taught" (Guerra G. , 2019). Eva also developed and directed adult education classes in the Linn-San Manuel area.

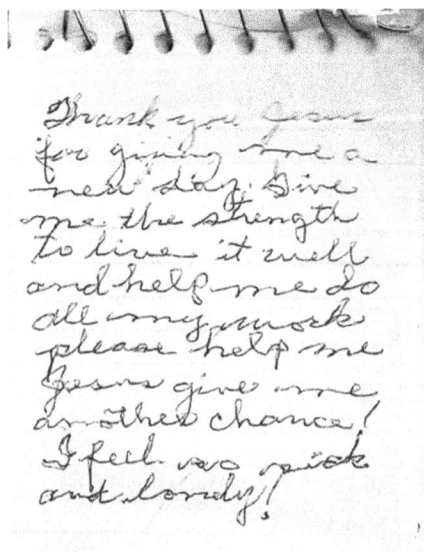

She was also very active in her community. She served as a choir director for St. Ann's Church for many years;

she taught religion classes; and she conducted pre-marriage seminars for young adults of the area. She loved to play the piano and taught many of the residents of the area how to play. Eva was very civic-minded, belonging to several organizations, one of which was the Pan American Round Table.

Leonardo Guerra was born on 17 Aug 1910 in San Manuel, Hidalgo, Texas (Rancho La Reforma) as the third child of Juan Nepomuceno Guerra and Carlota Vela Villarreal. He had six siblings, namely: Adolfo, Leonora, Juan N Jr., Enrique, Ernesto Conrado, and José Eugenio. He died on 02 Apr 2000 in Edinburg, Hidalgo, Texas (in a house fire). When he was 33, he married Evangelina Guerra, daughter of José Antonio Guerra and Tecla Guerra de Guerra, on 01 Dec 1943 in San Manuel, Hidalgo, Texas.

Juan Guerra and Carlota Villarreal family portrait, 1928.
Front (L to R): Virginia Villarreal Guerra (Wife of Adolfo Guerra), Reynaldo Guerra (Baby), Juan N Guerra, Carlota Villarreal Guerra. Back (L to R): Ernesto Conrado Guerra, Enrique Guerra (hit by car & died), Adolfo Guerra, Eugenio Guerra (struck by lightning & died), Leonardo Guerra, Leonora Guerra –photo from Leonard Guerra Jr. Collection.

Leonardo Guerra lived in Justice Precinct 6, Hidalgo, Texas in 1920 (Age 9; Able To Speak English: no; Attended School: yes; Enumeration District: 91; Marital Status: Single; Relation To Head of House: Daughter). He lived in Justice Precinct 6, Hidalgo, Texas in 1930 (Age 19; Able To Speak English: Yes; Attended School: Yes; Can Read Write: Yes; Enumeration District: 0042; Registration District: 42; Marital Status: Single; Relation To Head of House:

Son). He lived in San Manuel, Hidalgo, Texas in 1935. He lived in JP6, Hidalgo, Texas in 1940 (Age 29; Occupation: Salesman; Attended School: No; Class of Worker: Working on own account; Employment Code: 1; Employment Details: No; Employment History: No; Enumeration District: 108-42; Grade Completed: College, 1st year; Hours Worked: 70; Income: 0; Income Other Sources: Yes; Is Employed: Yes; Public Emergency Work: No; Seeking Work: No; Weeks Worked: 52; Marital Status: Single; Relation To Head of House: Son). He lived in Hidalgo, Texas on 01 Apr 1940. He served in the military between 1941–1945 at Fort Sam Houston, San Diego, and Germany (Age 31). In Jun 1941 in Linn, Hidalgo, Texas he was described as: Complexion: Light; Eye Color: Brown; Hair Color: Black; Height: 5'10" Weight: 189 lbs. He was employed as a rancher, Guerra's Grocery Market owner, and Guerra's Brand Chorizo producer in 1975 in Edinburg, Hidalgo, Texas. He had a medical condition of a mini-stroke (blocked carotid veins in neck) in May 1991 in Edinburg, Hidalgo, Texas. He was buried on 04 Apr 2000 in Mission, Hidalgo, Texas (Valley Memorial Gardens Sec O Lot 383 Space 2; Find A Grave #197169009). He was also known as Lalo. His cause of death was smoke inhalation from a house fire. Race: White.

Leonardo, known by his friends as "Lalo," was born on Rancho La Reforma, about twelve miles west of San Manuel, and lived in the vicinity of San Manuel, Texas most of his life. His father, Juan Nepomuceno Guerra was a farmer on Rancho La Reforma and his mother Carlota Villarreal was born, and later buried, on nearby Rancho El Rucio. Leonardo was a farmer, rancher and businessman in the Linn-San Manuel area. He also was actively involved as an election judge for many years.

Right: Leonardo Guerra (on left) poses in 1942 with his Uncle Arcadio Guerra and Cousin Rafael Guerra (on right) while serving in the U.S. Army during World War II –photo from Leonard Guerra Jr. Collection.

In 1941 during World War II, Leonardo, his brother Ernesto, and his cousin Rafael Guerra enlisted in the army and trained at Fort Sam Houston, Texas before being assigned a unit. His son Leonard Jr. says, "Dad was originally stationed in San Diego, but then he got shipped to Germany. He was an Infantry fighter. . . . One thing dad would never talk about (were) his experiences at war. He never really sat down and told us what it entailed and what he saw" (Guerra L. J., 2019). For his wartime service he received the American Defense and World War II medals.

In 1943 during the war he married Evangelina Guerra, a school teacher, who came from the **José Manuel Guerra** branch of the Guerra family. No one knows how or when they met but

Eva's son Leonard Jr. thinks it may have been at a dance. He says, "My father loved to dance. He always dressed-up real sharp, double-breasted suit, nice tie, and he had a real thin little moustache; very handsome man, and he always wore one of those little 'Al Capone' hats kinda sideways like this, and he would pose" (Guerra L. J., 2019).

According to his son Leonard Jr., before the war Leonardo started Guerra's Grocery and Meat Market in San Manuel,

"Dad started the business first by himself, and his mother (Carlota Villarreal) would help him, and between them both they developed and created that recipe to come up with a chorizo until they fine-tuned it. Then in '41 when the World War II started of course dad got drafted and Ernesto his brother. . . . So they asked another brother, Adolfo Guerra, if he could oversee the store while they were gone. After the war in '45 dad came back . . . and they became three partners and from then on they ran the store together" (Guerra L. J., 2019).

Chorizo de San Manuel, a Mexican sausage with cumin, pepper, and chili powder, created by Leonardo Guerra, is still sold in supermarkets throughout the Rio Grande Valley as "Guerra's Brand," 19 Jan 2019.

Leonardo's youngest son George remembers,

"That's where my dad and his brothers started Chorizo de San Manuel. It was a Mexican sausage. It was famous throughout the valley. My dad bought his brothers out and he ran it for a while and when he sold it the people who bought it went commercial and that's why you can get it at all these stores today. When my dad made it, it was more like a homemade product. . . . There was another item they used to make all the time that was very popular back in that area. It was called *chicherones*. . . It was kinda like fried pork rinds and a lot of it was tasty and very good and people would go there and buy this . . . it was very famous" (Guerra G. , 2019).

Leonardo owned and operated Guerra's Grocery and Meat Market in San Manuel for many years, retiring in 1975. He became known for his Mexican style chorizo, "Guerra's Brand" Chorizo de San Manuel which is still sold in the area. Lalo died in a house fire in 2000, four years after his wife Evangelina died of cancer in 1996. He was 89 years old.

Leonardo Guerra and Evangelina Guerra had the following children:

+2.   i.   ROSE MARIE[2] GUERRA was born on 01 Jan 1945 in Edinburg, Hidalgo, Texas. She married (1) ARTHUR FRANK SCHLICHTING on 16 Jun 1962 in Hidalgo, Texas. She married (2) MIGUEL GABRIEL GUZMAN-RAMIREZ on 26 Aug 1974 in McAllen, Hidalgo, Texas (George Guerra house). He was born on 24 Mar 1952 in Los Ángeles, Tamaulipas, Mexico.

+3.   ii. LEONARD GUERRA JR. was born on 28 Jun 1946 in Edinburg, Hidalgo, Texas. He married Sandra Espinosa, daughter of Rodolfo Espinosa and Delia Benita Salinas, on 21 Jun 1980 in Alamo, Hidalgo, Texas (St Joseph Catholic Church). She was born on 08 Sep 1952 in Alamo, Hidalgo, Texas (home birth).

+4.   iii. GEORGE XAVIER GUERRA was born on 12 Feb 1950 in McAllen, Hidalgo, Texas. He married Maria Del Rosario Treviño on 15 Jul 1972 in Edinburg, Hidalgo, Texas (St Joseph Catholic Church). She was born on 05 Jul 1951 in Edinburg, Hidalgo, Texas (Grandview Hospital).

Generation 2

2. ROSE MARIE[2] GUERRA (Evangelina[1], Leonardo, Juan Nepomuceno) was born on 01 Jan 1945 in Edinburg, Hidalgo, Texas (Edinburg General Hospital). She married **Miguel Gabriel Guzman-Ramirez** on 26 Aug 1974 in McAllen, Hidalgo, Texas (George Guerra house). He was born on 24 Mar 1952 in Los Ángeles, Tamaulipas, Mexico.

Right: Undated portrait of Rose Marie Guerra –photo from Leonard Guerra Jr. Collection.

Rose Marie Guerra graduated about 1963 in Edinburg, Hidalgo County, Texas (Edinburg High School). She lived in Edinburg, Texas in 1965 (Age 20). She received a BS Degree (Education) in 1966 in Pan American College, Edinburg. She was employed as an elementary school teacher between 1966 and 2019 in Edinburg, Hidalgo County, Texas. She lived in Linn, Hidalgo, Texas in 1996. She is also known as Miss Rose.

Rose Marie, or "Miss Rose" as her students call her, was Evangelina and Leonardo's first child and the only one named after a Princess. As Rose Marie recalls, "My mom said when she was dating dad they went to a drive-in movie and saw a movie about an Indian princess and her name was Rosemarie; and she said 'If I ever have a daughter I want to name her Rosemarie' " (Guerra R. , 2019).

Rose Marie has fond memories of her childhood: playing, bike riding, and especially family vacations. Every summer the family would go to Saltillo, Mexico to visit Eva's sister Tere Garza and their cousins. She remembers the steep mountains, winding roads, and stops in Monterrey. Rose Marie says about the family vacations, "Mostly Mexico are the ones I treasure the most because I always loved going to Mexico but my brothers hated it" (Guerra R. , 2019).

In fact she met her husband Miguel in Mexico,

> "I was on a bus with my mom and we were going to Saltillo to stay with Almita (cousin Alma). . . I'd go every summer, and when we were on the bus, I saw him, he saw me. . . even my mom thought he was handsome . . . and we just looked at each other and when we got off . . . he approached me and said, 'Can I have your aunt's phone number?' . . . I was so nervous I gave him everything wrong, and mom said, 'Oh well, you'll probably never see him again anyway.'. . . But the next day . . . he ended up at Almita's house! After that just back and forth then one time he came down and he said, 'Do you want to get married?' . . . And it's already been almost 45 years, and recently he became a U.S. citizen" (Guerra R. , 2019).

Left: Rose Marie (age 5) and Leonard Jr. (age 4) dressed for a Sunday outing at their home in Edinburg, Apr 1950 –photo from Guadalupe Guerra Collection.

Miss Rose always believed that she would become a teacher like her mother. She says, "My mom taught at Brewster. She taught me, she taught my brothers, then I taught my own kids at Brewster. . . . I would even teach school when I was young. The little neighbors would go to the house. Mom got me a little chalkboard, chalk, and I would hold school. It has always been in my blood" (Guerra R. , 2019). She has been teaching for 53 years so far!

Miguel Gabriel Guzman-Ramirez and Rose Marie Guerra had the following children:

5. i. ORLANDO[3] GUZMAN was born on 25 Jun 1976 in McAllen, Hidalgo County, Texas.
6. ii. CELINDA GUZMAN was born on 04 Jul 1979 in Edinburg, Hidalgo, Texas.

3. LEONARD[2] GUERRA JR. (Evangelina[1], Leonardo, Juan Nepomuceno) was born on 28 Jun 1946 in Edinburg, Hidalgo, Texas as the second child of Leonardo Guerra and Evangelina Guerra. He had two siblings, namely: Rose Marie, and George Xavier. When he was 33, he married **Sandra Espinosa**, daughter of Rodolfo Espinosa and Delia Benita Salinas, on 21 Jun 1980 in Alamo, Hidalgo, Texas (St Joseph Catholic Church).

Leonard Guerra Jr. had a medical condition of epileptic seizures due to football concussion in 1960. He graduated in 1964 in Edinburg, Hidalgo County, Texas (Edinburg High School). He lived in Edinburg, Texas in 1965 (Age 19). He was employed as a Hidalgo County Dept of Community Affairs Program Auditor between 1972 and 1980 in Edinburg, Hidalgo County, Texas. He was employed as a Hidalgo County Dept of Community Affairs acting Personnel Director in 1991 in Edinburg, Hidalgo County, Texas. He lived in Edinburg, TX in 1996 (Postal Code: 78539-8003 (1996); Street Address: 2113 Dolly St; Age 50). He tested his DNA on 10 May 2018 in Edinburg, Hidalgo, Texas (Ancestry DNA Kit). He is also known as Leo. He was employed as a Deputy Director, Amigos del Valle nonprofit in Edinburg, Hidalgo, Texas.

Right: Leonard Guerra Jr. family portrait, From left: Leonard Jr., Sandra Espinosa, Michael, Audrey –2015 photo from Leonard Guerra Jr. Collection.

Like his older sister and younger brother, Leonard Guerra Jr. was born in the Edinburg General Hospital, about twelve miles south of the family home in San Manuel which is still ranch country. When he was a child, Leonard Jr. says, "People would ask us, what do you all DO? There is nothing but the ranch, trees, and brush. We became creative. You know, make horses out of broom sticks. . . . We'd climb trees, play marbles, spin the top. We of course had BB guns. . . . We always found something to do" (Guerra L. J., 2019).

Leo and his brother George also had chores to do around home and at the grocery and meat market but they did get their rewards as he explained, "We were growing up helping our father. On Saturday mornings everyone else was at home watching TV. . . . We were up at six in the morning cleaning the store getting ready for the customers to come in . . . and dad would pay us fifty-cents a week. That was a lot of money for us. . . . . With a nickel we could go to the movies. With a quarter we could go to the movies, buy popcorn and buy a soda. We were thrilled to death" (Guerra L. J., 2019).

Leonard Jr. also remembers how as the older and bigger kid, he tormented his younger brother George, "We'd have our little scuffles in the grass you know, a little wrestling here and there. Most of the time I'd always win anyway because I would pin him down, and then mom would always come out with a belt, 'Leonard get off him, get off him!' Since I was older, I had a little more advantage and I was always taller than him. George was short, so sometimes I would take a little advantage over him and then dad would intervene, and he would say, 'You want to take advantage, take advantage of me' " (Guerra L. J., 2019).

After graduating from Edinburg High School in 1964, Leo attended the Pan American College for two years and he remembers, "But then the Vietnam War started getting hot, you know, and I wanted to join with what's called the buddy system with a cousin of mine where we would be shipped together anywhere the army would send us." (Guerra L. J., 2019). This was a similar program to the one his father Leonardo used when he joined the army in World War II. However when it came down to the physical exam, he was not allowed to join because of his epileptic seizures due to a football concussion in 1960.

So after Leonard Jr. attended McAllen Business College he started his business career by moving to Houston with a friend and working there for a year or so. He returned to Edinburg in 1972 and got a job with the Hidalgo County Department of Community Affairs as a Program Auditor. He met his future wife Sandra on April 9, 1979, a day he says he will never forget. Apparently that day Leo's sister Rose called him at work to ask if he could pick up her son Orlando at school and take him to the doctor as she was in the middle of giving exams at Whitney Elementary School where she and Leo's brother George's wife *Chiqui* were teachers.

As Leonard Jr. tells the story,
> "I drove up and my sister went back and I saw this foxy looking lady walking on the outside hall. . . . Long beautiful hair, beautiful blouse, and these tight-fitting white pants, and then I see these green eyes. I'm going Wow what a fox. I'd love to meet her one of these days. And then she went into her room. George's wife was behind Sandra and said 'That's Sandra.'. . . So I called her that night and her mother said she was at choir practice. . . . She says I can give you the number where she's at. So I called. . . . I heard a lot of music in the background –but it wasn't church music! . . . Oh I understand you are at choir practice. 'It's not choir practice, we say that because (we don't tell mom) it's a party. Why don't you come over?'. . . I'll never forget that day" (Guerra L. J., 2019).

Leonard Jr. and Sandra were married about a year later in June, 1980 in her family's church in Alamo, Texas. Together they raised two children and Leo retired after working many years for Hidalgo County and local non-profit organizations.

Left: Leonard Guerra Jr. family at the Guerra Primos Reunion. Front, from left: Grandson Lucas Garcia, Sandra Espinosa, Leonard Jr.; back: Michael Guerra, Audrey (Guerra) Garcia, 13 Apr 2019.

Sandra Espinosa was born on 08 Sep 1952 in Alamo, Hidalgo, Texas (home birth) as the first child of Rodolfo Espinosa and Delia Benita Salinas. When she was 27, she married Leonard Guerra Jr., son of Leonardo Guerra and Evangelina Guerra, on 21 Jun 1980 in Alamo, Hidalgo, Texas (St Joseph Catholic Church).

Sandra Espinosa lived in Alamo, TX in 1968 (Postal Code: 78516; Street Address: POB 2312; Postal Code: 78539-8003 (1995); Street Address: 2113 Dolly St; Postal Code: 78577-6130 (1993); Street Address: 1312 E Maurer St; Postal Code: 78516-2820; Street Address: 940 W Bowie Ave # 2312; Age 16). She lived in Edinburg, Texas in 1975 (Age 20). She received a BA degree in 1976 in Pan American College, Edinburg. She was employed as an Elementary Teacher in 1977 in Pharr, Hidalgo, Texas. She received a Master of Education Degree (Education Administration) on 15 May 1999 from Pan American College, Edinburg. She lived in Mission, Hidalgo, Texas in 2002 (Street Address: 1823 Fairway Cir). In 2015 she was employed as the Principal of Cayetano Cavasas Elementary School in Edinburg, Hidalgo, Texas.

Leonard Guerra Jr. and Sandra Espinosa had the following children:
   7. i.   MICHAEL ANTHONY[3] GUERRA was born on 10 Dec 1982 in McAllen, Hidalgo, Texas (McAllen General Hospital).
 +8. ii. AUDREY NICOLE GUERRA was born on 27 Feb 1984 in McAllen, Hidalgo, Texas (McAllen General Hospital). She married JESSIE GARCIA.

4. GEORGE XAVIER[2] GUERRA (Evangelina[1], Leonardo, Juan Nepomuceno) was born on 12 Feb 1950 in McAllen, Hidalgo, Texas as the third child of Leonardo Guerra and Evangelina Guerra. He had two siblings, namely: Rose Marie, and Leonard Jr. When he was 22, he married **Maria del Rosario Treviño** on 15 Jul 1972 in Edinburg, Hidalgo, Texas (St Joseph Catholic Church).

George Xavier Guerra graduated about 1968 in Edinburg, Hidalgo County, Texas (Edinburg High School). He lived in Austin, Texas in 1971 (University of Texas: Junior). He received a BS Degree (Pharmacy) in 1972 at the University of Texas, Austin. He was employed as a pharmacist at Klinck's in 1972 in McAllen, Hidalgo County, Texas. He lived in McAllen, Texas in 1993 (Postal Code: 78501-1827; Street Address: 404 W Jonquil Ave; Age 43). He is also known as Jorge Javier (on birth record). He was employed as a Pharmacist.

Actually 'George' was not his given name. Instead, he says, "I was born Jorge Javier Guerra. But I changed it in high school because . . . in social circles I was always George, George,

George. (On my) driver's license I even put George. . . But yet I would officially be Jorge. I asked my mom and dad. I said I'm never going to go by Jorge Javier so can I just change it? So I went to the courthouse and just changed it. I think I was a sophomore in high school. So that's how I became George Xavier" (Guerra G. , 2019).

George was the youngest of the three Guerra children and has many good childhood memories. He remembered the family's annual vacations, "The one place we would go as a family routinely was Gardner State Park close to San Antonio. I remember my dad and mom would take us there, Leonard, Rose and me. . . They had little cabins and we would swim in the Frio River which was really cold" (Guerra G. , 2019). Also almost every summer they would go to Saltillo, Mexico to see their cousins, the children of their mother Eva's sister Teresa Garza.

He also says that after his mother Evangelina became a full-time teacher, "My mom never cooked, rarely, because when I was five years old we got a housekeeper from Mexico . . . so she would do the cooking. Her name was Rosa and she is still alive today. . . When Rosa wasn't cooking Dad cooked." And of course dad (Leonardo) had his own meat market and more than a few recipes for beef, pork, and *cabrito* (baby goat). Otherwise, George says, "The one regret I have is growing up with my mother who was a piano teacher . . . and she always encouraged us, and she had a piano at home, and kids would come over and take lessons, and we didn't want to learn" (Guerra G. , 2019).

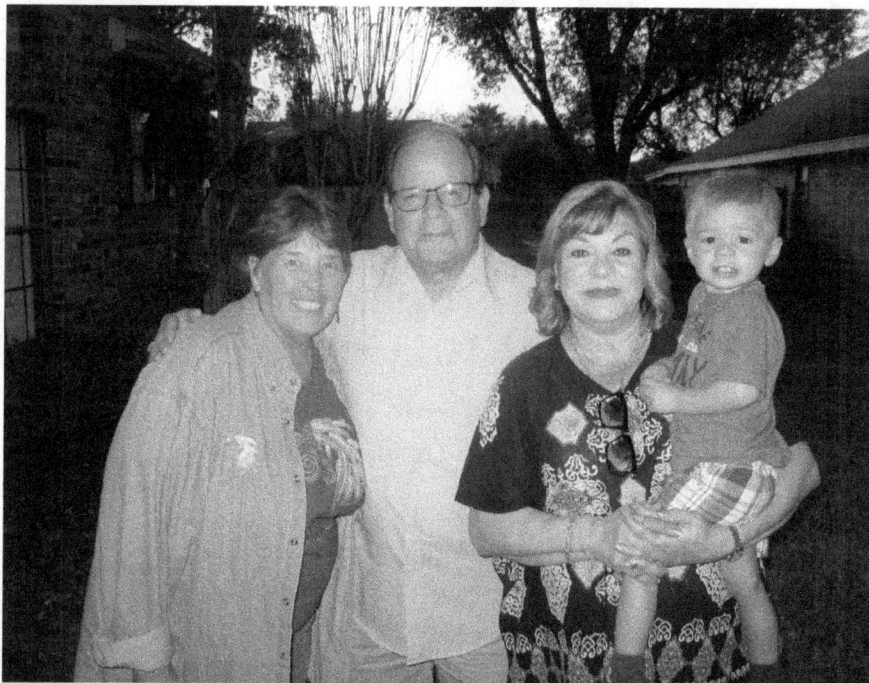

Mary (Guerra) Conklin (left) with her cousin George Guerra and his wife Maria del Rosario Treviño (Chiqui) and their grandson Cooper, 14 Jan 2019.

George attended the University of Texas in Austin where he graduated with honors and a BS Degree in Pharmacy in 1972. He also met and married his wife Maria del Rosario Treviño

(Chiqui) in 1972 who was also a school teacher and taught in the same schools as his mother and sister. Together they raised three children as well as pursuing careers as a pharmacist and school teacher.

Evangelina and Leonardo Guerra's children get together at Leonard Guerra Jr.'s home in Edinburg. From left: Leonard Jr., Rose Marie, George Xavier, 20 Apr 2019.

Maria del Rosario Treviño was born on 05 Jul 1951 in Edinburg, Hidalgo, Texas (Grandview Hospital). When she was 21, she married George Xavier Guerra, son of Leonardo Guerra and Evangelina Guerra, on 15 Jul 1972 in Edinburg, Hidalgo, Texas (St Joseph Catholic Church). Maria del Rosario Treviño is also known as Chiqui. She was employed as a 5th Grade Teacher for 27 years.

George Xavier Guerra and Maria del Rosario Treviño had the following children:

   9. i.   BRIAN JOSEPH³ GUERRA was born on 11 Jan 1977 in McAllen, Hidalgo, Texas (McAllen General Hospital).
  10. ii. LEANNE MARIE GUERRA was born on 24 Sep 1978 in McAllen, Hidalgo, Texas.
 +11. iii. STEVEN MICHAEL GUERRA was born on 03 Apr 1986 in Hidalgo, Texas. He married Sarah Marie Wright on 12 Oct 2013 in Bexar, Texas. She was born in 1987.

Generation 3

8. AUDREY NICOLE³ GUERRA (Leonard² Jr., Evangelina¹, Leonardo, Juan Nepomuceno) was born on 27 Feb 1984 in McAllen, Hidalgo, Texas (McAllen General Hospital). She married **JESSIE GARCIA**.

Pharr girl wins state honor as "Miss Texas American Princess"

by La-Nora McWilliams

Pretty little Audrey Guerra of Pharr is just seven years old. Like other seven-year-old girls she attends school, does her homework and all the other things most other little girls do.

Only Audrey's talents extend far beyond those of most of her peers. She is the daughter of Leonard and Sandra Guerra of Pharr and attends Canterbury Elementary in Edinburg where her mother teaches. Her father is acting personnel director for the Hidalgo County Department of Community Affairs.

Audrey was named Miss Texas American Princess in her age group (4-7) at the annual state pageant which took place in August in Houston. As the state winner, she will represent Texas in her age group at the National Miss America Princess Pageant to be held November 27-December 1 at the Hyatt Regency Hotel in Tampa, Florida.

She competed against 94 other

> ### She won the crown over 94 other contestants.

contestants for the state title and her awards include cash, an official state crown, banner, trophy and travel expenses to the national pageant. She and one parent will also join state winners and family winners for a day in Disneyworld.

Audrey appears to be a natural for competition of this type. She has appeared in television commercials here in the Valley when Chevrolet first introduced their 1991 Lumina series. She appeared in the commercial running toward the car yelling "Wait for me" as the family was loading up for a trip to Disneyworld. She will soon appear in a commercial for the South Texas Organ Bank that will be seen in both English and Spanish in The Valley as well as across the River into Mexico.

She started modeling school at the age of five. In talking with Audrey, she has the beauty, style, mannerisms and mature vocabulary of a young lady in her late teens. It's easy to see why she won from a field of 94 contestants to represent the state of Texas at the Florida pageant.

She likes to read and swim and has taken both dancing and piano lessons. She also wants to take gymnastics classes.

> ### Audrey is looking forward to competing at the next age level.

In addition to her official state crown, banner and trophy, she received flowers and a $500 cash award, plus her airfare to Florida to compete in the National Miss American Princess Pageant.

She won the Texas event based on interview, interview appearance and

appearance in evening gown. Contestants were also able to compete in several optional contests such as the Talent Contest, Photogenic Contest and Miss Princess Honors Contest.

The pageant is open to all young girls between the ages of 4-7 and offers contestants an opportunity to meet new friends and to perform on stage in front of an audience, thereby developing poise and self-confidence.

Audrey is looking forward to the win. But even if she doesn't place the event, she said she still feels like a winner because she had the opportunity to make the trip and to compete in the pageant. Audrey has a brother nearly her age and the entire family supports her in her quest for another crown.

As a seven-year-old she is at the top of the 4-7 age bracket for competition. However, the Pageant has other age brackets above the age level which includes girls through age of 19. Thus, Audrey will be eligible to compete in higher age levels after she reach the age of eight, she is looking forward to competing

> ### WINNER
> *Cont'd. from pg. 1*

at the next age level.

The Miss Texas Princess Hostess for 1991 was Leslie Robinson of Brownsville. She received the official state hostess crown, banner and trophy and will represent Texas until the following year's pageant. Leslie also had the most ticket sales.

Good luck Audrey. Win, lose or draw in Florida, you'll always be a winner in The Rio Grande Valley!

***

SCHOOL ASSIGNMENT — Even a princess has to do her homework. Here Audrey is cutting yarn for hair to make a three-dimensional self image project for school.

Left: News article about Audrey Guerra being named "Miss Texas American Princess" –from The Valley Monitor, McAllen, Texas Aug 1991.

Audrey Guerra is the younger of Sandra and Leonard Jr. Guerra's two children. She grew up in Pharr, Texas and went to school in Edinburg and Canterbury Elementary School. When she was five years old she began taking modeling lessons. By the time she was age seven, she had appeared in several television commercials. In August 1991 she competed and won state honors against 94 other contestants for the title of "Miss Texas American Princess" in the 4-7 age group in Houston. She married Jessie Garcia and had a son, Lucas Garcia, born in 2017.

Jessie Garcia and Audrey Nicole Guerra had the following child:

  12. i. LUCAS ROBERTO[4] GARCIA was born on 25 Aug 2017 in Austin, Travis, Texas (St David's Hospital).

11. **STEVEN MICHAEL[3] GUERRA** (George Xavier[2], Evangelina[1], Leonardo, Juan Nepomuceno) was born on 03 Apr 1986 in Hidalgo, Texas. He married Sarah Marie Wright on 12 Oct 2013 in Bexar, Texas. She was born in 1987.

Steven Michael Guerra and Sarah Marie Wright had the following child:

  13. i. COOPER KEHLET[4] GUERRA was born in 2019 in McAllen, Hidalgo, Texas.

Evangelina Guerra's hand-written family tree from her family bible
–from Leonard Guerra Jr. Collection.

Appendix 1. Mary Guerra Ancestors Pedigree Chart

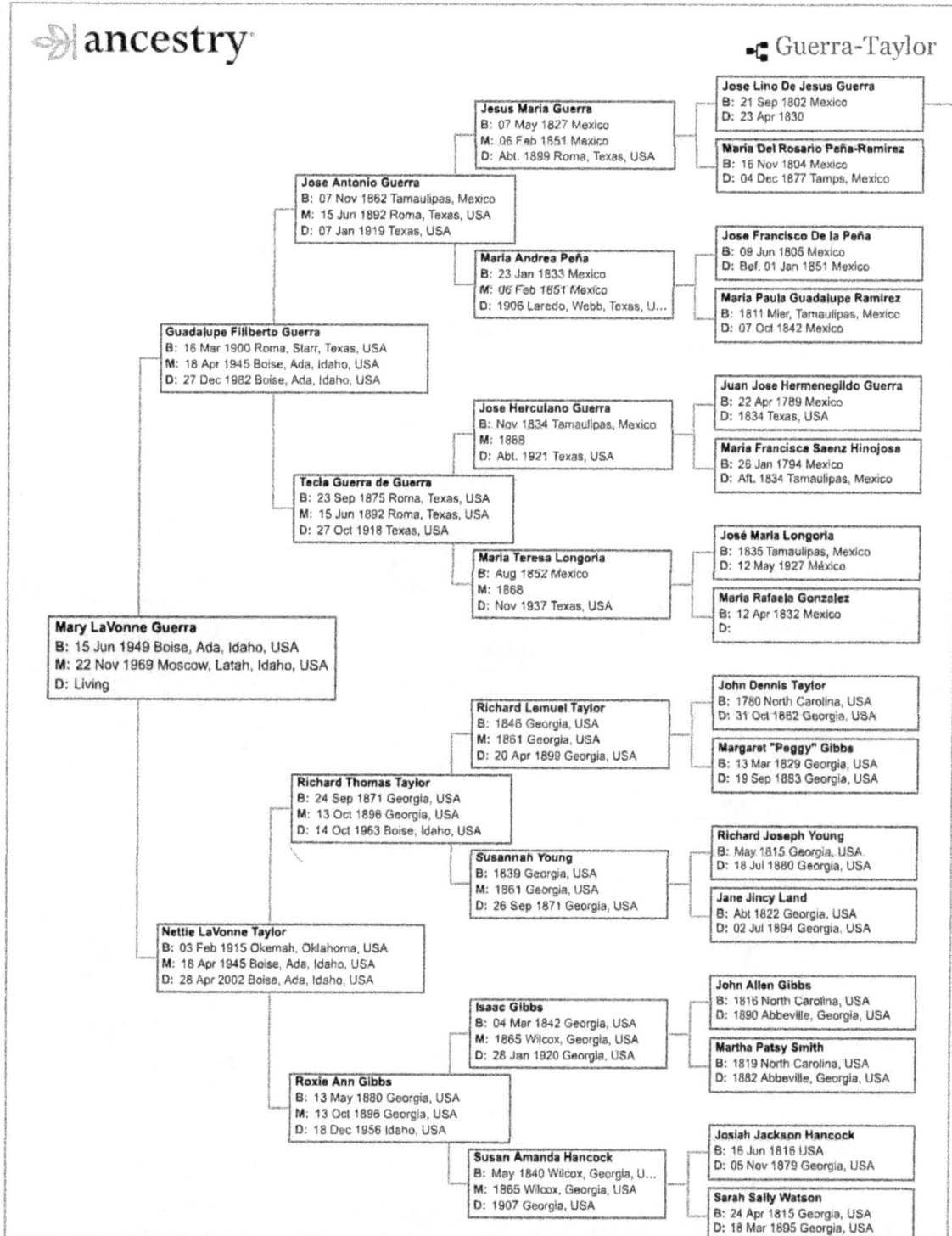

ancestry   Guerra-Taylor

Jose Lino De Jesus Guerra
B: 21 Sep 1802 Mexico
D: 23 Apr 1830

Jesus Maria Guerra
B: 07 May 1827 Mexico
M: 06 Feb 1851 Mexico
D: Abt. 1899 Roma, Texas, USA

Maria Del Rosario Peña-Ramirez
B: 16 Nov 1804 Mexico
D: 04 Dec 1877 Tamps, Mexico

Jose Antonio Guerra
B: 07 Nov 1862 Tamaulipas, Mexico
M: 15 Jun 1892 Roma, Texas, USA
D: 07 Jan 1919 Texas, USA

Jose Francisco De la Peña
B: 09 Jun 1805 Mexico
D: Bef. 01 Jan 1851 Mexico

Maria Andrea Peña
B: 23 Jan 1833 Mexico
M: 06 Feb 1851 Mexico
D: 1906 Laredo, Webb, Texas, U...

Maria Paula Guadalupe Ramirez
B: 1811 Mier, Tamaulipas, Mexico
D: 07 Oct 1842 Mexico

Guadalupe Filiberto Guerra
B: 16 Mar 1900 Roma, Starr, Texas, USA
M: 18 Apr 1945 Boise, Ada, Idaho, USA
D: 27 Dec 1982 Boise, Ada, Idaho, USA

Juan Jose Hermenegildo Guerra
B: 22 Apr 1789 Mexico
D: 1834 Texas, USA

Jose Herculano Guerra
B: Nov 1834 Tamaulipas, Mexico
M: 1868
D: Abt. 1921 Texas, USA

Maria Francisca Saenz Hinojosa
B: 26 Jan 1794 Mexico
D: Aft. 1834 Tamaulipas, Mexico

Tecla Guerra de Guerra
B: 23 Sep 1875 Roma, Texas, USA
M: 15 Jun 1892 Roma, Texas, USA
D: 27 Oct 1918 Texas, USA

José Maria Longoria
B: 1835 Tamaulipas, Mexico
D: 12 May 1927 México

Maria Teresa Longoria
B: Aug 1852 Mexico
M: 1868
D: Nov 1937 Texas, USA

Maria Rafaela Gonzalez
B: 12 Apr 1832 Mexico
D:

Mary LaVonne Guerra
B: 15 Jun 1949 Boise, Ada, Idaho, USA
M: 22 Nov 1969 Moscow, Latah, Idaho, USA
D: Living

John Dennis Taylor
B: 1780 North Carolina, USA
D: 31 Oct 1862 Georgia, USA

Richard Lemuel Taylor
B: 1846 Georgia, USA
M: 1861 Georgia, USA
D: 20 Apr 1898 Georgia, USA

Margaret "Peggy" Gibbs
B: 13 Mar 1829 Georgia, USA
D: 19 Sep 1883 Georgia, USA

Richard Thomas Taylor
B: 24 Sep 1871 Georgia, USA
M: 13 Oct 1896 Georgia, USA
D: 14 Oct 1963 Boise, Idaho, USA

Richard Joseph Young
B: May 1815 Georgia, USA
D: 18 Jul 1880 Georgia, USA

Susannah Young
B: 1839 Georgia, USA
M: 1861 Georgia, USA
D: 26 Sep 1871 Georgia, USA

Jane Jincy Land
B: Abt 1822 Georgia, USA
D: 02 Jul 1894 Georgia, USA

Nettie LaVonne Taylor
B: 03 Feb 1915 Okemah, Oklahoma, USA
M: 18 Apr 1945 Boise, Ada, Idaho, USA
D: 28 Apr 2002 Boise, Ada, Idaho, USA

John Allen Gibbs
B: 1816 North Carolina, USA
D: 1890 Abbeville, Georgia, USA

Isaac Gibbs
B: 04 Mar 1842 Georgia, USA
M: 1865 Wilcox, Georgia, USA
D: 28 Jan 1920 Georgia, USA

Martha Patsy Smith
B: 1819 North Carolina, USA
D: 1882 Abbeville, Georgia, USA

Roxie Ann Gibbs
B: 13 May 1880 Georgia, USA
M: 13 Oct 1896 Georgia, USA
D: 18 Dec 1956 Idaho, USA

Josiah Jackson Hancock
B: 16 Jun 1816 USA
D: 05 Nov 1879 Georgia, USA

Susan Amanda Hancock
B: May 1840 Wilcox, Georgia, U...
M: 1865 Wilcox, Georgia, USA
D: 1907 Georgia, USA

Sarah Sally Watson
B: 24 Apr 1815 Georgia, USA
D: 18 Mar 1895 Georgia, USA

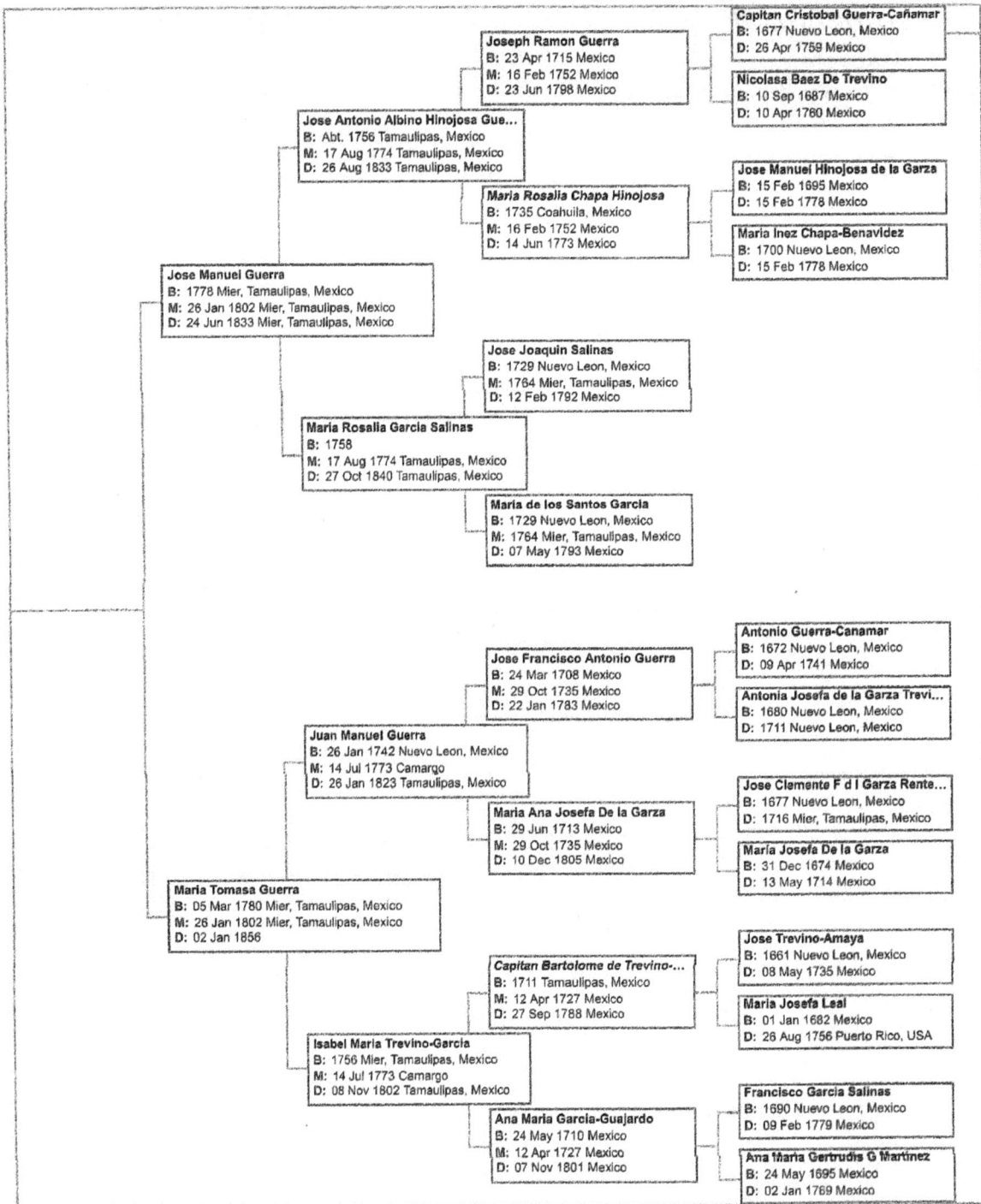

```
                                                              ┌─────────────────────────────┐
                                                              │ Capitan Cristobal Guerra-Cañamar │
                                                              │ B: 1677 Nuevo Leon, Mexico    │
                                            ┌─────────────────┤ D: 26 Apr 1759 Mexico         │
                                            │ Joseph Ramon Guerra      └─────────────────────────────┘
                                            │ B: 23 Apr 1715 Mexico    ┌─────────────────────────────┐
                                            │ M: 16 Feb 1752 Mexico    │ Nicolasa Baez De Trevino     │
                                            │ D: 23 Jun 1798 Mexico────┤ B: 10 Sep 1687 Mexico        │
          ┌─────────────────────────────┐   │                          │ D: 10 Apr 1780 Mexico        │
          │ Jose Antonio Albino Hinojosa Gue...│                        └─────────────────────────────┘
          │ B: Abt. 1756 Tamaulipas, Mexico │
          │ M: 17 Aug 1774 Tamaulipas, Mexico │
          │ D: 26 Aug 1833 Tamaulipas, Mexico │ ┌─────────────────────────────┐  ┌─────────────────────────────┐
          └─────────────────────────────┘   │ Maria Rosalia Chapa Hinojosa │  │ Jose Manuel Hinojosa de la Garza │
                                            │ B: 1735 Coahuila, Mexico      │──┤ B: 15 Feb 1695 Mexico         │
                                            │ M: 16 Feb 1752 Mexico         │  │ D: 15 Feb 1778 Mexico         │
                                            │ D: 14 Jun 1773 Mexico         │  └─────────────────────────────┘
                                            └─────────────────────────────┘  ┌─────────────────────────────┐
                                                                             │ Maria Inez Chapa-Benavidez    │
                                                                             │ B: 1700 Nuevo Leon, Mexico    │
                                                                             │ D: 15 Feb 1778 Mexico         │
                                                                             └─────────────────────────────┘
```

Jose Manuel Guerra
B: 1778 Mier, Tamaulipas, Mexico
M: 26 Jan 1802 Mier, Tamaulipas, Mexico
D: 24 Jun 1833 Mier, Tamaulipas, Mexico

Jose Joaquin Salinas
B: 1729 Nuevo Leon, Mexico
M: 1764 Mier, Tamaulipas, Mexico
D: 12 Feb 1792 Mexico

Maria Rosalia Garcia Salinas
B: 1758
M: 17 Aug 1774 Tamaulipas, Mexico
D: 27 Oct 1840 Tamaulipas, Mexico

Maria de los Santos Garcia
B: 1729 Nuevo Leon, Mexico
M: 1764 Mier, Tamaulipas, Mexico
D: 07 May 1793 Mexico

Jose Francisco Antonio Guerra
B: 24 Mar 1708 Mexico
M: 29 Oct 1735 Mexico
D: 22 Jan 1783 Mexico

Antonio Guerra-Canamar
B: 1672 Nuevo Leon, Mexico
D: 09 Apr 1741 Mexico

Antonia Josefa de la Garza Trevi...
B: 1680 Nuevo Leon, Mexico
D: 1711 Nuevo Leon, Mexico

Juan Manuel Guerra
B: 26 Jan 1742 Nuevo Leon, Mexico
M: 14 Jul 1773 Camargo
D: 26 Jan 1823 Tamaulipas, Mexico

Maria Ana Josefa De la Garza
B: 29 Jun 1713 Mexico
M: 29 Oct 1735 Mexico
D: 10 Dec 1805 Mexico

Jose Clemente F d l Garza Rente...
B: 1677 Nuevo Leon, Mexico
D: 1716 Mier, Tamaulipas, Mexico

Maria Josefa De la Garza
B: 31 Dec 1674 Mexico
D: 13 May 1714 Mexico

Maria Tomasa Guerra
B: 05 Mar 1780 Mier, Tamaulipas, Mexico
M: 26 Jan 1802 Mier, Tamaulipas, Mexico
D: 02 Jan 1856

Capitan Bartolome de Trevino-...
B: 1711 Tamaulipas, Mexico
M: 12 Apr 1727 Mexico
D: 27 Sep 1788 Mexico

Jose Trevino-Amaya
B: 1661 Nuevo Leon, Mexico
D: 08 May 1735 Mexico

Maria Josefa Leal
B: 01 Jan 1682 Mexico
D: 26 Aug 1756 Puerto Rico, USA

Isabel Maria Trevino-Garcia
B: 1756 Mier, Tamaulipas, Mexico
M: 14 Jul 1773 Camargo
D: 08 Nov 1802 Tamaulipas, Mexico

Ana Maria Garcia-Guajardo
B: 24 May 1710 Mexico
M: 12 Apr 1727 Mexico
D: 07 Nov 1801 Mexico

Francisco Garcia Salinas
B: 1690 Nuevo Leon, Mexico
D: 09 Feb 1779 Mexico

Ana Maria Gertrudis G Martinez
B: 24 May 1695 Mexico
D: 02 Jan 1769 Mexico

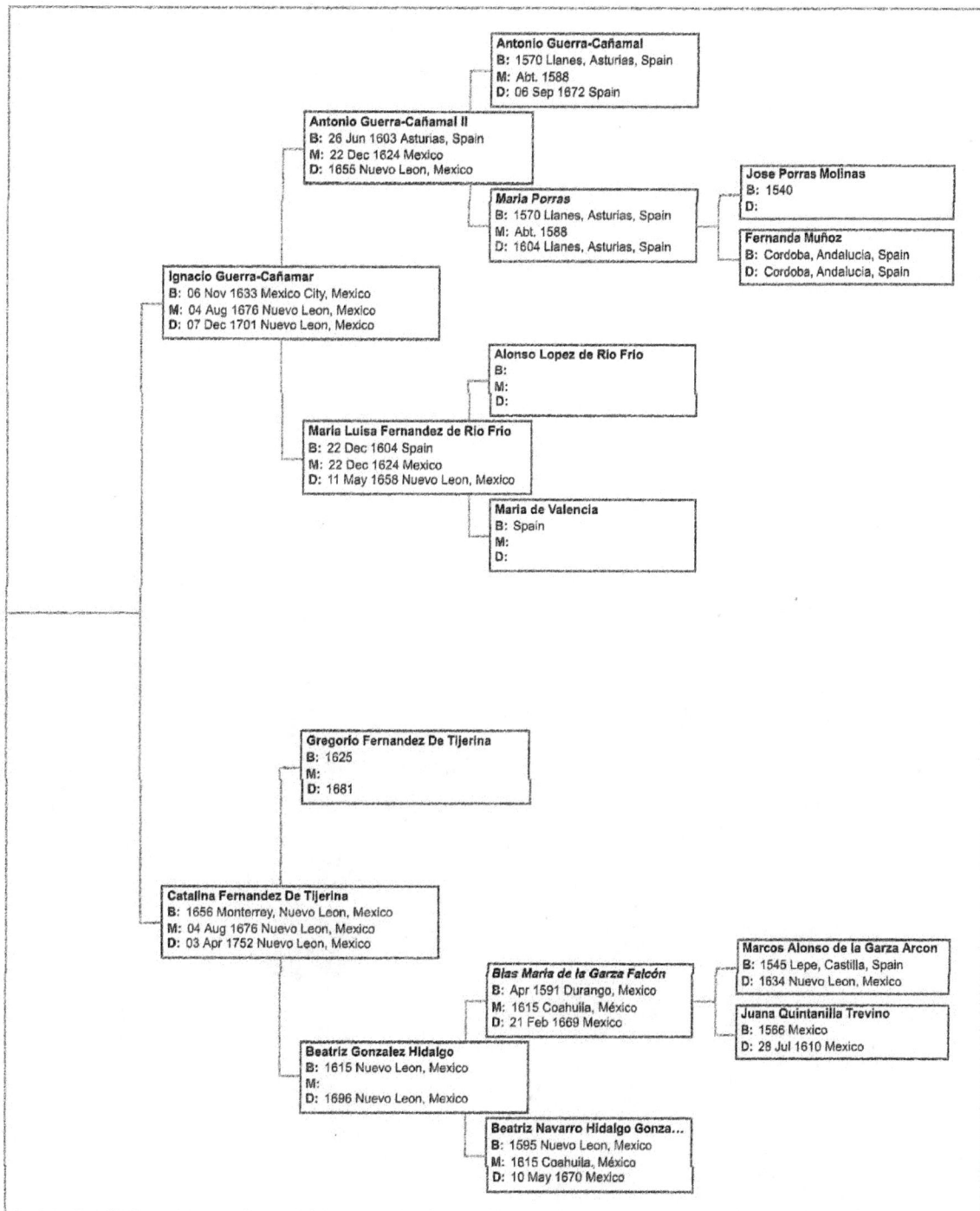

Antonio Guerra-Cañamal
B: 1570 Llanes, Asturias, Spain
M: Abt. 1588
D: 06 Sep 1672 Spain

Antonio Guerra-Cañamal II
B: 26 Jun 1603 Asturias, Spain
M: 22 Dec 1624 Mexico
D: 1655 Nuevo Leon, Mexico

Jose Porras Molinas
B: 1540
D:

Maria Porras
B: 1570 Llanes, Asturias, Spain
M: Abt. 1588
D: 1604 Llanes, Asturias, Spain

Fernanda Muñoz
B: Cordoba, Andalucia, Spain
D: Cordoba, Andalucia, Spain

Ignacio Guerra-Cañamar
B: 06 Nov 1633 Mexico City, Mexico
M: 04 Aug 1676 Nuevo Leon, Mexico
D: 07 Dec 1701 Nuevo Leon, Mexico

Alonso Lopez de Rio Frio
B:
M:
D:

Maria Luisa Fernandez de Rio Frío
B: 22 Dec 1604 Spain
M: 22 Dec 1624 Mexico
D: 11 May 1658 Nuevo Leon, Mexico

Maria de Valencia
B: Spain
M:
D:

Gregorio Fernandez De Tijerina
B: 1625
M:
D: 1681

Catalina Fernandez De Tijerina
B: 1656 Monterrey, Nuevo Leon, Mexico
M: 04 Aug 1676 Nuevo Leon, Mexico
D: 03 Apr 1752 Nuevo Leon, Mexico

Marcos Alonso de la Garza Arcon
B: 1545 Lepe, Castilla, Spain
D: 1634 Nuevo Leon, Mexico

Blas Maria de la Garza Falcón
B: Apr 1591 Durango, Mexico
M: 1615 Coahuila, México
D: 21 Feb 1669 Mexico

Juana Quintanilla Trevino
B: 1566 Mexico
D: 28 Jul 1610 Mexico

Beatriz Gonzalez Hidalgo
B: 1615 Nuevo Leon, Mexico
M:
D: 1696 Nuevo Leon, Mexico

Beatriz Navarro Hidalgo Gonza...
B: 1595 Nuevo Leon, Mexico
M: 1615 Coahuila, México
D: 10 May 1670 Mexico

Appendix 2. Guerra Y-DNA Tree

4 December 2017

The Y-DNA test

AncestryDNA is not a Y-DNA test. Only men have a Y chromosome which is what the Y-DNA test examines. The AncestryDNA test looks at autosomal DNA. We get half of that from each parent. So it is typically the most useful DNA test for genealogical purposes as it allows one to find cousins from every branch of our trees through recent generations. Autosomal DNA recombines every generation. So we end up having less and less autosomal DNA in common with our ancestors and cousins. Y-DNA on the other hand stays mostly the same for centuries. The Y chromosome is passed down strictly from father to son similar to how surnames are these days. So it is ideal for focused research into a surname. A group interested in this Guerra lineage noticed that there were two separate groups of results of those few who had taken a Y-DNA test.

Ancestry does not sell Y-DNA tests so they have been using FamilyTreeDNA (FTDNA) test kits. There are different types of tests and even different levels for Y-DNA tests. For this however, the minimum (such as the Y37) is more than enough. Basically the Y-DNA tests like Y37 look at certain locations in the Y chromosome with repeating DNA patterns. The number in the test name like Y37 tells you how many of these STR markers are examined. The results end up being a string of numbers of the repeats in each STR marker. The usefulness comes in how they compare with others in the database. More closely related cousins will have similar or even exact values.

What is the Direct Paternal Lineage?

Your direct paternal lineage is the line that follows your father's paternal ancestry. This line consists entirely of men. It traces your father, his father, his father's father, and so forth back to our shared common paternal ancestor. For genealogists, this clear line means that they can trace two or more descendants of a single man many generations back and compare their Y-DNA results with the expectation of a match. For those interested in deeper ancestry, tracing the modern geographic origins of exact and close matches means that they can discover with great certainty the origins of their own line. Note that because Y-DNA follows exclusively the direct paternal line, common ancestors between you and your matches on other parts of your pedigree are coincidental.

The Human Family Tree Genographic Project
In October 2014 The Genographic Project revealed interesting findings about Asturias, Spain, or Espana Verde (Green Spain). Genetic results from the region go deep. From low hominin ancestry to high numbers of unique European lineages, the Genographic Project shed new light on the history of Espana Verde.

Before modern humans arrived in Iberia about 40,000 years ago, **Neanderthals** ruled Spain. And although most anthropologists agree that humans and Neanderthals mixed, a point of interest among the participants was the unusually low percentage of Neanderthal in their DNA. The people from Asturias on average carried only 1.5% Neanderthal DNA, compared to the 2.5% average observed among most other modern European groups.

Haplogroup R1b was the reoccurring lineage for paternal ancestry, accounting for nearly 75% of male participants in this group. R1b is the most common European Y-chromosome branch, and nearly 60% of European men carry this lineage. One interesting finding revealed, however, was that many of the men came from lesser known branches of the R1b, suggesting their exact origin remains a mystery. Among the paternal lineages only one had ties to Europe's fist modern humans.

Maternal haplogroup H was the most common branch among participants, accounting for more than a third of lineages. Interestingly, the ancestral haplogroup HV, with ties to early agriculturalists from the Middle East or possibly Europe's earliest settlers, was found in eleven Asturians present. Overall, the maternal results showed a high frequency of some of Europe's oldest lineages, a pattern similar to their Basque neighbors, also from northern Spain (Brutan, R. & NGS Newsroom, 2014).

The Guerra Project
The purpose of this project is to help anyone who descends from someone with the Guerra surname. This includes people with different surnames as well as people that match other Guerra's but don't know a lot about their paternal line. You can learn more about the project by visiting the main web site: https://www.familytreedna.com/groups/guerra.

There are two sets of Guerra descendants that trace their surname back to Capitan Antonio Guerra-Cañamal-II. This ancestor was born in Asturias, Spain and lived in present day Mexico in the early 1600s where he started a family. When these descendants took Y-DNA tests they had different predicted Haplogroups. One set was R-M269 and if tested further found out to be R-M153. The second group was J-M267 and if tested further found out to be J-L816. Both sets cannot descend from the same Spaniard through a paternal line.

They may still be related to this Spaniard through other branches of their trees. A group led by David Reta and Crispin Rendon put the pieces together to figure out where the break in the Guerra line took place and which Haplogroup this Spaniard belongs in. Above is the first Guerra Y-DNA tree. The Y-DNA tested kits are shown at the bottom. The blue boxes are the R-M153 kits and the red boxes are the J-L816 kits. Their surnames and kit numbers are shown. The names above them are of their Guerra ancestors.

Not all ancestors are shown, just enough to show the splits between the tested individuals. Based on what was gathered, it looks like the R-M153 (blue) kits are likely to be the true paternal line descendants of the Spaniard that brought over the Guerra surname. We are still narrowing down where the NPE (non-paternal event) took place for the J-L816 (red) kits.

Y-DNA37 results have been uploaded for kit MK36622, Carlos A Guerra. Y-DNA37 test results are at the intermediate-level for tracing direct paternal lineage. They include information about geographic origins on this line. Matches who share the Guerra surname are genealogically relevant.

Carlos Guerra's results shown in the chart below match that of Guerra group 1 (shown in blue). These are the descendants of Antonio Guerra-Cañamal-II. The ones in red are group 2. Their paper trail leads them to the same ancestor but their Y-DNA results clearly indicate that they do not match group 1. Which means group 2's ancestor was given the Guerra surname without being a biological son of someone in group 1.

The latest Guerra Y-DNA Tree is shown on the following page.

Guerra Y-DNA Tree
Descendants of
Conquistador Antonio Guerra Cañamar

Prepared by Nanis Guerra Wallace (nanis.wallace@gmail.com)
updated: 10/10/2019
sources:
1) Descendants of Capt. Ignacio Guerra Cañamar by José René Escobar y Sáenz, 2005
2) Antonio Guerra Cañamar descendant report by Erasmo Eduardo Pulido, 2016
3) modified after mtDNA chart by David Peña

Gen

Generations: 13, 12, 11, 10, 9, 8, 7, 6, 5, 4, 3, 2, 1

DNA Haplogroup =>
Guerra group =>
member

Legend:
- Paternal ancestors not confirmed to be related to either red or blue descendants
- Y-DNA tested person w/ R haplotype
- Y-DNA tested person w/ J haplotype
- Relationship to ancestors in tree unknown
- Break in paternal line
- born/died

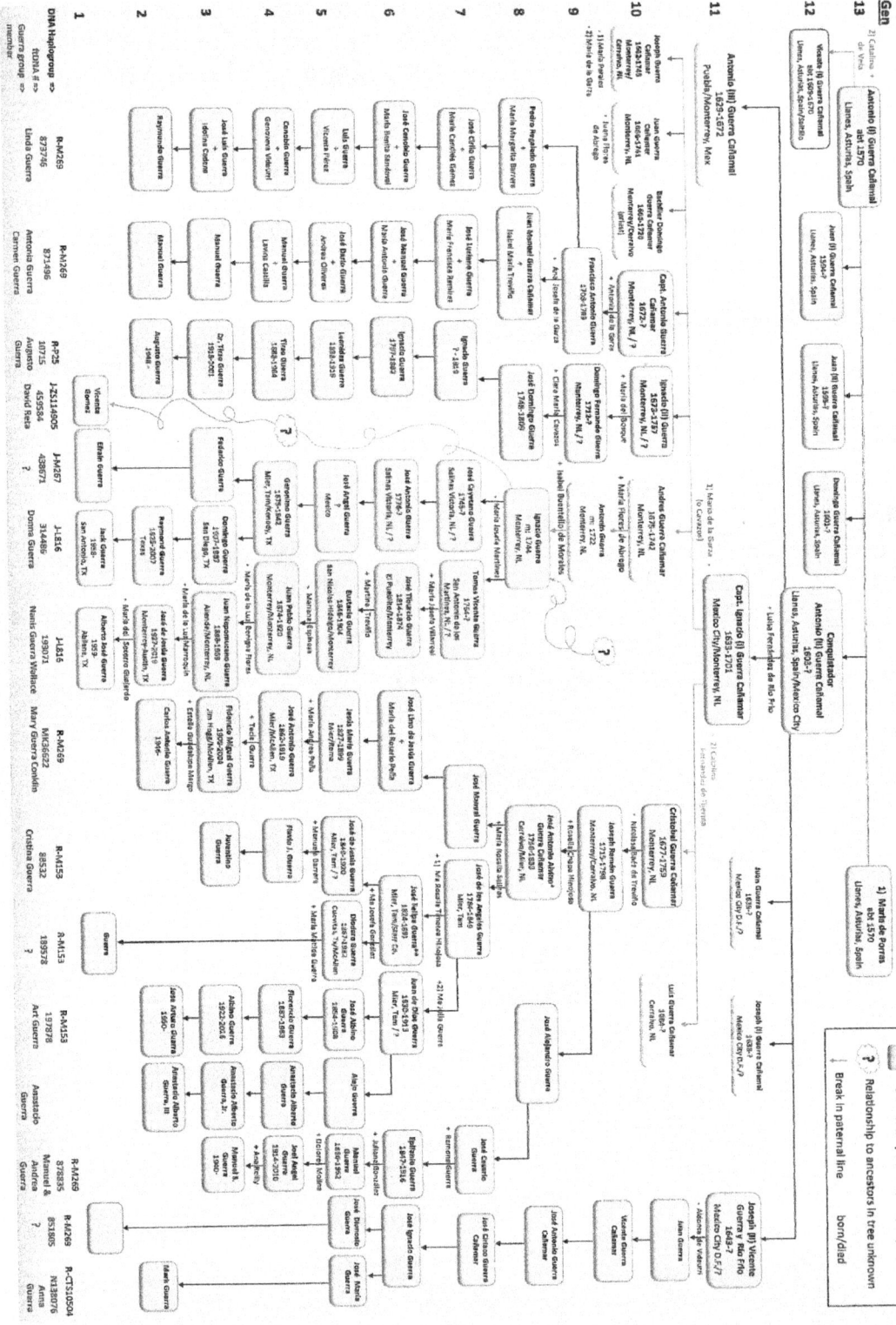

* Moises Guerra
** Gabby Guerra

Conquistador
Antonio (II) Guerra Cañamar
1633-1701
Llanes, Asturias, Spain/Monterrey, NL

1) María de Porras
abt 1570
Llanes, Asturias, Spain

Appendix 3: DNA Ethnicity Reports

Introduction to Guerra Family DNA Ethnicity Reports

Each of the following DNA ethnicity reports include information on: 1) an Actual *versus* Predicted Relationship to the home person, Mary Guerra (Ancestry Kit #A022185), based on documentation *versus* DNA analysis; 2) the approximate amount of shared DNA (in centimorgans (cM), a unit used to measure the length of DNA) in the relationship. and 3) a DNA Ethnicity Estimate that graphically shows which regions of the world the approximate percentage of DNA for that person is estimated to be from.

Although the AncestryDNA web page shows that Mary Guerra currently has more than 1000 4th cousins or closer, only 3 DNA reports are included at this time. These reports were selected for the following reasons: 1) they all used the same AncestryDNA test and results display; 2) they all have separate documentation as to their actual location in the Guerra family tree; and 3) they all have given permission to view their reports.

AncestryDNA Match Confidence Score:
When AncestryDNA compares your DNA to the DNA of one of your matches, they calculate a confidence score for you. This score lets you know how much DNA evidence there is for you and your match actually being related.

The confidence score is based on the amount and location of the DNA that you share with your match. AncestryDNA shows the shared amount using centimorgans (cM), a unit used to measure the length of DNA. The higher the number, the higher the confidence, and in general, the closer the relationship. Since you can share DNA with your match on one or more segments in different locations in the genome, AncestryDNA shows you how many. Note that the number of segments and number of centimorgans that they show reflects only those segments that they believe were inherited from a recent common ancestor (in other words, segments that are likely to be identical by descent).

Confidence Score	Approximate amount of shared centimorgans	Likelihood of a single recent common ancestor	Description
Extremely High	More than 60	Virtually 100%	You and your match share enough DNA to prove that you're both descendants of a common ancestor (or couple)--and the connection is recent enough to be conclusive.
Very High	45—60	About 99%	You and your match share enough DNA that we're almost certain you're both descendants of a recent common ancestor (or couple).

Confidence Score	Approximate amount of shared centimorgans	Likelihood of a single recent common ancestor	Description
High	30—45	About 95%	You and your match share enough DNA that it is likely you're both descendants of the same common ancestor or couple, but there's a small chance the common ancestor(s) are quite distant and difficult to identify.
Good	16—30	Above 50%	You and your match share some DNA, probably from a recent common ancestor or couple, but the DNA may be from distant ancestors that are difficult to identify.
Moderate	6—16	15—50%	You and your match might share DNA because of a recent common ancestor or couple, share DNA from very distant ancestors, or you may not be related.

The amount of centimorgans you share with a match can also help you understand your relationship to them. For example, you'll usually share about 120 centimorgans with a 3rd cousin, but it's possible to share as few as 90 or as many as 200. Be aware that the precise amount of shared DNA can vary beyond the ranges shown in the table below (Ball, Catherine. et al., 2016).

Approximate amount of shared DNA (in centimorgans)	Possible relationship
3,475	Parent, child, or identical twin
2,400—2,800	Full sibling (including fraternal twins)
1,450—2,050	Grandparent, aunt, uncle, half sibling
680—1,150	1st cousin, great grandparent
200—620	2nd cousin
90—180	3rd cousin
20—85	4th cousin
6—20	Distant cousin: 5th cousin — 8th cousins

AncestryDNA Ethnicity Estimate:
AncestryDNA uses two different processes to determine the regions provided in your DNA Story: a reference panel and Genetic Communities™.

Building a reference panel
One way AncestryDNA create estimates of your genetic ethnicity is by comparing your DNA to the DNA of other people who are native to a region. The AncestryDNA reference panel contains 40,017 DNA samples from people from around the world.

AncestryDNA builds the reference panel from a larger reference collection of 97,000 DNA samples collected from people whose genealogy suggests they are native to one region. Many of these samples were originally collected by the Sorenson Molecular Genealogy Foundation. Each panel member's genealogy is documented so we can be confident that their family is representative of people with a long history (hundreds of years) in that region.

Each volunteer's DNA sample from a given region is then tested and compared to all the others to construct the AncestryDNA reference panel. In the end, 40,017 samples were carefully selected to represent 60 global regions for the reference panel (Ball, Catherine. et al., 2019, p. 10).

Comparing your DNA to the reference panel
AncestryDNA then compares your DNA to the DNA in the reference panel to see which regions your DNA is most like. The ethnicity estimate you see on the web site is the result of this comparison.

Your AncestryDNA Results reveal your unique story —
who your ancestors were and where they came from.

Results as of:
21 Sep 2020

DNA Results Summary for Mary Guerra

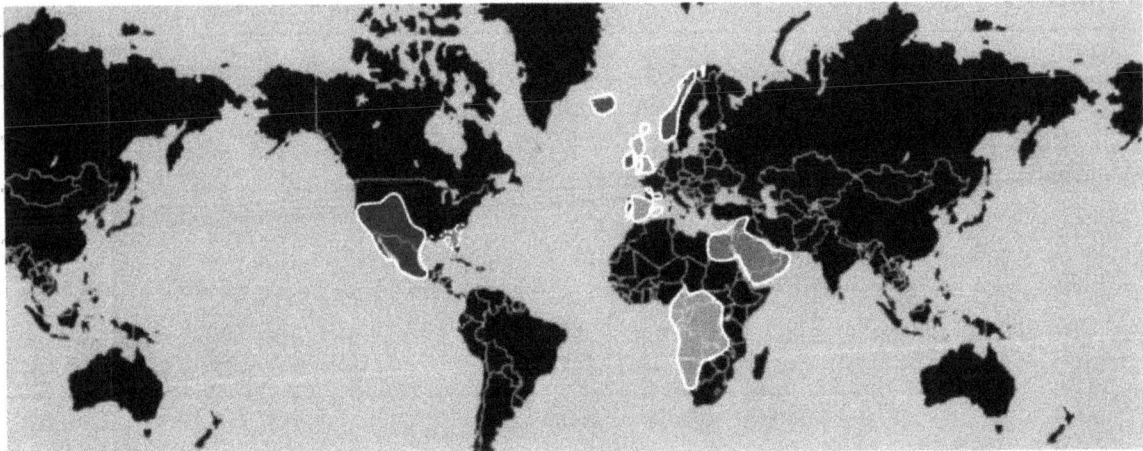

© Mapbox, © OpenStreetMap

Ethnicity Estimate

Spain	33%
England & Northwestern Europe	28%
Scotland	13%
Wales	6%
France	5%
Indigenous Americas—Mexico	5%

- Nuevo León, Tamaulipas & South Texas
  - Northeastern Nuevo Leon & South Texas
  - Rio Grande Valley

Portugal	4%
Norway	2%
Ireland	2%
Middle East	1%
Cameroon, Congo & Western Bantu Peoples	1%

Additional Communities

- Georgia & Florida Settlers
  - Southeast Georgia Settlers
  - Central Georgia Settlers
- South Carolina Settlers
  - Coastal Carolinas Settlers

Leonard Guerra Jr.—Paternal 1ˢᵗ Cousin (actual)

Amount of Shared DNA: 1,062 centimorgans shared across 44 DNA segments
Possible range: 1st - 2nd cousins
Confidence: Extremely High
Ancestry Kit #

Relationship Info: 1st Cousin (Predicted)

Our analysis of your DNA predicts that this person you match with is your first cousin.
The exact relationship however can vary. It could be a great nephew or great-great grandmother.

While there may be some statistical variation in our prediction, it's likely to be a four-degree separation. However, the relationship could range from three to five degrees of separation.

Here are some examples of possible relationships separated by 4 degrees:

1st Cousins

1st Cousins share your grandparents

Grandparent (Jose Antonio Guerra)
2 degrees

Parent (Guadalupe Guerra)
1 degree

Aunt (Evangelina Guerra)
3 degrees

You (Mary Guerra)
0 degrees

1st Cousin (Leonard Guerra Jr.)
4 degrees

Your AncestryDNA Results reveal your unique story — who your ancestors were and where they came from.

Results as of:
06 Mar 2020

DNA Results Summary for Leonard Guerra

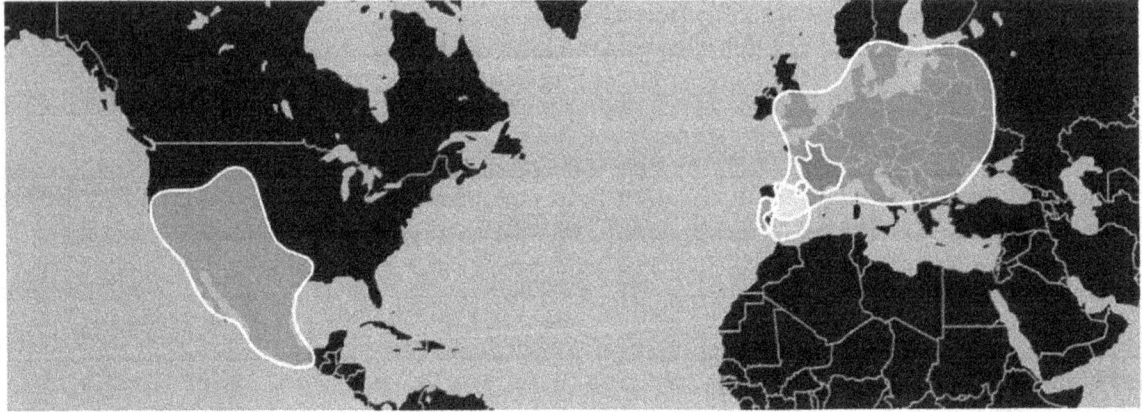

© Mapbox, © OpenStreetMap

Ethnicity Estimate

Spain	46%
Portugal	28%
Indigenous Americas—Mexico	15%
Nuevo León, Tamaulipas & South Texas	
Northeastern Nuevo Leon & South Texas	
Nuevo Leon, Western Tamaulipas & South Texas	
Rio Grande Valley	
European Jewish	6%
Basque	3%
France	2%

Daniel Guerra—Paternal 1ˢᵗ Cousin (actual)

Amount of Shared DNA: 932 centimorgans shared across 34 DNA segments
Possible range: 1st - 2nd cousins
Confidence: Extremely High
Ancestry Kit #

Relationship Info: 1st Cousin (Predicted)
Our analysis of your DNA predicts that this person you match with is your first cousin.
The exact relationship however can vary. It could be a great nephew or great-great grandmother.

While there may be some statistical variation in our prediction, it's likely to be a four-degree separation. However, the relationship could range from three to five degrees of separation.

Here are some examples of possible relationships separated by 4 degrees:

1st Cousins
1st Cousins share your grandparents

Grandparent (Jose Antonio Guerra)
2 degrees

Parent (Guadalupe Guerra)
1 degree

Uncle (Fidencio Guerra)
3 degrees

You (Mary Guerra)
0 degrees

1st Cousin (Daniel Guerra)
4 degrees

Your AncestryDNA Results reveal your unique story —
who your ancestors were and where they came from.

Results as of:
19 Apr 2020

DNA Results Summary for Daniel Guerra

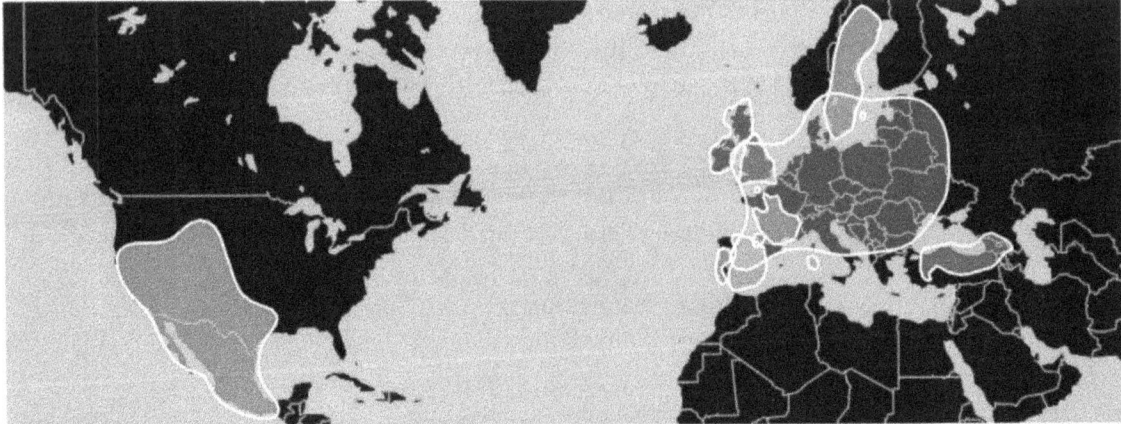

© Mapbox, © OpenStreetMap

Ethnicity Estimate

Spain	53%
Portugal	12%
Indigenous Americas—Mexico	9%
Nuevo León, Tamaulipas & South Texas	
Northeastern Nuevo Leon & South Texas	
France	7%
England, Wales & Northwestern Europe	7%
European Jewish	5%
Ireland & Scotland	2%
Basque	2%
Turkey & the Caucasus	1%
Sweden	1%
Sardinia	1%

Gloria Garza—Paternal 1st Cousin (actual)

Amount of Shared DNA: 874 centimorgans shared across 38 DNA segments
Possible range: 1st - 2nd cousins
Confidence: Extremely High
Ancestry Kit # TB5818962

Relationship Info: 1st Cousin (Predicted)

Our analysis of your DNA predicts that this person you match with is your first cousin.
The exact relationship however can vary. It could be a great nephew or great-great grandmother.

While there may be some statistical variation in our prediction, it's likely to be a four-degree separation. However, the relationship could range from three to five degrees of separation.

Here are some examples of possible relationships separated by 4 degrees:

1st Cousins
1st Cousins share your grandparents

Grandparent (Jose Antonio Guerra)
2 degrees

Parent (Guadalupe Guerra)
1 degree

Aunt (Teresa Guerra)
3 degrees

You (Mary Guerra)
0 degrees

1st Cousin (Gloria Garza)
4 degrees

DNA Results Summary for Gloria Garza

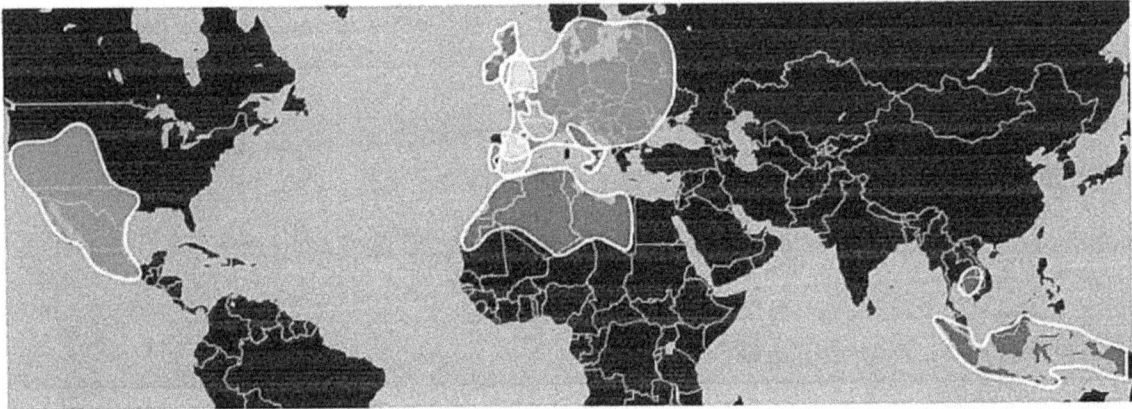

© Mapbox, © OpenStreetMap

Ethnicity Estimate

Spain	38%
Indigenous Americas—Mexico	23%
Nuevo León, Tamaulipas & South Texas	
Northeastern Nuevo Leon & South Texas	
Portugal	20%
European Jewish	6%
Ireland & Scotland	4%
Basque	3%
Italy	2%
Northern Africa	1%
Southeast Asia	1%
France	1%
England, Wales & Northwestern Europe	1%

Appendix 4. Guerra Ancestors Grave Locator

Guerra Ancestors Grave Locations
Online Find A Grave Memorials (www.findagrave.com)

as of 21 Sep 2020

NAME: FIRST	MIDDLE	MAIDEN	LAST	MEMORIAL #
Jose	Lino	De Jesus	Guerra	
Maria	Rosario	Pena	Guerra	
Jesus	Maria	Pena	Guerra	
Maria	Andrea	Pena	Guerra	
Herculano			Guerra	
Maria	Teresa	Longoria	Guerra	
Jose	Antonio		Guerra	197162561
Tecla		Guerra	Guerra	197162984
Jacobo			Garza-Hinojosa	197163566
Maria	Florinda		Guerra	197164087
Herlinda (Linda)		Guerra	Babb	197164330
Elmer	Libbey		Babb	
Teresa		Guerra	Garza	199515115
Leonel			Garza	
Ciria	Luz	Portilla-Martinez	Guerra	ashes scattered
Abel	Eulalio		Guerra	ashes scattered
Bernardo			de la Garza	177488081
Reuben	Gabriel		Valle	197169455
Victoria		Guerra	de la Garza/Valle	197169262
Guadalupe (Lupe)	Filiberto		Guerra	193540388
Nettie	LaVonne	Taylor	Guerra	193540239
Antonio	Richard		Guerra	132078861
Daniel	Oakley		Blood	24849229
Harold	Clifton		Blood	24849237
Marjorie	Alene	Jones	Blood	24849241
Margarita			Guerra	
Fidencio	Miguel		Guerra	12636155
Estela	Guadalupe	Margo	Guerra	111728886
Diana	Maria	Guerra	Levesque	111728451
Leonardo			Guerra	197169009
Evangelina (Eva)		Guerra	Guerra	197168847
Juan	Nepomuceno		Guerra	46070178
Carlota	Vela	Villarreal	Guerra	145764073
Ruperto	Reymando		Margo	197185372
Sofia		Clarke	Margo	197185083
Jesus	Maria		Guerra Jr	
Manuela		Cruz	Guerra	
Diodoro	Vidal		Guerra	199518656
Maria	Matilda	Guerra	Guerra	199518284
Florentino			Beddinghous	
Maria	Adelaida	Guerra	Beddinghous	
Jesus			Pena	
Maria	Concepcion	Guerra	Pena	

References

Alonzo, A. C. (1998). *Tejano Legacy: Rancheros and Settlers in South Texas, 1734-1900.* Albuquerque, NM: University of New Mexico Press.

Altman, I., & Lockhart, J. (1976). *Provinces of Early Mexico: Variants of Spanish American Regional Evolution.* Los Angeles, CA: University of California Latin American Center Publications.

Alvarez, A. (2017). "Un Nuevo Amanecer" (A New Dawn) [Recorded by A. Alvarez]. On *Un Nuevo Amanecer.* Baton Rouge, LA. Retrieved from https://www.angelaalvarez.com.

American Studies Class. (1975). *McAllen: A Bicentennial Reflection.* McAllen, TX: McAllen High School.

Anders, E. (1982). *Boss Rule in South Texas: The Progressive Era.* Austin, TX: University of Texas Press.

Anders, E. (2010, Jun 15). *Manuel Guerra.* Retrieved Nov 30, 2019, from Handbook of Texas Online: http://www.tshaonline.org/handbook/online/articles/fgu14.

Arteaga, M., & Guerra Jr., R. J. (1996). *Thirteen Generations of Guerra in the New World.* Edinburg, TX: San Antonio Press, University of Texas Rio Grande Valley. Published privately by the authors.

Ball, Catherine. et al. (2016). *AncestryDNA Matching White Paper.* AncestryDNA. Retrieved Mar 6, 2020, from https://www.ancestry.com/corporate/sites/default/files/AncestryDNA-Matching-White-Paper.

Ball, Catherine. et al. (2019). *Ethnicity Estimate White Paper.* AncestryDNA. Retrieved Mar 3, 2020, from https://www.ancestrycdn.com/dna/static/pdf/whitepapers/ EV2019_white_paper_1.

Browning, Arnold J. & Justin W. Wilder. (2009). *The Descendants of Emory R. Wilder (1889-1967.* Camas, WA: Arnold J. Browning.

Brownsville Herald. (1936, May 10). Ranches of Hidalgo County. *Brownsville Herald*, pp. 61-62.

Brutan, R. & NGS Newsroom. (2014). *DNA Results from Asturias, Spain Add to the Genographic Project Human Family Tree.* National Geographic Society. Retrieved Jul 2, 2019, from https://blog.nationalgeographic.org /2014/10/10/dna-results-from-asturias-spain-add-to-the-genographic-project-human-family-tree/.

BYU. (2018). *Spanish Documents.* (Brigham Young Univ.) Retrieved Nov 2018, from Center for Family History and Genealogy: https://script.byu.edu/Pages/ Spanish/en/given.aspx.

Chance, J. E. (1991). *The Mexican War Journal of Captain Franklin Smith.* Oxford, MS: University of Mississippi Press.

Chapa, J. B. (1997). *Texas and Northeastern Mexico, 1630-1690.* (W. C. Foster, Ed., & N. F. Brierley, Trans.) Austin, TX: University of Texas Press.

Conklin, D. (1975). *Montana Historic Preservation Plan.* Helena, MT: Montana Dept of Fish, Wildlife & Parks.

Conklin, D. (2002). *Montana History Weekends: 52 Adventures in History.* Guilford, CT: Globe Pequot Press.

Conklin, D. G. (2018). *Conklin-Marinkovic Family History.* Kalispell, MT: David G. Conklin. Published privately by the author. Moore Graphics, Youngtown, Arizona. 177pp.

Conklin, D. G. (2020). *The Descendants of Richard Thomas Taylor.* Kalispell, MT: Unpublished Manuscript.

Diaz, G. T. (2015). *Border Contraband: A History of Smuggling Across the Rio Grande.* Austin, TX: University of Texas Press.

Elmore, J. L. (2010, Jun 15). *Guerra, Texas.* Retrieved Jan 14, 2019, from Handbook of Texas Online Web Site: http://www.tshaonline.org/handbook/online/articles/hlg38.

Figueroa, B. (2004). Antiguos Pobladores: Ancient Colonizers de la Nueva Espana, Nuevo Reyno De Leon, and Nuevo Santander, The Guerra Canamar History. *Hispanic Organization for Genealogy and Research (HOGAR) Journal, V7*, p79.

Figueroa, B. (2009, Sep 16). Tejanos: Where We Came From. *Kingsville Record.* Retrieved Jul 1, 2018, from http://www.kingsvillerecord.com/opinion/tejanos-where-we-came-from/article.

Garcia, C. P. (1984). *Captain Blas Maria De La Garza Falcon: Colonizer of South Texas.* Austin, TX: The Jenkins Publishing Co. San Felipe Press.

Garza, G. (2019, Apr 24). Gloria Garza Family History Video Interview. (D. G. Conklin, Interviewer)

Garza, M. (2018). *The Founding Families of Mier, Tamaulipas, Mexico and Their Descendants.* Mission, TX: Moises Garza. Published privately by the author.

Guerra, B. (2019, Apr 14). Brenda Guerra Family History Video Interview. (D. G. Conklin, Interviewer)

Guerra, C. (2018, Apr 21). Carlos Guerra Family History Video Interview. (M. G. Conklin, Interviewer)

Guerra, D. (2019, Jan 10). Daniel Guerra Family History Video Interview. (D. G. Conklin, Interviewer)

Guerra, E. (1969, Oct 18). Evangelina Guerra letter to Guadalupe and Nettie Guerra. San Manuel, TX: from Evangelina Guerra Collection in author's Guerra Family History files.

Guerra, F. (2019, Apr 14). Florencio Guerra Family History Video Interview. (D. G. Conklin, Interviewer)

Guerra, F. J. (2019, Apr 20). Abel Guerra Jr. Phone call Video Interview. (D. G. Conklin, Interviewer)

Guerra, F. J. (2019, Jan 17). Fidencio Guerra Jr. Family History Video Interview. (D. G. Conklin, Interviewer)

Guerra, G. (1978, Oct 8). Guadalupe Guerra Family History Audio Interview. (D. G. Conklin, Interviewer)

Guerra, G. (2019, Jan 12). George Guerra Family History Video Interview. (D. G. Conklin, Interviewer)

Guerra, J. (2019, Jan 10). Judy Guerra Family History Video Interview. (D. G. Conklin, Interviewer)

Guerra, J. O. (1997). *Descendants of Ignacio Guerra Canamar*. Retrieved Apr 7, 2019, from https://www.hispanicgs.com/igg.html

Guerra, L. J. (2019, Apr 16). Leonard Guerra Jr. Family History Video Interview. (D. G. Conklin, Interviewer)

Guerra, M. (2015, Nov 28). Mary Guerra Family History Video Interview. (D. G. Conklin, Interviewer)

Guerra, R. (2019, Jan 9). Roberto Guerra Family History Video Interview. (D. G. Conklin, Interviewer)

Guerra, R. (2019, Apr 20). Rose Guerra Family History Video Interview. (D. G. Conklin, Interviewer)

Guerra, T. (2018, Aug 17). Tecla Guerra Family History Video Interview. (D. G. Conklin, Interviewer)

Hebbronville. (1963). *Fiftieth Anniversary: Jim Hogg County. Texas.* Hebbronville, TX: Hebbronville Chamber of Commerce.

Hordes, S. (2005). *To the End of the Earth: A History of the Crypto-Jews of New Mexico.* New York: Columbia University Press.

Inman, R. (1997). *Spain: Eyewitness Travel Guide.* (R. Inman, Ed.) London: Dorling Kindersley Ltd. p. 108.

Laredo Daily Times. (1927, Feb 16). Young Laredo Man Commits Suicide. *Laredo Daily Times, Laredo, TX,* p. 1.

MacKiev. (2019). Family Tree Maker. Boston, MA. Retrieved from https://www.mackiev.com/ftm/index.html.

Monitor. (1939, Mar 21). Buyers Leave on Trip to Markets. *The Valley Monitor, McAllen, TX,* p. 2.

Monitor. (1943, Oct 4). Herlinda Babb Reports Train Wreck. *The Valley Monitor, McAllen, TX,* p. 4.

Monitor. (1943, Mar 7). Herlinda Guerra Becomes Bride of Washington Man at Simple Rites Here. *The Valley Monitor, McAllen, TX,* p. 8.

Monitor. (1944, Jul 2). Herlinda Babb in Saltillo. *The Valley Monitor, McAllen, TX,* p. 2.

Monitor. (1944, Jan 30). Herlinda Babb trip to Trinidad. *The Valley Monitor, McAllen, TX,* p. 4.

Monitor. (1950, Mar). Helping March of Dimes. *The Valley Monitor, McAllen, TX.*

Monitor. (1974, Jun 1). Judge Fidencio M. Guerra Administers Lawyer's Oath To Son. *The Valley Monitor, McAllen, TX,* p. 8.

Monitor. (2001, Jun 24). Marcos Alonzo Garza y del Arcon. *The Valley Monitor, McAllen, TX,* p. 8E.

Salinas, M. I. (2018). My Guerra Ancestors from Antonio Guerra & Maria de Porras. *Kingsville Record,* p. 8. Retrieved Jan 4, 2019, from http://www.kingsvillerecord.com/opinion/tejanos-where-we-came-from/article.

Santa Maria Times. (1952, Sep 12). Soviets Free Three Allies. *Santa Maria Times, Santa Maria, CA,* p. 5.

Santos, J. P. (2010). *The Farthest Home is in an Empire of Fire: A Tejano Elegy.* NY: Penguin Books.

Somos Primos. (2010, Sep 6). *Family Line of Vicente Guerra Canamar y Vela.* Retrieved from Hispanic Heritage Web Site: http://www.somosprimos.com/sp2004/spfeb04/.

The Daily Review. (1954, Sep 14). Fidencio Guerra Picked as 139th Court Judge. *The Daily Review, Edinburg, TX,* p. 1.

Weber, D. J. (1982). *The Mexican Frontier, 1821-1846.* Albuquerque, NM: Univ. of New Mexico Press.

Wikipedia. (2019). *Guerra.* Retrieved Sep 9, 2019, from Wikipedia: https://en.wikipedia.org/wiki/Guerra.

Wikipedia. (2020). *Infintilism.* Retrieved Jan 20, 2020, from Wikipedia: https://en.wikipedia.org/wiki/Infantilism.

Index of Individuals

Females are indexed under both maiden and married names. Dates of birth/baptism and death (where available) are provided for many of the numerous same names to help the reader find a specific individual.

A

Abrego, Juana Flores de, 23
Aguirre de Aguirre, Soledad, 58, 60
Aguirre Sr, Joaquin, 58, 60, 63, 64
Aguirre, Belinda, 63
Aguirre, Eduardo Joaquin, 61, 62, 64, 101
Aguirre, Joaquin, 58, 60, 63
Aguirre-Garza, Alma Norma, 64
Aguirre-Gonzalez, Kiara, 65
Aguirre-Gonzalez, Ricardo, 65
Aguirre-Gonzalez, Rodrigo Alejandro, 64
Alvarez, Angela, 71
Arnold, Mark Edward, 111, 118, 120
Arnold, Natalie Colleen, 120, 122
Asturias, Rodrigo Alvarez de, 17

B

Babb, Elmer Libby, v, 101, 103, 104
Babb, Linda. *See* Guerra, Herlinda
Blood, Casey Guerra, 95
Blood, Cathy. *See* Woo, Cathy Hui-Ju
Blood, Daniel Oakley, 87, 88, 90, 91
Blood, Ellery Abner, 96
Blood, Harold Clifton, 87, 88, 90
Blood, Marjorie. *See* Jones, Marjorie Alene
Blood, Tecla. *See* Guerra, Tecla Ann
Braughton, Alexa, 91, 96
Braughton, William, 91, 96
Brooke, Bennett Franklin, 111, 117, 118
Brooke, Brenda. *See* Guerra, Brenda Estela

C

Castro, Catarina Gomez de, 24, 28
Cavazos del Campo, Juan, 19, 20
Cavazos Montemayor, Elena, 23
Cavazos, Linda, 63, 65
Cavazos, Maria de la Garza, 21, 22
Chapa, Juan Bautista, ii, 9, 11
Chapa, Maria Luisa, 27
Chapa, Maria Matiana Hinojosa de, 31
Chapa-Benavidez, Maria Inez, 25, 28

Chen, Nancy Fong Ju, 91, 95
Clarke, Sofia, 52, 105, 107, 108, 109, 115
Conklin, Charles Franklin, 93
Conklin, Christopher Andrew, 98
Conklin, Dacia Marie, 96, 97, 98
Conklin, David Gene, iv, 87, 91, 93, 94, 96, 97
Conklin, Mary (Guerra). *See* Guerra, Mary LaVonne
Cruz, Bartolo, 43
Cruz, Manuela, 43

D

De la Garza Jr., Bernardo, 80, 81, 82
De la Garza Rodriguez, Elena, 19, 20
De la Garza, Maria Ana Josefa, 6, 24, 26, 27
De la Garza, María Josefa, 24, 26
De la Garza, Ygnacio, 52, 79, 81
De la Peña, José Antonio, 31, 34
De la Peña, José Dionicio Garcia, 34, 36
De la Peña, José Francisco, 31, 34, 36, 40
De Maya, Catalina, 22, 25
De Tijerina, Catalina Fernandez, 21, 22, 25
De Tijerina, Gregorio Fernandez, 20
De Treviño, Francisco Baez, 22, 25
De Treviño, Nicolasa Baez, 22, 25
Dewey Sr., Eloy, 63
Dewey, Belinda, 63, 65
Dewey, Eloy, 60, 63, 65
Dewey, Galwin, 63, 65
Dewey, Linsay, 63, 65
Dickenson, Zena Marie, 91, 96
Dominga, 9, 20

E

El Cid. *See* Vivar, Rodrigo Diaz de
English, Dacia. *See* Conklin, Dacia Marie
English, Randal William, 96, 97, 98
Espinosa, Rodolfo, 128, 129, 132
Espinosa, Sandra, 128, 129, 130, 132
Estrada, Alonso de, 10

F

Fernandez, Gregorio, 20, 21

Fernandez-Godoy, Mardana, 64, 66

G

Garcia, Ana Maria, 27, 35
Garcia, Jessie, 135
Garcia, José Joaquin, 30
Garcia, Juanita, 43
Garcia, Maria de los Santos, 30, 31
Garcia, Maria Lugarda Salinas, 30, 33
Garcia-Barrera, Maria Petra, 31, 34
Garcia-Guajardo, Ana Maria, 27, 30
Garza Arcón, Marcos Alonso de la, 9, 10
Garza Falcón, Blas Maria de la, 11, 13, 24, 28
Garza Falcón, Juan José de la, 28
Garza Falcón, Juan José De la, 24
Garza Falcón, Maria Rita de la, 31
Garza Falcón, Micaela Geronima de la, 23
Garza Falcón, Miguel Gonzalez de la, 11
Garza Renteria, José Clemente Falcón de la, 26
Garza, Alejandra Flores, 63, 65
Garza, Alma Ninfa, 60
Garza, Carlos Javier, 63
Garza, Gloria Estela, 55, 56, 58, 60, 61, 62, 63, 64, 92,
    153
Garza, Launa, 63
Garza, Leonel, 58, 59
Garza, Sabrina S., 111, 120, 122
Garza, Tacoleo, 63
Garza, Teresa. *See* Guerra, Teresa
Garza, Victoriano, 58, 61, 62
Garza-Cantu, Matias, 55, 56, 58, 60, 61
Garza-Hinojosa, Jacobo, v, 52, 55, 56, 58, 60, 61, 62
Garza-Montemayor, Antonio, 58, 61, 62, 63
Gasque e Sol, Susana Blanca, 72, 73, 77
Gibbs, Roxie Ann, 52, 83, 87
Gonzalez Hidalgo, Beatriz, 20
Gonzalez, Angel, 61, 64
Gonzalez, Basilia, 45
Gonzalez, Maria Josefa, 35, 37, 39, 42, 44
Gonzalez, Prudencio, 38
Gonzalez-Muzquiz, Consuelo Yolanda, 61, 64
Good, Elizabeth Susan, 111, 114, 116
Gross, Kurt David, 120, 122
Guerra Jr., Fidencio Miguel, 73, 100, 106, 116, 117
Guerra Jr., Leonard, 92, 123, 124, 125, 126, 128, 130,
    132, 134, 136, 149
Guerra y Guerra, Abel. *See* Guerra, Abel Eulalio
Guerra y Peña, Matilde. *See* Guerra, Maria Matilde
    Guerra de
Guerra, Abel Eulalio, ii, v, 67, 68, 69, 70, 71, 72
Guerra, Abel Luis, 73, 77
Guerra, Adolfo, 125, 127
Guerra, Antonio. *See* Jose Antonio Guerra

Guerra, Antonio Richard, 87
Guerra, Arcadio, 126
Guerra, Arturo, 106
Guerra, Audrey Nicole, 135
Guerra, Brenda Estela, 117, 118
Guerra, Carlos Antonio, 114, 116, 143
Guerra, Chiqui. *See* Treviño, Maria del Rosario
Guerra, Cooper Kehlet, 1, 135
Guerra, Daniel José, 57, 59, 92, 120, 122, 151
Guerra, Diana Maria, 111, 112, 113
Guerra, Diodoro Vidal, 34, 39, 42, 44, 45, 67
Guerra, Donaciano Ernesto, 37
Guerra, Estela. *See* Margo, Estela Gueadalupe
Guerra, Evangelina, v, 89, 123, 124, 125, 126, 128, 129,
    132, 134, 136, 149
Guerra, Fidencio Miguel, v, 105, 107, 111, 113, 114, 116,
    117, 118
Guerra, Florencio Antonio, 76
Guerra, Florencio Ignacio, 52, 67, 71, 73, 74, 75, 77
Guerra, Florinda. *See* Guerra, Maria Florinda
Guerra, Francisco. *See* Guerra, Jose Francisco Antonio
Guerra, George Xavier, 2, 132, 134
Guerra, Guadalupe Filiberto, 1, 2, 18, 40, 57, 59, 67, 70,
    72, 73, 79, 81, 82, 83, 84, 85, 86, 87, 88, 90, 91, 92,
    99, 101, 102, 103, 110, 112, 113, 114, 129, 149, 151,
    153
Guerra, Herlinda, v, 101, 102, 103, 104
Guerra, Jesus Maria, 8, 9, 34, 37, 39, 41, 42, 43, 47, 51
Guerra, Jorge Javier. *See* Guerra, George Xavier
Guerra, José Alejandro Hinojosa, 33, 41
Guerra, José Angel. *See* Guerra-Cañamar, José de los
    Angeles
Guerra, José Antonio, i, ii, v, 1, 8, 17, 25, 34, 37, 43, 47,
    51, 52, 55, 56, 67, 71, 79, 81, 83, 84, 87, 99, 101, 103,
    105, 108, 115, 120, 123, 125
Guerra, José Antonio Albino Hinojosa, 7, 30, 31, 32, 34
Guerra, José de Jesus, 39
Guerra, José Francisco, 39
Guerra, José Francisco Antonio, 6, 26, 27
Guerra, José Herculano, 37, 42, 47, 51
Guerra, José Lino de Jesus, 9, 34, 36, 40, 41
Guerra, José Manuel, 7, 29, 30, 31, 34, 36, 40, 126
Guerra, Joseph Ramon, 6, 25, 26, 28, 29, 51
Guerra, Juan José Hermenegildo, 35
Guerra, Juan Manuel, 30, 32, 34, 35
Guerra, Juan Nepomuceno, 14, 52, 123, 125, 126
Guerra, Judith Ann, 119, 120
Guerra, Leonardo, v, 47, 52, 73, 99, 123, 124, 125, 126,
    127, 128, 129, 132, 134
Guerra, Lulu. *See* Portilla-Martinez, Ciria Luz
Guerra, Lupe. *See* Guerra, Guadalupe Filiberto
Guerra, Manuel (1856-1915), 34, 43, 44
Guerra, Margarita, 52
Guerra, Maria Candida Francisca, 28

Guerra, Maria Emeteria, 39
Guerra, Maria Emilia, 39
Guerra, Maria Florinda, v, 99, 100
Guerra, Maria Julia, 35
Guerra, Maria Matilde Guerra de, 39, 43, 44, 45, 85
Guerra, Maria Tomasa, 32, 34
Guerra, Mary LaVonne, iii, v, 1, 10, 11, 26, 28, 31, 34, 50,
    51, 63, 68, 80, 92, 93, 94, 96, 97, 124, 137, 145, 149,
    151, 153
Guerra, Nettie. *See* Taylor, Nettie LaVonne
Guerra, Rafael, 14, 15, 126
Guerra, Raul Jr, 4
Guerra, Roberto Miguel, 113, 114
Guerra, Rose Marie, 124, 128, 129
Guerra, Sandra. *See* Espinosa, Sandra
Guerra, Steven Michael, 135
Guerra, Tecla Ann, 88, 90, 91
Guerra, Tecla Guerra de, 34, 42, 47, 50, 51, 52, 55, 56,
    67, 71, 79, 81, 83, 87, 99, 101, 103, 105, 108, 123,
    125
Guerra, Teresa, v, 55, 56, 57, 58, 59, 60, 61, 62, 153
Guerra, Victoria, ii, v, 79, 81, 82
Guerra-Barrera, Jesús, 43
Guerra-Cañamal, Antonio (b1570), 1, 3, 5, 10, 17, 18, 19
Guerra-Cañamal-II, Antonio (b1603), 5, 6, 9, 18, 19, 21,
    142, 143
Guerra-Cañamar, Antonio, 24
Guerra-Cañamar, Cristobal, 25, 26
Guerra-Cañamar, Ignacio, 6, 21, 22, 25
Guerra-Cañamar, José de los Angeles, 31, 34, 35
Guerra-Cañamar, Juan, 9, 20, 23
Guerra-Cañamar, Vicente, 5, 9, 20
Guerra-Cañamar-II, Juan, 23
Guerra-Hinojosa, José Felipe, 38, 39, 42, 44, 48
Guerra-Muller, Mariel Alexana, 76
Guzman, Rose Marie. *See* Guerra, Rose Marie
Guzman-Ramirez, Miguel Gabriel, 128, 129

H

Hinojosa de Chapa, Maria Matiana, 28
Hinojosa de la Garza, José Manuel, 25, 28
Hinojosa, Gervacio, 32, 35
Hinojosa, Isidra, 55, 56
Hinojosa, Maria Francisca Saenz, 33, 35
Hinojosa, Maria Gregoria, 33, 35
Hinojosa, Maria Rosalia Chapa, 25, 28, 29
Hinojosa, Rafaela, 37
Hinojosa, Rosalia Timotea, 35
Houston, Ezra B., 38

J

Jones, Marjorie Alene, 87, 88, 89, 90

K

Kunz, Myron Logan, 94, 96
Kunz, Myron Troy, 96, 98

L

Levesque, Jon Michael, 122
Levesque, Roger J., 111, 113
Longoria, Herminia L., 52, 79, 81
Longoria, Maria Teresa, ii, 36, 37, 42, 47, 51

M

Margo, Estela Guadalupe, v, 10, 52, 105, 106, 107, 108,
    110, 111, 113, 114, 116, 117, 118
Margo, Robert, 108
Margo, Ruperto Reymundo, 52, 105, 107
Marinkovic, Betty, 93
Martinez, Aurora, 79, 81
Martinez, Rurara, 52
Martinez-Morales, Elvira, 67, 71
Mendel, David, 63, 65
Montemayor, Petra, 58, 61, 62
Muller-Gandolfo, Evelyn Audrey, 72, 73, 75, 77
Muñoz, Fernanda, 17
Muzquiz, Olga, 61, 64

N

Nelson, Sandra Lucille, 94, 96

P

Parra de Rubio, Carmen, 58
Peña, Maria Andrea, ii, 9, 36, 37, 39, 40, 41, 42, 43, 47,
    51
Peña-Ramirez, Maria del Rosario, 9, 34, 36
Porras Molinas, José, 17
Porras, Maria, 17, 18
Portilla, Lulu. *See* Portilla-Martinez, Ciria Luz
Portilla-Bolado, Manuel, 67, 71
Portilla-Martinez, Ciria Luz, 52, 67, 69, 71, 72

R

Ramirez, Jesus, 38
Ramirez, José Cristobal, 28, 31
Ramirez, José Eugenio, 28, 31
Ramirez, Maria Leonarda Chapa, 35, 36
Ramirez, Maria Paula Guadalupe, 34, 36, 40
Raygadas, Adan Rubio, 58
Regules-Rojas, Manuel, 75, 76
Rio Frio, Maria Luisa Fernandez de, 5, 9, 19, 21

Rubio-Raygadas, Carmen Aurora, 58, 59

S

Saenz, José Antonio, 33, 35
Salinas, Delia Benita, 128, 129, 132
Salinas, Joaquin, 31
Salinas, José Angel, 38, 39
Salinas, José Joaquin, 30, 31
Salinas, Maria Rosalia Garcia, 30, 31, 32, 34, 35
Salinas, Maria Rosalia Peña, 30
Santos-Aguirre, Adrian Matias de los, 64
Santos-Aguirre, Melchor de los, 64, 66
Santos-Ordonez, Melchor de los, 60, 64, 66
Santos-Ordonez, Melissa de los, 64
Smith, Brittany, 98

T

Taylor, Arlene, 92
Taylor, Dennis, 92
Taylor, Nettie LaVonne, v, 1, 10, 83, 86, 87, 88, 90, 91
Taylor, Richard Thomas, 52, 83, 87
Treviño, Antonia Josefa de la Garza, 23, 24
Treviño, Bartolome, 35
Treviño, Isabel Maria, 27, 30, 35

Treviño, Juana Quintanilla, 9
Treviño, Maria del Rosario, 132, 133, 134
Treviño, Maria Teresa, 32, 35
Treviño, Teresa Maria, 35
Treviño-Garcia, Isabel Maria, 27, 30, 32, 34
Treviño-Leal, Capitan Bartolome de, 27, 30

V

Valle, Cedric, 52, 79, 81
Valle, Ruben Gabriel, v, 79, 80, 81, 82
Valle, Victoria. *See* Guerra, Victoria
Vanessa, Rebeca Alessandra, 76
Vela, Catalina de, 18, 19
Vidaurri, Ildefonsa de, 20
Villa, Pancho, 50, 57
Villarreal, Carlota Vela, 53, 123, 125
Vincik, Tracy Ann, 113, 122
Vivar, Rodrigo Diaz de, 17

W

Wilkinson, Nora Elizabeth, 104
Woo, Cathy Hui-Ju, 91, 95
Woo, George Tai Mei, 91, 95
Wright, Sarah Marie, 134, 135

www.ingramcontent.com/pod-product-compliance
Lightning Source LLC
Chambersburg PA
CBHW080623030426
42336CB00018B/3056